Alan Silverstein's

HOME BUYING STRATEGIES

Alan Silverstein's

HOME BUYING STRATEGIES

NEWLY BUILT HOMES

First published in 1987 by
Stoddart Publishing Co. Limited
34 Lesmill Road
Toronto, Canada
M3B 2T6

Canadian Cataloguing in Publication Data

Silverstein, Alan, 1951-
    Alan Silverstein's home-buying strategies for newly-built homes

ISBN 0-7737-2089-8

1. House buying — Canada. I. Title. II. Title:
    Home-buying strategies for newly-built homes

HD1379.S53 1987 643'.12'0971 C86-094941-9

Design: Brant Cowie/Artplus
Typesetting: Jay Tee Graphics Ltd.

Printed in the United States

TABLE OF CONTENTS

Preface

Buying a house should be one of the happiest and most exciting times in anyone's life. The enthusiasm begins when the decision is first made to go house-hunting, and escalates once an offer is signed and accepted. Emotions peak on closing day, when the deed and key are delivered. To some people, the passion they have for their new home during this time is intoxicating. Why not? Their home contains all their hopes and dreams for the future.

But unless the decision is well thought out and planned, this bubble called optimism could burst at any time, and totally demoralize a purchaser. It is even more unfortunate when you consider that few of the problems purchasers face need be unanticipated, unexpected and unforeseen. The key is to recognize and deal with the potential surprises and disruptions well ahead of time, so it's smooth sailing until closing day. Otherwise, problems could cause emotional strain and hardship on purchasers, at untold cost.

Traditionally, buying an owner-occupied house has been a "learn-by-doing" experience. How many home owners wish they had known at the start what they knew at the end! It used to be that the first step in buying a house was to sign an offer to purchase. Only then did buyers ask the important questions and deal with issues that really should have been examined well before any commitment was made.

In recent years, more and more Canadians have turned the old-fashioned approach on its head. Once they begin to look for a house, they pose fundamental questions and make key decisions *before they sign the offer.* Their areas of inquiry include needs, wants, location (the biggest single factor affecting real estate), selecting a lawyer plus their financial ability both to buy and carry the property. Everything is planned out and arranged ahead of time, and nothing is left to chance. They know what to expect every step of the way. These Canadian home buyers are creating and then following their own unique game plan — a Home-Buying Strategy or HOBS — in order to find the "right" house that best satisfies their particular needs and wants, and the one they can afford to own.

With a home-buying strategy, signing an offer is the climax to the process, and never the beginning. Only by creating and implementing a home-buying strategy can buyers understand what they are committing to before making those commitments. Only with a home-buying strategy will they know the questions to ask and the answers to seek, the issues to consider and the trap doors to avoid, before signing an offer to purchase. The more information the buyer has, the easier it is to make an informed decision. HOBS takes the guesswork out of buying a house.

A home-buying strategy will explain what to do when buying a newly-built house, and more significantly, how to do it. It not only tells purchasers the rules, but more importantly it explains the strategies needed to best apply those rules.

Buying a newly-built house is different in many respects from purchasing a resale home. Probably the most marked difference is that the house hasn't been built yet. The expression used in the industry is "presold." Because the house doesn't exist, you can't see it, measure it or touch it. This means unique issues, problems and concerns must be addressed from the time *before* the contract is signed until well after closing. New home buyers need answers to different questions and need to apply different strategies than those buying a resale home.

Many potential pitfalls lie between deciding to buy a house and actually moving in. What risks are involved? What should purchasers look for and, more importantly, look out for? What is the best way to buy a house from plans? How can buyers find out what the neighborhood and community will look like? Rarely does work on a house begin as soon as the offer is signed. What preliminary work must be completed first? And what kind of problems could jeopardize the entire transaction?

Newly-built home buyers are not accompanied by a real estate agent when they look at houses. Without that expert, how does the buyer know what builder to deal with (the second most important factor when buying a newly-built home)? Is the house protected by any form of new home warranty? How does the warranty work? Are the mortgage terms guaranteed?

What about some of the uncertainties associated with buying a newly-built home? Everyone has heard horror stories of hidden costs when buying a newly-built home. What is the true cost of closing, and when can it be determined? The same holds true for the printed form contract. How can purchasers protect themselves against clauses so heavily weighted in favor of the builder? And what are your rights and obligations if closing is delayed or even cancelled, something resale purchasers seldom face? Sometimes, it appears to be just a matter of luck when everything is done properly and promptly. But the only way to learn the true answers to these questions and eliminate the need for luck is with a home-buying strategy.

New home buyers are always concerned that they have overlooked or forgotten something important. But where could they turn for help? *Alan Silverstein's Home-Buying Strategies for Newly-Built Homes* was written to fill that need, to address the major concerns people have when they buy a newly-built home. It was designed to provide Canadians with a straightforward, step-by-step approach through every step of the transaction. The central focus of this book is the most typical of new home purchases — buying from a builder in a new subdivision.

The format of the book parallels the way your home-buying strategy is applied. Most of the crucial decisions must be made before even considering, let alone signing, any offer. This means a large part of the book is devoted to establishing and applying your HOBS, and key concerns you should be addressing, before putting pen to paper.

To assist purchasers, most chapters are followed by a series of Tips and Pointers that summarize the key points of what was discussed. Where appropriate, checklists and charts appear in the book to help you organize relevant information.

Alan Silverstein's Home-Buying Strategies for Newly-Built Homes completes a series of three books dealing with Canadian home ownership. Purchasing an existing home using a HOBS is examined in *Alan Silverstein's Home-Buying Strategies for Resale Homes*. And financing or refinancing a mortgage in Canada — what to know, what features to include, how to pay it off as soon as possible (the POPS principle) and what to do afterwards — is the basis of *Hidden Profits in Your Mortgage*. The message in all three books is the same — whether buying a newly-built home, an existing home or arranging a mortgage, a sound personalized strategy is essential before any commitment whatsoever is made.

Experience is a great teacher, and gaining experience is a very difficult process. In large part, this book reflects the trials and tribulations other people have faced in buying an unbuilt home, and the home-buying strategies they developed as a result. Just as you are about to benefit from their experiences, can we also benefit from yours? Do you have a home-buying strategy other people should know about? Do you have any suggestions about how the purchase of a newly-built home can be improved? Let's hear from you. Address your correspondence to: Alan Silverstein, c/o Stoddart Publishing, 34 Lesmill Road, Toronto, Ontario M3B 2T6. Please enclose copies of any relevant documents that will help us understand the situation and your solution.

Acknowledgments

For the past three years, I have been writing books to help the Canadian public buy a resale home, buy a newly-built home and arrange the best possible mortgage. To be able to do this while still maintaining my legal practice, I am most grateful to my secretary, Donna Boisselle, a dynamo of a person; and to my receptionist, Connie Romanyshyn, who makes sure the office functions properly each day. Thanks for technical help go to Ian Woods, chartered surveyor, my good friend Jack Haft, and to the Ontario New Home Warranty Program, for the specimen Warranty Certificate. To the staff at Stoddart Publishing, who have become my friends over the years, a special thanks.

Most importantly, I offer my sincerest appreciation and gratitude to the three people who made this book possible, my loving sons Elliott and Darryl and especially my dear wife, Hannah. I dedicate this book to them, for their inexhaustible encouragement, understanding and support.

Part One

YOUR HOME-BUYING STRATEGY

1

Why Buy a Newly-built Home?

In many ways buying a house is like buying a car. Some people prefer to purchase a new car, while others regularly buy used ones. Whether cost, value, potential headaches or simply "newness" steers buyers in one direction or the other, shopping for a new car is a totally different ball game than searching for a good used vehicle. Different strategies are needed for each type of purchase.

The same holds true in the residential real estate industry, where buying a newly-built home differs markedly from purchasing a "used" resale home. With a resale home, buyers like Dwayne and Emma easily can see what they get, and wind up getting what they see. Rooms can be measured, operating systems can be inspected, and costly items like fences, driveways and landscaping can be negotiated into the deal. Just as with cars, some buyers believe they get much better value buying an item that has been previously owned.

Yet many people are powerfully attracted by the prospect of owning a newly-built home. What captivates them are the enchanting thoughts of a home that is bright, fresh, clean, modern looking and, of course, brand new. By being the first occupants, purchasers of a newly-built home will not have to inherit someone else's headaches, concealed problems or color schemes. So irresistable is this yearning for freshness and newness that it overrides most concerns people have about buying a home from a builder. Probably this is the single most important reason for the popularity of newly-built homes in Canada today.

What a thrill it is to see your new house being constructed! It becomes your own private tourist attraction, a place to visit two, three or even more times each week. After all, it represents your future, your hopes and your aspirations. Every bit of progress brings a smile to your face. Many people take pictures of their house at various stages of construction — vacant land,"hole in the ground," installed foundation, framing, bricking, finished product. They want a permanent record of what the house looked like, from start to finish.

All the latest equipment and features are found in a newly-built house, which is expected to be trouble-free for years to come. Greater energy efficiency is promised as well, the house being constructed and insulated according to the most up-to-date building code standards. This alone will save home owners hundreds of dollars annually.

Today's homes have a more modern look and design than their predecessors. Interior layouts have greatly changed over time. Newly-built homes have a roomier, more open feeling, and often include the increasingly popular multi-purpose family room. Compared to their plain, modest role in older homes, kitchens and bathrooms have become focal points and even showpieces. Practically every newly-built home today has an outdoor patio, ready for that first barbeque of the season. Even a simple necessity like the stairs has been transformed into the "staircase" where the type of handrail, picket and surface-covering has taken on added importance.

Newly-built homes are the first choice of many people like Rob and Laura because they can have some influence on how their house will eventually look. With a resale home, the purchaser has little room to maneuver. Except for possible cosmetic changes, the way the house looks today is the way the house will *always* look. While the exterior colors of a newly-built home may be decided by the builder, most purchasers still can choose the interior color scheme and decor, and customize the house in many other ways. Depending on the builder, Rob and Laura can select their own floor coverings, fireplace style, cupboards and plumbing fixtures, just to name a few. Even walls can be moved and room sizes rearranged, if the house is still unbuilt. All this is possible in many cases at no extra cost, being part of the purchase price for the home.

If Rob and Laura are willing to spend extra money, the sky's the limit on further customizing their house. Each builder offers numerous extras, options and upgrades, so the house can better suit and reflect the owner's taste and lifestyle. Everything from upgraded carpeting to fully tiled bathtub enclosures are available

— for a price. Just as with a new car, few people buy a new home "stripped." Most buyers include some "option" the "dealer" offers. This is not surprising, since most people take great pride in their homes. Being able to personalize a house and to have some say in its final appearance, especially when it can be done at little or no additional charge, is part of the allure of the newly-built home.

In the resale market, buyers may find the selection of homes somwhat limited. Few homes may be listed in a certain community or neighborhood, or a particular type or size of house may not be readily available. Not so with new homes. Builders not only market different models of homes, but they offer different variations or "elevations" of each model, too. Purchasers have another type of choice as well, since builders operate in clusters in new subdivisions. Just count the number of sales trailers greeting visitors to new developments. At times, it seems there is too much of a good thing available — too many possibilities to choose from.

Only in the rarest of cases can the purchaser of a resale home choose from two or more identical properties. Not so with a newly-built home. Once all the key decisions have been made on which model and elevation to buy, the purchaser is left with one important final choice — which lot to select. This is one of the most important yet complicated decisions buyers of newly-built homes must make.

Peer pressure is a very powerful reason why some people buy newly-built homes. Prospective buyers often follow the lead of friends and acquaintances who are buying homes in desirable developing areas.

It's not just buyers of resale homes who can get very good value for their money. For starters, the basic rules of supply and demand apply to newly-built homes, too. With so much construction going on, builders must price their homes competitively. Depending on the state of the market, a builder may be flexible on price, or may include certain "extras" in the deal, just to make a sale.

Purchasers of resale homes always run the risk of being saddled with hidden defects that only are discovered after closing. To the resale purchaser, it's still *caveat emptor* — let the buyer beware. One way to minimize these risks and reveal the potential problems is to have a home inspector thoroughly investigate an existing property before it is bought. But even when problems are uncovered early, the cost of correcting them usually falls on the buyer, if he decides to proceed with the deal at all.

On the other hand, some (but not all) newly-built homes are

covered by a warranty covering defects in materials and workman-ship for a limited period of time. It's comparable to the "parts and labor" warranty on new cars. Rarely, if ever, is this type of coverage seen in the resale home market. Many people find it reassuring to know that problems will be repaired during the war-ranty period at the builder's expense. Money saved on maintenance and repairs is part of the "better value" that buyers of newly-built homes expect.

Resale homes are generally located in fully developed areas where the necessary support services, transportation facilities, schools and shopping are all in place. Purchasers of newly-built homes will find out, however, that they are modern-day pioneers in those grow-ing neighborhoods and communities! Many of the facilities they once took for granted just won't be there for years to come. As compensation for the inconveniences they face in the immediate future, purchasers in developing areas demand either more value for their money or a lower price for a comparable home. Why pay the same price as in an established area, they ask, to get the same type of house but fewer amenities? This "new home mentality" is another key reason why people expect better value buying from a builder.

Most new homes are constructed in areas that were vacant land just a few short years — even months — ago. It is not uncommon, though, for a new home to be built in an established area, on a lot where an older home was torn down. Occasionally, one or more houses may also be built in an existing area on an oversized lot subdivided into smaller building lots, a practice known as "in-filling." Since most newly-built houses fall into the first category, our focus of attention will be on new homes being built in new subdivisions and developments.

The debate over the merits of buying a resale vs. a newly-built home will never cease. Clearly, as long as Canadians buy houses, a market exists for both. The type selected is strictly a matter of personal preference. But to many people, there is nothing like buy-ing a newly-built home. It is new, fresh — and exciting!

Tips and Pointers

- Chart the progress of your newly-built home. Your pictures and notes will be a great keepsake for years to come.
- Find out what features of your new house the builder will allow you to select.
- Remember that new developments lack important amenities for years to come.

2

HOBS for the Newly-built Home

What is HOBS, and why is it so important for purchasers of newly-built homes? Simply put, HOBS means *home-buying strategies,* the game plan that every person *must* have when buying a house. In its simplest form, HOBS emphasizes the need to carefully plan and arrange every stage of a purchase transaction, *before signing any Offer to Purchase.* Without HOBS, buyers could find themselves signing an offer before all the important details are in place. With HOBS, the heady enthusiasm and excitement most people experience at house-hunting time can be maintained and even enhanced until well after they take possession of their house. With a home-buying strategy, many of the problems purchasers of newly-built homes face can be anticipated, planned for and eliminated.

Look at any professional or amateur sports team. Before commencing play, teams prepare a detailed strategy or game plan for their upcoming encounter. Advance planning and preparation is the key to victory.

The same holds true for buyers of newly-built homes, especially since selecting and purchasing one has become so complex. It takes considerable time, thought and preparation. Much preliminary work is necessary before you even consider signing an offer to purchase. Taking a tip from the Boy Scouts, developing and applying a home-buying strategy means buyers must "be prepared" for their purchase.

To effectively design this game plan or strategy, buyers must be prepared to ask many pointed questions and seek detailed answers, and take a careful look at *themselves* first, before they even start to seriously look at houses.

All too often, less time and attention is given to the purchase of a home than other consumer products. It's amazing that people will spend hours researching the purchase of a car, television or VCR — items worth only a fraction of a home's price, and items which depreciate in value over time. Perhaps people feel intimidated when buying a house. If they do, then they're making a sizeable five- or six-figure commitment to purchase with only several hours' thought. Anyone buying a house this way leaves himself exposed to problems later on, many of which could have been dealt with even before the offer was signed. One way to avoid this intimidation factor, and to give buyers the confidence they need when buying a home, is to have a home-buying strategy.

One of the first questions to answer is whether to buy at all. Home ownership is not for everyone, especially people like Paul and Joy who dislike the chores associated with owning a home — shovelling snow, cutting the grass and repairing the little problems every house presents. Paul and Joy's mobile lifestyle is best served by a rental apartment, although owning a condominium unit has become a viable alternative. As tenants, no long-term mortgage obligations or commitment of funds are necessary. Yet renting does not offer them much security, stability, privacy or feeling of permanence, either.

Once the decision has been made to buy, the next step is to begin preparing a "needs" (must have) and a "wants" (would like to have) shopping list. This involves a little personal stock-taking followed by a little informal house-hunting — to look and to learn, but not to buy. Items on the list should be recorded in order of priority, a type of personalized ranking system. Remember to be realistic in analyzing your needs and wants in a house. Have reasonable expectations. Be prepared to compromise and even lower your standards, if necessary, to avoid buying a house beyond your means.

At the same time, carefully examine your financial ability to buy the house, plus whether you can afford to "carry" it (or pay its ongoing monthly costs). Be sure to spend some time *now* comparing different mortgages in the marketplace. Otherwise, the opportunity to shop for a more attractive mortgage package could be lost. If time is pressing after the offer is signed, you may have to accept whatever financing the builder has arranged, simply because it is available.

Never lose sight of the fact a home is an investment just like term deposits, stocks and bonds, mutual funds and Registered Retirement Savings Plans. Money paid to purchase a home could well be placed in a host of different investments. Although buying a home doesn't yield cash dividends, you eventually expect to see growth and capital appreciation. Besides this, homes are not "liquid" investments like Canada Savings Bonds and term deposits, since they cannot be readily converted into cash on short notice. To recover your funds, it is necessary either to sell the property or mortgage it, both of which are time consuming and costly. Creating a home-buying strategy means carefully researching the financial side associated with the purchase of an owner-occupied home too.

Another important factor to consider in designing your HOBS is location — assessing the community, neighborhood and specific site features. Since a new home purchase is an investment in your future, always take into consideration the resale potential of a home. After all, *every* property will eventually be resold. Resale value for homes in a new development may be difficult to calculate when the homes aren't even built yet. But the resale value is bound to be higher if your house possesses desirable features and is in a location that will make it easy to sell in the future.

Once these factors have been considered, the prospective buyer must identify the key players in the new home purchase. One of the most obvious differences between buying an existing home and one from a builder is the absence of a separate real estate agent. Many resale purchasers rely on an agent to introduce them to different properties. Purchasers of a newly-built home must shop the market themselves. This does not mean they are totally on their own, as if there was no one to represent and protect their interests. (As will be seen in Chapter 11, nothing could be further from the truth.) But the lack of a separate sales agent does increase the importance of creating, updating and properly applying a home-buying strategy.

It's also imperative to select a lawyer and home inspector long before you actually buy a house. After all, how can a lawyer best represent the purchaser if the offer is signed, sealed and delivered before the lawyer is even chosen?

A home inspector is another indispensable ally when buying from a builder. Too often, though, his role in protecting buyers of newly-built homes is not clearly understood.

As part of their home-buying strategy, buyers should demand complete disclosure of *all* costs to be faced in closing the deal, including the numerous so-called hidden costs *before an offer is signed*. So many additional charges are tacked on that mask the purchase price, that buying a newly-built home today resembles ordering dinner in a fine restaurant *a la carte!* Without knowing all the costs now, how can a buyer properly budget his funds for closing, or know how large a mortgage to arrange?

As a prospective buyer of a newly-built home, you should also be aware of expenses to be incurred *after* closing. These can include the cost of window coverings (sheets covering windows are never very appealing!) and appliances, which are rarely included in a newly-built home. Over time, money may also have to be spent erecting a fence, laying a driveway, and landscaping the lot.

With the preliminary work completed, prospective purchasers are ready to look more seriously at houses, but not to make a final decision! That's right! It's still premature to buy that dream house! Looking again at our sports team, while it follows the game plan as best as it can, the squad must be able to adapt. Depending on how the game is going, it may have to change or vary the strategy.

So too with a purchaser's home-buying strategy, which should never be etched in stone. Your HOBS game plan will be modified, refined and updated over time as you look at more and more homes. Items may be shuffled between the needs and wants lists; you may expand or reduce the number of communities and neighborhoods that interest you; or you may decide to lower your expectations after you realize what the house will cost to purchase and maintain. With time, you'll find the right house — one that satisfies all of your needs and as many wants as possible, and one that you can afford.

Just as every prospective home buyer's circumstances are different, so too with each person's home-buying strategy. As you look at houses, learn more about mortgages and closing costs, and gain more experience about buying a newly-built home, you'll make decisions and develop strategies unique to your circumstances. The final result will be your own home-buying strategy — the master plan that is best for you.

With HOBS, all relevant information affecting the *entire* transaction has been obtained, and *all* key decisions have been made before any contract is signed. Signing the offer is the culmination of your home-finding expedition and not its starting point. The interval between acceptance and closing should be anti-climactic.

As important as a HOBS is to all home purchasers, it takes on added significance in the new home market. When buying from a builder, purchasers must be sold on that builder. This means spending considerable time to research and investigate builders, their products, their reputations and past performance, and their after-sales service *before making any commitment*. Signing an offer is just the beginning of a long-term relationship with the builder/seller, something resale purchasers never have to face. Now is the time to do your homework checking out a builder, as this could well be *the* determining factor in selecting one home over another (see Chapter 12).

Purchasers of newly-constructed homes face other potential problems and uncertainties that resale buyers do not. Most new homes today are bought from plans and an "artist's rendering," without a model home to view. Determining exactly how the completed home will look is a difficult task that requires visualizing, speculating and asking many detailed questions. There is a technique to doing this properly, examined in chapter 9.

One of the most serious problems facing buyers of newly-built homes is the delayed or missed closing. What happens if the deal doesn't close on time because the house isn't ready? What are the legal rights and obligations of the builder and the buyer? Once again, before they make any commitment whatsoever, purchasers of newly-built homes must fully understand what the contract says — and doesn't say. Of course, purchasers of resale homes don't face this problem, since their house already exists. More information about delayed closings is in Chapter 25.

The offer to purchase a newly-built home is totally different than its resale counterpart. A buyer's nightmare, this lengthy, complex legal document imposes onerous restrictions and responsibilities on newly-built home purchasers, and is laden with pitfalls for the unwary. Unlike the resale market, builders' offers to purchase are not standard. All the more reason, as part of your HOBS, to take the offer to a qualified real estate lawyer for review and comment before it is signed.

Buying a home from a builder means anticipating a certain level of frustration in the weeks and months after closing. Rarely is a house totally completed when title changes hands. Usually some interior and considerable exterior work remains unfinished, to be completed by the builder once you are in possession. Over time, defects and problems may begin to appear as well. Getting the repair work done means telephone calls and even letters to the builder's service department. You may need to take some time off work to meet with the builder's service representative at the house to address the problem. While this is a headache and an inconvenience, you should prepare for it as part of your home-buying strategy.

Until the sod is laid, expect your front lawn and the surrounding area to turn into "Mud City" after every rainfall. Many homes in a development must be constructed and occupied, with the lots properly graded, before the grass is put down. This means you may have to put up with mud and dust, unpaved driveways, messy roads, dirty cars and clothes for months to come. Bricks and paint cans lying about, and similar types of garbage will also mar the look of your development for some time. By knowing what to expect, you can be prepared for these unpleasant aspects for the first few months after closing.

Time is often a purchaser's greatest enemy. Important decisions may have to be made on short notice and under great pressure. By following the home-buying strategy approach, prospective buyers of newly-built homes will objectively develop and refine their game plan early on. All this is taking place at at time when they really don't face any serious pressure. Key decisions can be made both comfortably and (if necessary) quickly to capitalize on a good opportunity.

Developing your HOBS will require considerable homework before doing any serious house-hunting. But it's a simple, inexpensive way of ensuring that the home you buy is the right one *for you*. Armed with a home-buying strategy, you will know what you are committing to before you actually make that commitment.

Tips and Pointers

- Establishing your unique home-buying strategy should be the first step you take in buying a newly-built house.
- Carefully analyze your needs, wants and ability to pay for the house of your choice.
- Your home-buying strategy should not be etched in stone. For it to be most effective, you must review and modify it over time.

3

Timing Your Purchase

After "location," the most commonly used word when buying a house is "time" (or "timing"). There can be a "good" time, the "right" time, and even a "bad" time to buy. Like most things in life, timing is everything. And it's never a good time to buy a house if key decisions are being made without first being carefully thought out and researched — items such as needs and wants, and financial ability to pay for it both on closing and in the future. In other words it's never a good time to buy if your HOBS isn't in place first.

Timing can be looked at in a number of different ways: the time of year when you are buying; the time the home will be completed and ready for occupancy; the extent of development of a new subdivision. These factors, combined with the number of unsold homes a builder has, all affect the "timing" of a purchase. By carefully examining these timing factors, buyers will have a much better understanding of when to buy and who to buy from.

Both Mother Nature and the real estate market have different seasons that seem to parallel each other. Without question, winter is the quietest time in the new home market. From early December until mid-February, when holidays and the weather are on people's minds, new home sales pavillions resemble desolate camps in a remote part of the Arctic.

But an old cliché says that it pays to shop for a car on a rainy day, when no one else is out looking. When business is quiet, salesmen are anxious to make a sale and more apt to give a break on price or features. It's a simple application of the rule of supply and demand.

The same holds true when buying a newly-built home. Builders tend to be more accommodating during the dead of winter because fewer people are out looking for homes. With financial commitments to meet on serviced lots they've bought, builders would love to emerge from the winter doldrums with a long list of signed offers to purchase. To do this, builders must be more willing to negotiate and make concessions on price, features and extras, to the obvious benefit of purchasers. In one respect, the right time to buy is when everybody else isn't. Following the crowd to that same sales office later in the year will probably cost you money.

During the slack winter market, new home sales agents have plenty of time on their hands, so it's an excellent opportunity for buyers, especially first-time purchasers, to learn more about the market and develop their HOBS. Sit down with different builders' agents. Ask them the many questions you have about buying a newly-built home. Compare what different builders offer. Using that information, start making many of the decisions that will form the basis of your home-buying strategy.

Builders emphasize that most home construction, including pouring concrete and laying bricks, can continue during the winter. But keep in mind this work is being done on homes sold the previous fall. Construction won't start on homes sold during the winter until late winter or early spring. People concerned with winter construction will shy away from a fall purchase and opt to buy in midwinter instead.

Come one nice day in February, all of a sudden people start thinking of home buying again. Interest in both the resale and the new-home markets blossoms quickly with each passing day. Just look at the number of people visiting new home sales trailers each weekend in late winter and early spring. Muck and dirt plague all new subdivisions, but the problem is especially bad during the spring thaw. Anyone going to new home sites at this time of year would be well advised to take along moisture-proof boots and wear a pair of old, washable slacks.

Without question, spring is the most popular time of the year to buy a newly-built house, or any home for that matter. Traditionally this is the time of the "seller's market," when builders tend to be less accommodating and take the upper hand in negotiations. Simply because of the increased interest, builders reason that it won't take long for an interested buyer, or a less demanding one, to appear.

Sales activity peaks in June and then falls off during the summer. Most people would rather spend a beautiful weekend or their time off work resting, relaxing or frolicking in the nice weather, rather than house-hunting. Just as in winter, purchasers may find builders a little more willing to dicker when business is slow. And just as in winter, agents have more time to spend with buyers answering their many questions.

In September, life seems to return to normal in more ways than one. Once again, interest builds in both the resale and newly-built home markets during this Indian summer. A flurry of buyers flock to sales trailers during late summer and early fall, signing contracts with "long closings," since houses will not be ready for occupancy until the following spring.

Today most newly-built homes are sold from plans, dubbed in the industry "pre-sales." In other words, the houses still have to be constructed! Because new homes today are pre-sold, it becomes even more important to consider timing — but in reverse. To do this, first consider when you want to move to the new home. Then work backwards from the anticipated closing date in order to decide when to start house-hunting. Timing your purchase this way is an important part of a HOBS — your unique home-buying strategy.

This gap between signing an offer and closing the deal also helps explain why early spring is the busiest time in the new home sales market. Most real estate transactions are closed between the middle of June and the beginning of September. The reason is simple. Home buyers like Jeff and Joanne with school-aged children want to close their purchase and move to their new home during the summer. Some prefer to move right after school ends, so their children can make new friends over the summer. Others prefer to move just before school starts.

Finding the right house takes time. And time is needed while the offer is considered by the builder, and any conditions such as getting mortgage approval or selling an existing home are satisfied. And, of course, don't forget it will take time for the builder to construct that pre-sale house. In a normal market, at least four months will pass between the time a building permit is issued and the day a newly-constructed home is ready for occupancy. Strikes, materials shortages, a scarcity of tradesmen plus inclement weather could mean a delay in closing. Buyers who want a summer closing should actively begin to look for a house no later than the middle of spring.

Glen and Donna found it very practical to time their new home purchase this way. Anxious to close in mid-July, and knowing how long construction would take, their house-hunting expedition began shortly after the New Year. By late February, when other people were getting the new-home itch, Glen and Donna had signed a contract for a pre-sale house on very favorable terms. Working backwards from their preferred closing date meant everything came together for Glen and Donna exactly when they expected.

Beware that signing an offer is not necessarily the final step before a house can be built! Depending on the subdivision's present stage of development, it may be some time before the first shovel can go into the ground. To get a better idea when construction can begin and more importantly when the house can be completed, prospective buyers should have a basic understanding of the development process before submitting an offer to purchase. (See Chapter 8.)

Bill and Vivian were among the first people to buy a home from their builder. "Early" purchasers like Bill and Vivian are very important to a builder in establishing a track record and a good reputation with the home-buying public. So builders are often willing to "throw in" certain items to generate those crucial first sales. What's more, the earlier you buy, the greater the number of lot locations to choose from. Once demand increases for a particular builder's product or for homes in a certain area, prices invariably begin to creep upwards. Items that were previously included in the purchase price now become extras. The selection of homes and the availability of certain models becomes quite limited. Like the early bird, it's the early buyer who benefits.

Stores going out of business often cut their prices to promote the quick sale of merchandise. The same holds true in the newly-built home market. Builders want to sell off their remaining homes as quickly as possible because a good portion of their profits may be tied up in those last few houses. Keep in mind of course, that the selection of homes may not be as great as before. Still, to encourage prospective purchasers to take this remaining inventory off their hands, builders once again may be willing to negotiate and "throw in"extras. Like any other "clear-out" sale, buyers must be prepared to act fast. That's all the more reason why advance preparation of your HOBS is essential.

Never overlook your future intentions for the house in considering the question of timing. Buying a house and holding it for only a year or two could work against you if development in the immediate vicinity will be taking place for years to come. Selling a "used" home when your own builder is marketing the same home "new" could prove very difficult, especially if he is offering features such as a full new home warranty and total color selection. Whenever possible, avoid competing with your own builder in this way.

Finally, the whole question of timing depends to a large extent on the state of the real estate market in a particular community at a given point in time. Where the market is flat or stagnant, the value of a house will not rise appreciably before it is built. Yet in a strong market, when the time-gap between signing the offer and delivery of the home is lengthened due to the heightened demand, house prices may increase considerably. Properly timing your purchase then takes on added importance. As part of your HOBS, check the newspapers and talk to sales agents to learn more about the current state of the new home market in your area. How else can you know if the time is right to buy?

Timing your purchase is one of the most important aspects of purchasing a newly-built house. While your individual circumstances will dictate precisely when to buy, developing a home purchase timetable early on, before any commitments are made, is fundamental to the success of your HOBS. If you already own a home, your timetable will be further complicated by the need to sell your present home. The question of when do you sell is examined in the next chapter.

Tips and Pointers

- Be different. To save money, buy when the market is quiet.
- When buying a house that is yet to be built, first consider when you want to close. Then work backwards from that date to decide when to begin house hunting.
- Being among the first or last buyers in a development can save you money.

4

Buy First or Sell First?

What a dilemma. Do you buy your new house first and then worry about selling the existing home, or vice-versa? It's the old "chicken and egg" question, repackaged for the 1980s. Is there any way to reduce the uncertainty and anxiety people face in these "back-to-back" or "double-ender" transactions? How does the state of the market affect their decision?

If you are a first time home buyer, don't just skip over this chapter. Eventually you too will be selling the home you're about to buy.

Consider Howard and Sheila, who faced the classic buy-first or sell-first dilemma. What they did was typical. Once they had decided to move, they directed all their energy into finding a new home. Applying their home-buying strategy, Howard and Sheila began analyzing needs and wants, communities and neighborhoods, mortgage packages and financial commitments. Of course, this focus on the future sharpened dramatically once they found their ideal home. The sale of their present house was almost an afterthought, a foregone conclusion. Surely *someone* would want to buy that property, presumably at the price Howard and Sheila were hoping to get for it.

Once the new home offer was signed, selling the present home quickly their number-one priority. As the clock ticked away, though, and their house remained unsold, Howard and Sheila became increasingly nervous. Even though closing still was four months away, each passing day reduced their chance to haggle over price and other terms. Howard and Sheila eventually just wanted to get their house sold to end their self-made nightmare!

Finally, after substantially reducing their price and including all appliances in the deal, Howard and Sheila were able to rid themselves of their old home. They learned the hard way of the danger in buying first. If you cannot sell your current home before the new-home purchase is scheduled to close, you will have only two choices: lower your expectations to complete the sale, or wind up owning two houses!

The other side of the coin is to sell first and buy later, as Gord and Connie did. Knowing their house was sold gave them considerable peace of mind. They could then concentrate their efforts on buying the newly-built house, knowing as well the appropriate price range for that purchase.

Still, selling before buying does have its own shortcomings. Jim and Kathy encountered a different type of time constraint — finding a suitable new home before completing the sale of their present home. As that closing inched closer, the pressure on Jim and Kathy to make a decision and sign a new home offer increased. No longer could they leisurely dicker over price and other features. They faced the distinct possibility of having no place to live! Eventually Jim and Kathy ended up buying that newly-built home — and spending more than they had planned!

Rob and Ellen's problem was slightly different. Although they sold first and bought later, completion of their newly-built home was delayed because of a strike in the construction industry. After carefully examining the different temporary accommodations that were available — renting an apartment on a short-term basis, living in a hotel, or staying with family or friends — they decided to move in with Ellen's parents. It was an experience none of them will forget.

In "back-to-back" or "double-ender" transactions, regardless of whether the sale or purchase comes first, a legitimate concern is what happens to the purchase if the sale doesn't close? Does this mean the existing home should not be sold until the new home purchase is completed? Realistically, that isn't practical. Few people have the financial resources to close and take possession of their new home, and only then start to work at selling their current home. Although it may be small consolation to home owners facing this dilemma, remember that few residential resale transactions do not close as scheduled. Most problems that arise are not insurmountable. And a buyer's reluctance to proceed with the deal usually can be detected early. The seller then should have enough time to resell the property to someone else.

Since most people think buy first instead of sell first, some mechanism is needed to protect overzealous purchasers from themselves. The solution is the "conditional on sale" offer, the cautious route Steve and Ruth chose to follow. When they bought their new home from the builder, the offer was made conditional on their existing home being sold within a short, specified period of time, usually 30 to 60 days. If no one bought their present home in this time, Steve and Ruth could back out of the new home deal, and have their full deposit refunded.

Long conditional periods benefit buyers, giving them more time to sell their current homes. Besides this, most builders today will not even start to work on the new house until the "conditional on sale" clause is removed. Together this means buyers can have a lengthier period, even 90 days and more, in which to list and sell their current home without prejudicing the builder.

Yet conditional offers are not always the great cure-all for buyers they first appear to be. Builders prefer unconditional offers, since a firm and binding contract is immediately created once the offer is accepted. For the buyer, an advantage of selling first is that they can "go in firm" with the new home offer, and not be concerned with a conditional offer to purchase.

Whether or not a builder will accept a conditional offer largely depends on the current state of the real estate market. When the market is soft and demand for houses is weak, builders are anxious to get *any* offer on their homes. In this market, an offer made conditional on selling your present home is more likely to gain acceptance. In a strong "seller's market," when the demand for homes is high, builders are unwilling to tie up a property this way. Before long, another buyer will submit an unconditional offer to buy that same house. Consequently, to get the house you really want in a seller's market, it may be necessary to "go in firm," whether or not you have already sold your house. All the more reason why finding out more about the real estate market before making any commitments is a key component of your HOBS.

Timing and the current state of the market also influence the decision whether to buy first unconditionally, or sell first. Two rules of thumb are to buy first in a rising market, and to sell first in a falling market. Of course, this begs the question: How can you tell if the market will rise or fall in the immediate future?

Larry and Wendy decided to buy first in a rising market. Not only were they able to fix the price for their new home, but the strong resale market also gave them the chance to get the best possible price for their current house. Up to closing, their newly-built house rose in value too — an added plus.

The reverse would apply in a declining market. Again, buying first fixes the price for the new home. However, the drop in prices means a lower-than-anticipated sale price for the present home. Purchasers who bought first faced this crisis during the severe economic down-turn of 1981.

Purchasers of pre-sale homes face a sizeable time-lag between acceptance of the offer and closing. When considerable preliminary work is needed before construction of the house can even begin, the time between acceptance and closing is even longer. This makes purchasers unintentional speculators, as they try to determine where the market is heading four months, six months, or possibly even a year down the road. Not an easy task for the average purchaser, especially when the experts themselves are divided about what the future holds in store.

Good arguments exist both for selling and buying first, so there is no "right" answer. Prudent purchasers applying their home-buying strategy will sell first for the security and stability it brings. Human nature being what it is, though, most people will buy first, and assume there will be no problem disposing of the current residence at a good price. Making the purchase "conditional on sale" is an excellent compromise, if the builder and market conditions permit.

Tips and Pointers

- Buying first assumes the existing house can be sold on favorable terms; is the market strong enough to make this assumption?
- While selling their present home first is comforting to home owners, it can create its own pressure situations.
- "Conditional on sale" offers may not always be accepted. Asking for them in a seller's market could jeopardize your purchase.

5

Different Types of Homes

It goes without saying that it's easier to find something when you know what to look for! Today, there's a broad range of different types of houses, styles of homes and forms of legal ownership available in the marketplace. Never before have buyers had such a great array to choose from. One of the first steps in developing your HOBS is to know what the alternatives are, and to examine them. Only by knowing what's out there can you start applying that home-buying strategy.

Types of Homes

a) Single-Family Detached Dwelling — Still the most popular type of home, resale or newly-built. The house is not joined to any other dwelling. More expensive than other types of homes, since detached homes occupy larger lots. They offer the greatest amount of privacy.

b) Semi-Detached Dwelling — "Semis" are two houses attached by a common wall. The connection may run the length of the house, or there may simply be a common wall between garages.

c) Linked Dwelling — This is a variation of the semi-detached dwelling. Two houses that appear detached above ground are actually attached underground. A very popular type of home in suburban areas, where land values are very high.

d) Duplex or Triplex — Two or three dwelling units stacked one above the other, in one building. Two buildings are often attached to create a four-plex or six-plex. Fewer of these are being built today compared to years ago.

e) Row Housing — A number of homes with similar designs are

joined together with common walls. Sometimes called "freehold townhouses," row housing is *not* the same as a condominium complex. Each home owner owns both the building as well as the lot on which the building sits.

f) Street Townhouses — While it visually resembles row housing, all the land in the townhouse complex is owned by a condominium corporation, not the individual home owners. All the owner acquires is the unit and an interest in the land. This "non-high-rise" type of condominium is very popular today.

Styles of Homes

a) Bungalow — A one-story house. Not too popular today, not being overly energy efficient.

b) Two-story — The entire property is two stories high.

c) Split-level — Sometimes called a one and a-half, part of the house is one-story high, and part of it is two stories high. In a side-split, the second story is on the side of the house. In a back-split, the second story is at the rear.

d) Condominium Apartment — A condominium apartment looks exactly the same as a rental apartment building. However, the units are individually owned, each owner also having an interest in the common areas. "Condos" are rapidly increasing in popularity.

Forms of Legal Ownership

a) Freehold — Where the home owner owns both the building and the land on which it sits. Far and away the most desired form of legal ownership.

b) Leasehold — In a leasehold parcel of land, the home owner owns the building. The land on which it sits is rented, often from a government agency.

c) Condominium — Here a specific unit is owned, together with a proportionate interest in the common areas. It is usually situated in a condominium apartment building or townhouse complex. For more information on condominiums, see Chapter 20.

d) Co-op — Instead of owning a specific unit, the co-op owner is a shareholder in the corporation that owns the entire building. In a co-op sale, the share and not the unit is transferred to the new owner. The owner only has the exclusive right to use and occupy that specific unit. Restrictions on selling the share may exist, or prior approval may be needed from the Board of Directors. Do not confuse private co-ops with government subsidized co-ops, where the units are rented, not owned. Not too popular as new owner-occupied housing.

e) Co-ownership — Instead of being a shareholder in a corporation as in a co-op, or owning a specific unit like a condominium, co-owners only own a percentage interest in the building with everyone else. Again, the co-owner has the exclusive right to use and occupy a specific unit, but the title is not registered in his name. Co-ownership rarely applies to newly-built buildings. It is used most often as a means of avoiding registration as a condominium when an existing rental apartment building is being converted. There are many problems inherent in this type of ownership.

With a HOBS in hand, and a better understanding of housing types and ownership options, purchasers are now ready to begin the pleasant task of house-hunting. But remember, at this stage it's only to look and learn, and not to buy.

Tips and Pointers

- Different types and styles of homes are available today.
- Make sure you understand fully the type of legal ownership that interests you.
- If you're in doubt about any of the differences among types of ownership, consult your lawyer.

Part Two

PUTTING YOUR STRATEGY TO WORK

6

Needs and Wants

One of the key components in designing and applying your own HOBS is a careful examination of your needs and wants. This self-analysis must be done *before* you ever start seriously looking for a newly-built home. As with any game plan or strategy, it will be modified with time, as you view more and more houses.

Too often the first question sales agents ask buyers is: How much do you want to spend? This looks at the home purchase from the wrong perspective — the spending side. The proper question to ask yourself is this: What do I need to buy? It's so important, it bears repeating. WHAT DO I NEED TO BUY? This question emphasizes what a house must provide — the buying side. As everyone's situation is different, only *you* can properly analyze your own requirements. But the points raised in this chapter will go a long way in helping purchasers answer this fundamental question.

You must be realistic in your expectations. Everyone would like to buy the biggest and nicest property available, but that's not practical. Rarely is the first home you buy the last home you'll ever buy. That's why the real estate industry refers to some properties as "starter homes." These properties, typically 1,100 to 1,400 square feet in size, satisfy most buyers' basic needs. Their role is straightforward — to get first-time home buyers into the market, and into a home that satisfies their needs and wants for the present and foreseeable future. Of course, a starter home also must be affordable.

Circumstances change over time. Families grow in size, tastes change, and both incomes and savings increase. Home buyers often trade in their former homes to buy larger, more prestigious residences. Many home owners buy and sell several times until they find a "permanent" residence, a "dream home."

In creating their HOBS, purchasers of newly-built homes will find it helpful to prepare two different shopping lists before doing any serious house-hunting. The first should be a "needs" list, containing those essential features the house must have. The second should be a "wants" list, with those items you would like to have, if they are available and affordable. These optional features should be listed according to personal preferences, with the most important and desired features at the top.

Armed with these two personalized catalogues, the house you eventually buy should satisfy all your needs and as many wants as possible, while still remaining affordable.

The basic features in any house are the bedrooms and bathroom, kitchen, living room, dining room and storage space. After that, individual taste determines what the home should contain. How many bedrooms are needed or desired? How large should they be? How many bathrooms? How large a kitchen? Where is the laundry room?

To help answer these questions, measure your furniture, and size the rooms in your present house. How much room do the children need for play without disturbing anyone? What about the increasingly popular family room? How many levels of stairs are in the house? Is air conditioning needed or desired? One-car or two-car garage? Simply put, you have to decide what that house must provide.

Developing your unique HOBS — home-buying strategy — takes a considerable investment of time and effort. Each visit to a new home sales trailer will help refine your all-important needs and wants lists. Over time, the lists will be adjusted and polished up, eventually allowing you to quickly decide if a particular property is appropriate.

Begin preparing your shopping lists in the space below by recording what you consider to be both essential and desirable in a home.

	NEEDS	WANTS

Size of house
Bedroom
Bathroom
Kitchen
Living Room

Dining Room
Storage Space
Laundry Room
Garage
Other Rooms
(Family Room)
Other Features
(Air Conditioning)

Clearly defining your particular needs and wants is an important first step in buying a newly-built house. Now, the key is to find precisely what you are looking for. So far, HOBS has required purchasers to look inward, thoroughly examining themselves. Now the time has come to apply that same approach outwardly, to learn more about possible communities and neighborhoods where that newly-built home might be bought.

Tips and Pointers

- The all-important question is this: What do I need to buy, not how much do I want to spend.
- The right house is one that is both appropriate to your needs and wants, and that is affordable, too.
- Complete the checklist in pencil. Its contents will probably change over time.

7

Location, Location, Location

It may be a cliché, but it bears repeating. When buying real estate, there are only three important factors — location, location and location. But what does this emphasis on location really mean? In designing a HOBS, remember that each "location" represents a different geographical area that must be explored and considered before any decision on where to buy is made. Only when you know more about location-community; location-neighborhood within a community; and location-specific site, are you ready to make any kind of commitment to purchase. As resale potential and market appeal are important considerations in any home-buying strategy, the property selected should be the best possible location as defined in these three different ways.

This chapter will examine the items to consider in selecting a community and neighborhood. Factors affecting specific site locations are explored in the next chapter. This approach mirrors the way that most people buy newly-constructed homes. First they decide to move to a certain community, and then they focus on the neighborhood with the most desirable features. Specific site factors come into play at the very end, as the purchaser narrows down the various options.

So far, any ventures into the new-home market have been simply to look and to learn. Now your house-hunting expedition is about to become more serious, more enjoyable and more meaningful. Investigating different communities and neighborhoods takes on added importance, as you learn more about the housing market — house prices, values and price ranges — in areas that appeal to you. Be sure to check the ads for newly-built homes in the weekend edition of the local newspaper. Visit builders' sales trailers and pick up their literature and brochures. Start analyzing what each builder has to offer, and at what price.

A community and neighborhood should reflect your lifestyle and station in life. As part of your HOBS, spend some time driving and walking around those areas that capture your imagination. If possible, stop and talk with some of the residents to learn more about the district. Who better to advise you what an area is like!

Local residents can also tell you which builder constructed their homes, and if they encountered any serious problems either before closing or with after-sales service. Ask the locals: Are there any other builders with good reputations in the area? What has happened to house prices in the community and neighborhood since they bought? There's a great deal of information and experience at your fingertips — just inquire!

One of the biggest uncertainties in buying a newly-built home is not knowing what will be constructed in the surrounding area. As part of your HOBS, you should *independently verify* what is planned for the immediate vicinity before making any commitment to purchase. Never simply rely on what you are told, even by a sales agent. Most information about development and land use plans can be confirmed by a simple phone call to the municipal planning department or local school board.

Danny and Marilyn, for example, were very concerned about a medium-sized vacant tract of land only four lots away from the home they considered buying. Although the land was zoned residential, rumour had it that a small plaza would be built there. As the prospects of a plaza greatly bothered them, Danny and Marilyn visited the local municipal offices. Yes, the property was zoned residential, but an application was pending to rezone the land for commercial use. Danny and Marilyn bought elsewhere in the community.

Some municipalities have made life easier for purchasers of newly-built homes by requiring that land-use plans for new subdivisions, drawn to scale and *approved by the municipality,* be displayed in every sales pavillion. The plan will help you visualize how the area will look when fully completed. Proposed and future land use such as parks, schools, church sites and commercial locations, transit routes and bus loops must be clearly marked. So must proposed road extensions and highways, railway lines and hydro transmission towers. So too must sidewalks, walkways, bicycle paths, and the location and extent of any existing or proposed fences along lot boundaries. These land use plans go a long way in eliminating the uncertainty over how a new area will be developed.

New-home buyers who follow the HOBS approach should carefully review this general development plan before signing any offer. If the plans for the area you're considering are not available, keep on asking questions until you know how all the vacant land will be developed within a radius of at least one kilometre.

Remember too that a newer community and neighborhood will lack the maturity, charm and character of a more established area for years to come. In its place, though, developing areas project youthfulness, vitality and freshness. Growing communities will also lack the support services, transportation facilities, schools and shopping available in more established areas. Know what to anticipate. Don't expect full-grown trees, parks and nicely manicured lawns. Count on having construction vehicles, messy roads and young, newly-planted trees on the boulevard. These are just some of the trade-offs between the two types of areas.

Make notes as you go along, recording your thoughts and reactions to specific areas. How appealing is the existing development and the future plans? What makes this community and neighborhood different from other areas? Would you like to be part of it?

Be a thorough explorer. If possible, visit the community and neighborhood both on a weekday as well as on the weekend. See them by day and by night, since some areas take on a different character after sunset. Acceptable noise levels by day may turn out to be totally unacceptable at night, when sound travels much farther. Are the streets adequately lit? Does the area appear both safe and serene at night?

All this exploring has been just a preliminary hurdle to whittling down the list of potential candidates! By now, several communities and neighborhoods should have caught your imagination. Investigate them even further, this time measuring them against the features that follow. As many of these standards are very subjective, every potential buyer will rank and weigh them differently. Still, these factors should be viewed as objectively as possible, since they will greatly affect the all-important resale potential of a property. Never simply ignore or downplay the negative. The more positive factors a property has to offer, the greater its future marketability. And remember, *every* home will be resold eventually.

Distance to work and other activities

Check both travel time and distance to important places like work. Most new developments are located in outlying urban areas. This means newly-built home buyers must be prepared to spend more time commuting to work and travelling elsewhere (i.e., to theaters and restaurants, to family and friends, and to other activities in the urban core). More time spent commuting means less time with family or enjoying some of life's other pleasures. In return, commuter communities usually offer more reasonably priced homes. But rarely is this trade-off permanent. New facilities, features and employment opportunities soon move into a community as part of its growth.

Whenever possible, do a test run to work in rush hour. For comparison, try it as well during off-peak hours. Don and Aline did a rush-hour test before they moved to a new suburban community, and were satisfied with the results. No surprises for them the first day they headed for work after moving!

Transportation

It's a fact of life that new communities lack adequate public transportation. The reason is simple — the demand is just not present. Nonexistent, irregular or limited transit service is an important consideration for one-car families. Never rely too heavily on projected start-up dates for new transit routes, or the extension of existing lines into your area.

If public transit is available, find out how frequently it is provided, especially at night and on weekends. Will an extra fare be charged? Find out where the nearest transit or commuter stop is located. During the worst blizzard, the farthest anyone would want to walk to or from a bus or train is about one kilometer.

Besides public transportation, you should examine the network of roads and highways servicing the community. It's nice to be close to a highway or expressway, but not too close! Are there any plans for a new highway or an interchange in the general vicinity? Where will it be located, and when will it be built? Again, in many cases projected start-up dates are little more than educated guesses. Are the present roads wide enough to accommodate rush-hour traffic, especially when all planned development is completed? If not, traffic tie-ups may become part of your daily routine, followed by a major roads project that will cause snarls for months.

Schools

Probably the number-one concern of most home buyers in developing communities and neighborhoods is the proximity of schools. In contrast to older areas, newer communities lack the necessary "infill" of all types of schools — public and separate; primary and high schools. This means busing and portable classrooms are a way of life.

In many subdivisions you may see signs proclaiming "future school site." While the site may be set aside for a school, that designation is no guarantee a school will be built. Usually the construction date will not be determined for a number of years. In fact, if the need for the school never arises, homes could eventually be built on the site.

If being close to a school is important, find out from the school board where that school site sits on the priority list for construction. Never simply rely on signs, subdivision plans showing school sites or a sales agent's comments about a school. You may be surprised to learn that the likelihood of a school being built in a particular location is slim to none.

Also, investigate the school system itself. Different boards of education offer different types of programs (i.e., gifted child classes; services for the disabled; French Immersion). Find out before you buy whether the local board carries desired educational programs for your children.

Shopping

Commercial development trails the growth of new residential communities and neighborhoods. Businesses appear only when there are enough residents in an area to make a commercial project economically viable. Until then, plan to travel some distance for the kind of shopping you have been accustomed to.

This means part of your HOBS is to find out where *existing* shopping centers and plazas are located. That magnificent mall everyone is talking about for your area may be years in the making. The local municipality can give you a much better idea when construction is expected to begin.

As with schools, people like to be close to shopping — but not too close! Whether it's traffic congestion, noise, or just kids "hanging out," living near a commercial development, big or small, can be unpleasant. Even though it may not bother you, it could deter someone else from buying your property. Therefore, always look at a home from two different perspectives — your own, and that of a future buyer (its resale potential).

Support Services

Think of the health care people you rely on regularly — doctor, dentist, druggist, paediatrician. Rarely are they in the vanguard of development. Instead, like commercial development, they follow the leader, part of the "in-fill" that takes place once a large number of homes have been sold, built and occupied.

Adequate police protection, fire stations, ambulance depots, daycare centers, libraries, hospitals and frequent garbage pickups also follow slowly in the wake of residential development. Residents in new subdivisions can often be heard clamoring for these services shortly after they move in, especially if they have come from more established areas.

Recreational Facilities

Although communities and neighborhoods will eventually have modern, new recreational facilities, these amenities are not always in place for the first wave of residents. Typical facilities which appear over time are parks, playgrounds, tennis courts, skating rinks, swimming pools, libraries, community centers, theaters and museums.

Some municipalities, like the one George and Pauline moved to, recognize that new residents are anxious for high-quality recreational facilities. As part of the development agreement with the municipality, all the developers had to contribute money to a recreational fund which was used to build a major recreational complex in the heart of the community. The complex now is being maintained by user fees paid by people like George and Pauline who use the facilities for skating, swimming, or club meetings. With this approach, the community gained a state-of-the-art and fully-paid-for facility, which opened its doors just three years after the first house was sold.

To learn more about plans for recreational facilities, contact the local municipality.

Lot Levies

Lot levies are fees charged by municipalities to developers on a per lot basis in new subdivisions. This cost is passed on to the builder and then to the buyer, who ultimately pays the charge. In theory the levy is collected to provide a fund from which the municipality can provide the necessary "hard" services new developments need — highways, sewage treatment facilities and the like. What upsets developers and builders, however, is the use of these funds for so-called "soft" services, such as police stations, swimming pools, parks and libraries. How lot levies should be used is very much a political issue. Their impact on house prices is equally controversial.

For example, Maison Construction built identical homes in two subdivisions in two adjacent municipalities, Cheeper and Costley. Because of a higher lot levy, Maison had to charge $2,500 more to sell its homes in Costley.

Cheeper's lot levy was applied to hard services only, while the additional money Costley collected was used to provide soft services. In both areas Maison Construction made the same net profit. Predictably, the homes buyers perceived as being more reasonably priced in Cheeper were sold more quickly.

Try to discover how large a lot levy is being assessed in a community that looks promising to you. Compare that levy to those in other areas. Find out if the levy covers hard or both hard and soft services. This will give you a better indication of the "true cost" of the home.

Peer Pressure

More than any other reason, people are attracted to specific communities and neighborhoods to be with their peers. It may be the desire to live in an area with others from similar ethnic, cultural or religious backgrounds; to have children in the neighborhood similar in age to their children; to be close to good friends; or a combination of all three.

But moving to a certain community or neighborhood has to make good sense for all the right reasons — needs, wants and ability to pay. Never decide on a move simply because "everyone else is doing it." As pleasant as moving to a new area with friends might seem, resist the temptation if your home-buying strategy indicates the move is not appropriate for you. The head must do the talking and the heart must listen. Yet if everything else is in order, the desire to live with contemporaries could well be the deciding factor in buying a home in a particular community and neighborhood.

Other Factors

Many other factors must be explored and considered *before* making any decisions on a community and neighborhood.

a) *Postal Service.* As part of its Community Mailbox Program, Canada Post will *no longer* provide regular door-to-door mail delivery in new subdivisions. Instead, all new urban areas will have "Supermailboxes" from which residents can pick up their own mail, and deposit outgoing mail. To be located no more than 600 feet from any home, the new boxes have been designed to "fit right into the look of your street." While not as convenient as home delivery, community boxes are a marked improvement over the first stage of mail service in many new communities where residents must pick up their mail at the local post office. A far cry from the door-to-door service people who live in mature neighborhoods are accustomed to.

b) *Telephone Service.* Move from a major metropolitan area and you will quickly learn how small the local calling area is. What once was a local call now may be subject to long-distance charges. One of the small hidden costs of moving.

c) *Religious Facilities.* Some people find it important to live near a religious facility, be it a church, synagogue or religious school. Occasionally, a neighborhood centers around a religious facility and develops a distinct religious orientation.

d) *Potential Deterrants.* With land being such a valuable commodity today, homes are being built near major thoroughfares, industrial parks, airports, railway yards, cemeteries, and apartment buildings. Close proximity to an industrial park, for example, may seem unimportant to you, but may have a great impact on what your property is worth to someone else. Just as a newly-built house with a number of negative factors may cost less to buy, by the same token it will generate a lower price as a resale home. Look at these possible deterrants *objectively* in developing your HOBS, to avoid undermining the resale potential of a home.

A key reason for a HOBS is to help you realize when you have found "the right" house in "the right" area. In some respects, the experience is just like love. While it may be very difficult to express in words, when you have found your "right" house, you know it!

Use a form similar to the one below to record your observations about communities and neighborhoods that look interesting and promising.

COMMUNITY/NEIGHBORHOOD   NOTES
Proximity to work and
    other activities

Transportation
Schools
Shopping
Support Services
Recreational facilities
Other factors

It's one thing to examine communities and neighborhood and to start narrowing down the choices. Now you must think about particular sites within a community and neighborhood, and the many issues that will influence your decision.

Tips and Pointers

- Always bear in mind the resale potential of a house. Look at location factors as objectively as possible.
- Carefully explore appealing communities and neighborhoods, and verify what you are told. Leave nothing to chance.
- Record your thoughts and impressions as you go along. These notes will help you compare different areas more easily.

8

Factors Affecting the Home Site

In the last chapter, location was examined from two different viewpoints; the community and smaller neighborhoods within that community. When devising your home-buying strategy, you cannot overlook the many factors that will affect your selection of the actual home site. Just as with selecting a community and neighborhood, you must consider these specific site features as objectively as possible. Always remember their impact on the resale potential of a home.

Purchasers of newly-built homes have an advantage rarely available in the resale market. Deciding where to buy in terms of community and neighborhood is not the final "location" question to be answered when buying from a builder. In most cases, the buyer also is given a choice of lots from the builder's inventory. This means factors affecting the home site take on added importance.*Before* you finally decide where your newly-built home will be located, carefully consider the following points as part of your HOBS.

Lot Size

Shorter, narrower lots are one way of keeping the cost of new housing affordable. Lot sizes are usually quoted in terms of street frontage, such as 30-foot and 40-foot lots. Too often, lot depth is overlooked; how large (or small) are the front and rear yards? As land values have increased, lot depths in urban areas have shrunk from 120 feet to 100 feet, allowing developers to build more homes per acre. Shorter lots mean shorter driveways too, cutting down the number of cars that can be accommodated. This has resulted in serious street parking problems, especially in developments with narrow lots. When comparing lot sizes, *don't forget about depth.*

Part of the impact from the conversion to metric measurements has been the further reduction in lot sizes. Today's "metric" 35-foot by 100-foot lot is often 10.5m by 30m. Converted to Imperial measure, you wind up with a lot 34.45 feet by 98.43 feet!

How large a house can be built on a lot depends on the size of the lot itself, a feature called "coverage." Coverage is extremely important to anyone planning to build an addition or extension in the future. For example, sixty percent coverage means the size of the house cannot exceed 60 percent of the size of the lot, all calculated in square feet. The 1,800-square-foot house Arnold and Hyla bought sits on a lot 40 feet by 100 feet. As the maximum allowable coverage is 60 percent, the largest house permitted on the lot would be 2,400 square feet (60 percent of 4,000 square feet). Lots of room to construct an addition in the future. Obviously, bigger lots can support bigger houses.

Parking

Having a two-car garage is very important to many people. But a big garage requires a wide lot and increases the price for that newly-built home. Ask yourself if a two-car garage is absolutely necessary. Will a one-car garage be adequate? Is a longer driveway a practical alternative?

Road Allowance

Like most people, Ron and Jennie were shocked to learn that much of their front yard does not belong to them! That's right, it's owned by the municipality. In Ontario, for example, the typical road allowance — the strip of land owned by the municipality — is 66 feet wide. Since the paved portion of the roadway on Ron and Jennie's street is only 26 feet wide, an additional 20 feet on each side of the curb is municipal property. Included here are the grassy boulevard, the sidewalk, and the underground municipal services. The rest of the 66-foot-wide strip looks like part of Ron and Jennie's (and their neighbor's) front yard, and they treat it as part of their front yard. But it is actually owned by the municipality.

In addition to this road allowance, the municipality also owns triangular pieces of property at all four corners of a street intersection in new subdivisions, called "sight triangles." Rick and Phyllis wisely checked this out before planting shrubs and trees in the front yard. Otherwise, the municipality could trim or even cut down the shrubs and trees on its sight triangle, if the line of vision for motorists approaching the intersection was being obstructed.

To learn where the municipally owned road allowance or sight triangle begins on a lot, measure the distance from the building to the lot line based on the information in the survey. Surveys are examined later in this chapter.

Municipal Easements

Years ago, service corridors of telephone and hydro wires usually ran above ground across the width of a lot at the rear. Often five feet wide, these strips of land are known as municipal easements or rights-of-way. In some areas, these services were buried at the back of the lot.

In today's new subdivisions, electricity, natural gas, water, cable TV and telephone service corridors are located underground, buried below the municipal road allowance at the front of the house. One easement, though, that runs across the rear of many newly-built homes, like the one Howard and Bonnie own, is for a drainage pipe and catch-basin. Although Howard and Bonnie own the rear five feet of the lot where this easement is located, municipal employees have access to that portion of the property, without being considered trespassers.

Increased concern over storm water management has resulted in detailed drainage plans for new subdivisions. Catch-basins play an important role as the external outlets for the overland flow of water into the storm sewer system. Catch-basins are those unsightly grates at the rear of some properties, where the terrain slopes downwards to direct the flow of water. Detailed agreements registered on title require that the area surrounding the catch-basin be kept clear of buildings, structures, improvements and land-scaping. If necessary the municipality can trim trees and shrubs — even remove them — so that the catch-basin and drainage pipe can be dug up if a problem occurs. Many people consider a catch-basin detrimentally affects the use and enjoyment — and value — of their property.

Make any specific plans to use part of the rear yard (such as a swimming pool) well known to the sales agent and your lawyer so the proper precautions can be taken before you sign an offer to purchase. Examine the "plot plans" discussed later in this chapter for any catch-basins. Check with the local municipality to learn if any are planned at the rear of your proposed lot. If necessary, add a clause to the offer that no catch-basins will be located on your property. Now is the time to explore, examine and protect yourself, not later.

Party Walls

Jack lives in a semi-detached home; his neighbor is Nick. The wall that runs the entire length between their homes is called a party wall. The middle of the party wall is the lot line. Neither Jack nor Nick can remove his part of the wall without the other's consent, since it provides structural support for both homes. This same principle applies to units of row housing as well.

Noise from the adjoining property is sometimes a concern with party walls. Inadequate soundproofing could mean that you unwillingly overhear much of what your neighbor says and does. Be sure to inquire about the amount of soundproofing to be installed. The transmission of noise through a party wall may be annoying, and could affect the resale potential of the house.

Zero Lot Lines

Municipal zoning by-laws require that homes have specified "setbacks," the prescribed distance between the house and the front, side and rear yard property lines. Very often the side yard set-back is four feet, so that the minimum area between two houses is eight feet.

Faced with skyrocketing land prices in urban and suburban areas, builders looked for new ways to increase densities for each acre of land, and thus keep the cost of newly-built homes down. To accomplish this goal, a new planning concept was developed in the 1960s and 1970s called "zero lot line."

Zoning requirements were changed, so developers in some areas could reduce the gap between houses. Instead of having two homes four feet from the lot line, with zero lot line one house has a four foot set-back from the lot line, while the other is built just inches away from it, so the set-back is virtually nil. The total distance between the houses is cut almost in half, the developer gaining almost four feet per lot this way. Zero lot line is an ingenious way for developers to do the impossible — create more land!

As an example, all houses on the following survey sketch have a zero lot line on their southern boundary. No house is built right on the boundary line, since the below-ground footings plus the above-ground eavestroughs, downspouts and roof overhangs must not encroach on the adjoining property. The area between the houses, marked 5, 6, 7 and 8, are called "maintenance easements." These areas of common usage are a necessity with zero lot line properties.

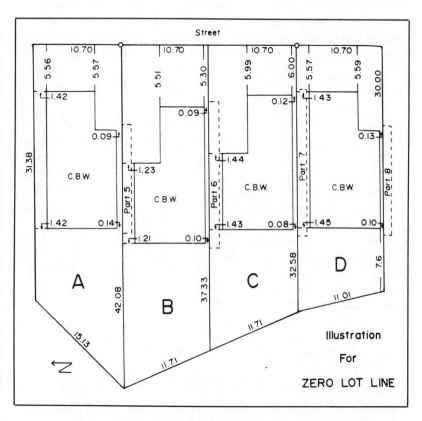

Bert owns Lot A. Lot B, which includes Part 5 between their two homes, is owned by Ernie. Bert's deed gives him access over Part 5 *only* of Ernie's property, without interference from Ernie. This allows Bert to maintain his property without being considered a trespasser. Ernie's deed confirms this right. Practically speaking, Bert can use the area between the two houses as if he owned it, to paint his house, clean the eavestroughs and downspouts, gain access to his roof, and repair, replace and otherwise maintain his property. Ernie, in turn, has a similar right of access over Part 6 on Lot C owned by Oscar.

Zero lot lines have been severely criticized in recent years, and have begun to fall into disfavor. Homes packed so tightly together produce a claustrophobic "army barracks" look. Smaller areas between houses are a potential fire hazard as well. It would not take much of a wind for a fire in one home to spread to adjoining properties. Because maintenance easements receive very little sun, grass will rarely grow between the houses. Unless they are covered with crushed stones, patio stones or bricks, maintenance easements tend to be unsightly at the best of times and worse following a storm.

Corner Lots

It seems there is no middle ground here — either you love them or hate them. Why select a corner lot? They provide a feel and look of roominess, with portions of two road allowances available for the homeowner's use. Corner lots often are made wider for visual impact, to avoid giving a street a tunnel-like appearance. Windows are also practical on at least three sides of the corner-lot house, something not always possible on the narrow lots so prevalent today.

On the other hand, all that extra land means extra work cutting the grass and cleaning two sidewalks of snow. Erecting a fence will cost more, since there is no neighbor on one side to split the cost. Privacy and security concerns are heightened as well with corner lots. Unless the rear yard is totally enclosed with a privacy fence, patio furniture, lawn equipment, barbeques and other personal possessions are all open to public view and possible theft. Heating the corner-lot house will probably cost more too, since the dwelling is exposed to the elements on three sides.

On the Sunny Side of the Street

The title of a once-popular song is one of those small but important points to consider when buying any house. Most people overlook how the sun will shine on their property before buying it. Since you probably can choose your own lot, now is the time to take this factor into account.

Houses on the west side of the street receive morning sun at the front of the house, and afternoon sun in the rear yard. This is ideal for Mark and Helene, since the afternoon sunlight gives their two young children additional time for outdoor play. Mark and Helene also made sure the master bedroom did not face east or south, since they both dislike waking to bright morning sun. On the other side of the street, of course, the reverse holds true.

After one winter, Mick and Carol noticed that the snow on their front yard and driveway, located on the north side of the street, melted faster than the snow at Ted and Maureen's home across the street. But Ted and Maureen enjoy having breakfast in the morning sun as their kitchen is in the rear of the house. Also Maureen, who loves sunbathing, receives more sun in her yard than Carol's.

When you're deciding which side of the street to live on, carefully consider the amount of sunlight on both the inside and the outside of your house, and how it suits your own personal lifestyle.

Zoning By-laws

Few people think about zoning when buying a house. They assume a residential neighborhood must be zoned residential. Because of the great impact zoning can have on a community, its neighborhoods and even your own home, purchasers of newly-built homes should know more about zoning before they buy.

Zoning by-laws affect home ownership in three ways:

a) How a property can be used
b) Height restrictions and "set-back" requirements
c) Different densities (number of units permitted per acre), even within a so-called residential neighborhood.

Unless a proposed use appears in the zoning by-law, it is not permitted. Changing the by-law involves rezoning the property, an expensive, lengthy procedure that usually requires an application to the local municipal council. Therefore, if you plan to use the property in a particular way, check the zoning with the local municipality early, before signing any offer to purchase. Do not rely on what the builder's sales agent may tell you. To learn afterwards could be too late.

Installing a satellite dish in their backyard was uppermost in Michael and Judy's minds. By doing their homework early, they learned that the zoning in a certain community prohibited dishes. Michael and Judy ended up buying their newly-built home elsewhere.

Set-backs are dealt with somewhat differently. Often a proposed change to the house would only slightly violate the zoning requirements. When the general intent and purpose of the zoning will be maintained, exceptions to the zoning by-law called "minor variances" are granted. The proposed addition to Lewis and Lily's home would result in the north wall being four feet eight inches from the lot line, rather than the required five feet. They sought, and were granted, a minor variance. A significant departure from the zoning requirements, however, would have required a rezoning of the property. So if you're planning any changes to the external shell of the building (called the "building envelope") in the near future, find out early about the set-back requirements.

Minor construction errors that result in set-back violations are quite common with newly-built homes. This is most likely to occur if the house is built on a curve, if the lot shape resembles a parallelogram, or if the lot is "pie-shaped" (wider at one end and tapering to a point). In Sam and Helen's case, the house was built three inches too close to the boundary line. A minor variance was required to "legitimize" the zoning infraction. But getting it meant closing was delayed for almost two months.

Although a property may be zoned "residential," the by-law may permit different density levels, which in turn allows different types of buildings to be built. Imagine how shocked Terry and Evelyn were to learn the "medium density" zoning in one community allowed single-family or semi-detached homes, townhouses, condominiums and apartment buildings. That doesn't leave too much that can't be built!

Keep in mind that zoning by-laws are not retroactive. Just because zoning standards are constantly being altered and tightened does not mean that a formerly legal use of a property is now illegal. If that was the case, homes would have to be torn down and businesses closed every time a zoning by-law was changed. When a zoning by-law is passed or amended, it exempts both buildings and uses that complied with the old zoning requirements. Even though they violate the current zoning, these prior legal uses known as "legal nonconforming uses,"can be continued indefinitely.

Knowing how zoning by-laws work can save considerable aggravation in the future. Robert installed a satellite dish in May, when the zoning permitted them. Marvin, his neighbor, decided to put it off for the summer. But a by-law prohibiting satellite dishes was passed in August, and now Marvin cannot install a dish without breaching the by-law. Since Robert's dish was installed before the by-law was passed, it can stay forever as a legal nonconforming use.

Part of your home-buying strategy should be to ensure that the attractive residential community and neighborhood you move into retains that character. Homeowners often complain about the impact any new development may have on property values in an area. This concern has added importance when buying a home in a new subdivision, where large tracts of undeveloped land exist. Geoff and Joan failed to make the appropriate inquiries, and were understandably irritated to learn after closing that a 20-storey apartment condominium would be built on their street just seven homes away. Never rely on a comment from the builder's sales agent about zoning matters. As we'll see in Chapter 18, agents are not accountable for any erroneous statements they make!

To best protect your future investment, call or visit the municipal offices *before you sign an offer*. Ask how the surrounding area for at least one kilometre from your proposed house is zoned, and what that zoning permits. Be sure to check the "official plan" for a general statement of land use policy and guidelines for future development. Also see if any rezoning or specific site development applications are pending that could affect the character of a neighborhood. Remember that the investment you're protecting is your own!

Registered Restrictions

While zoning by-laws are passed by municipalities to regulate the use of land, very often developers impose an even tougher set of restrictions. This ensures that the esthetic appearance of a subdivision remains appealing. Where lots are sold to different builders, these private restrictions may also regulate the type and size of homes that can be constructed.

Building restrictions or use covenants appear in a "building scheme," which is registered against the title to each lot in the subdivision. Typical registered restrictions include: no clotheslines; no permanent parking of campers, vans and trucks on the driveway; and no repairing cars on the driveway. Although the local municipality may not prohibit external TV antennae or satellite dishes, the developer's building scheme might. Most building schemes run for a fixed period of time, often 10 or 20 years, after which they automatically expire.

A clause stating that purchasers will accept title subject to any registered restrictions affecting the property is buried in most new home offers. As builders generally do not tell buyers about these restrictions, it's up to you to find out if they exist and if so, what they say. Ask the sales agent whether the developer plans to impose this type of building scheme. If he or she does not know, have your lawyer contact the builder's lawyer. Knowing this information is extremely important if you have a specific proposed use for the property in mind, even something as simple as the erection of a clothesline. In any case, how could you ever buy a newly-built home without first finding out about these registered restrictions? As part of your home-buying strategy, protect yourself properly now before making any commitment to purchase. Registered restrictions can easily become a trap for the unwary.

If no restrictions will be imposed, insert a condition into the offer to that effect, or delete the wording dealing with this point in the printed form. If title will be subject to any restrictions, get a copy of the building scheme before you sign any offer and review it carefully. Make sure you can live with the restrictions. Learn whether your proposed use is prohibited. To protect yourself further, add a condition to the offer stating that the specific use you intend is not prohibited either by by-law or registered restriction. This way, if you learn before closing that your proposed use will be prohibited, the decision whether to close the purchase is yours and yours alone.

Keep in mind that developers rarely police registered restrictions after the subdivision is sold out. Few building schemes prescribe penalties for violators, either. What's more, building schemes that allow the developer to exempt certain lots from the restrictions (as usually is the case) may not even be enforceable by law. Still, most new homes buyers honor building schemes, since they greatly enhance the appearance of the area in which they live.

State of Development

Just because a builder sells a house does not necessarily mean that the bulldozers and steam shovels move in the next morning. To understand fully why not, buyers of newly-built homes need a basic primer on how subdivisions are developed.

The most common scenario is for one company to develop a vacant tract of land by registering a plan of subdivision, "servicing" the land (as described below) and then selling those serviced lots to other companies that build the homes. In some cases, the developer is both developer and builder. After completing the preliminary work, it changes hats and constructs homes on its own land.

Newly-built homes are the end result of a planning process that does not exist in the resale market. New subdivisions today are carefully planned and heavily government regulated, a lengthy, time-consuming process. A subdivision or development agreement between the land developer and the municipality spells out the developer's responsibilities, imposes conditions that must be met before building permits will be issued, and states when homes can be occupied. Special terms deal with specific areas of the subdivision, such as the erection of fences bordering certain lots and the construction of walkways.

In many areas homes can be sold from "draft" or interim plans of subdivision, before the final subdivision plans are approved and registered. Before construction on any house sold this way (called a "pre-registration pre-sale") can begin, much needs to be done. First, the subdivision plans must be finalized. Then the developer must "service" the land *at its own expense*. Of course, these costs are passed on to buyers as part of the purchase price.

Servicing the land involves laying out and paving the streets; installing hydro and gas lines, watermains, sanitary sewers and storm sewers to the lot line, all to municipal specifications; erecting overhead street lights and other public works; constructing curbs, sidewalks and walkways; and setting aside land for parks, open spaces and school sites. The developer must provide financial security, usually letters of credit, to ensure the remaining work on the subdivision will be fully completed and all other obligations met to the municipality's satisfaction. Developers also must guarantee these services for a specified period of time, usually three years after the subdivision is completed. Only then does the municipality "assume" the subdivision, becoming the owner of the municipal services and public works, and accepting full responsibility for them.

Buyers of newly-built homes must recognize the great uncertainties they face, especially the earlier they buy in the development process. The more that needs to be done prior to construction, the less assurance there is that the house they bought will ever be built. Even if it is built there is no guarantee it will be ready for occupancy on the scheduled closing date. This explains why it is so important for purchasers of newly-built homes to find out exactly what remains to be done before construction can start.

Never rush in and buy a newly-built home without knowing more about the state of development of the subdivision. Before you sign any offer to purchase, be sure to get thorough and complete answers to the following questions dealing with the "timing" or status of the subdivision development. The points below will help you understand better both when *and if* the deal will close:

1. Is the subdivision registered yet? If not, the house being sold is a "pre-registration pre-sale." When is registration expected? Remember that with a pre-registration pre-sale, there is no assurance the subdivision will be registered, or that the lots will be the exact same size and configuration as in the draft plan. If the house cannot be built for one of these reasons, the deal is off. If the subdivision is registered, then get its registration number.

2. Has the land been serviced yet, a prerequisite before any work can begin on a particular house? If the roads have been laid, or are under construction, then you know servicing is underway. That is a sure sign as well that the proper steps have been taken to register the subdivision. Remember that delays in servicing the land usually mean a missed closing date.

3. Has a building permit been issued for the home? This is absolutely necessary before the builder can legally start to build. If one hasn't been issued, find out when will it be issued. Find out if it's been applied for. Besides subdivision approval and servicing, most offers to purchase newly-built homes are made conditional on a builder getting the permit, or else the deal is cancelled. This is one of the hidden and too-often overlooked hazards of buying an unconstructed home. Problems getting the building permit could delay the scheduled closing, not to mention jeopardizing the entire transaction.

On the surface, it seems that buying a home in the early stages of a subdivision development is fraught with risks, since so much can go wrong between signing and closing. Yet properly protected purchasers of newly-built homes can end up getting very good value for their money. The key, though, is for the purchaser to get particulars about the state of the development; to understand precisely what could happen if problems occur; and to prepare for those possibilities, all before any commitment to purchase is made.

The onus on getting this information rests with you, the buyer, and not anyone else. Expect the builder to be reluctant in volunteering these details, for fear of scaring off potential buyers. Never simply rely on a statement or comment made by the builder or its sales agent. What happens if they are wrong?

To best protect themselves, buyers of newly-built homes must independently verify the status of a lot or subdivision in the approval process at the local municipal office. There you can learn the truth about the subdivision, the servicing of the lands and the issuance of a building permit. These are the three key questions you must ask about the development of a new home subdivision, before putting pen to paper. In addition, a well-qualified real estate lawyer who reviews the offer *before it is signed* can offer invaluable information and protection to new home buyers. See Chapter 13 for further information on the role your lawyer can play.

If you are buying a house before a building permit is issued, check periodically with the builder on any progress in moving the subdivision through the development process. This will give you a much better idea whether your closing date is realistic.

Other Factors

Fire hydrants, overhead streetlamps, hydro boxes and stop signs are unimportant to some people, but may deter other buyers. Fire hydrants detract from the esthetics of a house, and prohibit parking in front of them. Getting to sleep in a bedroom near a streetlamp may be difficult but the bright light makes the house a less inviting target for night prowlers. Green hydro transformer boxes situated on the boulevard in front of some houses do not enhance the overall appearance of the home. Some people prefer to have their home close to a stop sign, since traffic should be travelling slower than normal as it approaches or leaves the intersection.

Purchasers of resale homes never face the problem of what may someday be installed in their home's vicinity. With one site inspection, they know precisely the location of hydrants, street lights and stop signs. Buyers of newly-built homes also want to know where these items will be located in a new subdivision, since it could influence their choice of a lot. But where can they get the details?

Before new homes are built, "plot" plans are prepared and receive municipal approval that show the exact location of the so-called "street hardware." Every house, every driveway, every fire hydrant, every stop sign, every hydro green box, every sidewalk, even every tree in the subdivision appears on these plans. The plans also reveal how the house will be "sited" on the lot (driveway to the right, door to the left, or vice-versa), and whether a sidewalk will be constructed at the front of the house. These subdivision blueprints should be available at the builder's sales pavillion. If not, make a quick trip to the municipal offices to see them.

As a prospective buyer of a newly-built home, and as part of your Home-Buying Strategy, it is absolutely essential that you carefully review these "plot" plans before you sign any offer to purchase. Examining these external plans is just as important as reviewing the blueprints for the house itself. Don't be afraid to ask questions about where various items are located and what the markings mean. If you have trouble reading these plans, bring along a friend or relative to help. Take as much time as you feel is necessary to ensure you fully understand the plans and how they affect your proposed lot. This is your chance to see on paper what purchasers of resale homes can see on the street. Unexpected and often unpleasant surprises can be avoided this way.

Survey

Obtaining a survey is a key element in your home-buying strategy. Surveys serve two purposes: i) they show the location of buildings and other structures (fence, garage, deck) on a property; and ii) they ensure you get what you bargained for, by graphically describing the exact dimensions or the "extent" of a property.

Surveys indicate the size of the lot and the exact location of its boundaries, plus items affecting the property such as fences, hedges, easements and road widenings. Only an up-to-date survey can assure a purchaser that the structures on the property are located completely within the lot lines, and whether any encroachments exist either onto this lot or an adjoining property. Municipalities also use the survey to confirm that the location of a building on a lot complies with the applicable zoning requirements. No survey is needed in condominium transactions as a copy of the survey for the complex is already on file with the registry office.

Tracking down a survey can be a real dilemma in resale transactions. According to the fine print in most standard form offers, sellers need only deliver any survey in their possession. Even then the survey is acceptable only if it is up-to-date and reflects current conditions. Often a seller will supply an affidavit confirming that the external shell or building envelope has not changed since the time the survey was drawn. If no survey exists, or if it is unacceptable, especially to the mortgage lender, the buyer bears the cost of a new survey — often upwards of $500.

Surveys are much more readily available in a newly-built home transaction. Builders receive money from their construction financing in stages, such as when work on the house commences above grade level. At this point a survey (like the one on page 43) is prepared and submitted to the municipal building department confirming that construction is proceeding according to the approved plans. This same survey is also delivered to the purchaser for his or her records. Sometimes it covers a number of properties, and might even be registered on title. What financial relief for a purchaser! And it also ensures that a survey is available for a subsequent sale of the property.

As strange as it sounds, few surveys drawn at this stage for newly-built houses are considered to be up-to-date for closing! Initials on the survey such as C.B.W. (sometimes referred to as C.B.F., C.B. or just C.F.), indicate that the survey was prepared at the concrete block wall, concrete block foundation, concrete basement or concrete foundation stage. All are different ways of saying the same thing — only the basement existed when the survey was drawn! Other surveys may state "dwelling incomplete," or that it is a D.U.C. (dwelling under construction). Whatever the initials, much has happened since the survey was drawn at the foundation stage — the house has been built! All it takes is the first row of bricks to be laid, and the survey, technically speaking, is out of date. A survey drawn at the C.B.W. state of construction obviously does not show the home itself, the eavestroughs, downspouts, a driveway, sidewalk or deck.

Still, virtually all institutional lenders rely on this type of survey when they advance funds to finance the purchase of a newly-built home. So do municipalities in deciding whether the property complies with the zoning by-law. Drawing another survey would add several hundred dollars to the cost of every house, at a time when holding down expenses is crucial.

Obtaining a survey that reflects the current state of the building and other structures on the property is critical in any real estate purchase. Practically speaking, it should not pose much of a problem when you are purchasing a newly-built home.

So far, your home-buying strategy has been concentrating on external location factors —community, neighborhood and specific site — in helping you decide where to buy that newly-built home. Now is the time to open the door and start considering features inside the house that will satisfy your pre-determined list of needs and wants.

A checklist summarizing the factors affecting the home site appears at the end of the next chapter, "Buying a Newly-Built Home From Plans."

Tips and Pointers
- Be sure you know how land in the adjacent area is zoned.
- Always review the development's plot plans to get a better idea of how a neighborhood will look when it has been completed.
- Find out at what stage a desirable property is in the development process, and what needs to be done before work on the house can actually begin.

9

Buying a Newly-built Home From Plans

Buying a home from a builder today is vastly different from buying a resale home. A resale home actually exists. You can see it, touch it, inspect and measure it. That's not the case with most "new" houses. Because of the extremely high financing costs involved in constructing and maintaining unoccupied dwellings, today's builders can no longer afford to have an inventory of unsold homes. To hold down costs even more, most builders may erect only one, or choose not to erect, a model home. The days of lavishly decorated model homes for each style being offered appear to be numbered.

Today, most "new" homes are sold by builders as "pre-sales" from a sales trailer. These homes are sold strictly from plans shown to buyers, before they are actually built. Only when all conditions in the offer have been satisfied, the subdivision registered, the land serviced and a building permit issued is the house actually built. Condominiums are also pre-sold this way, although the builder usually includes a clause in the offer that it can cancel the transaction if it is not satisfied with the "economic feasibility and viability" of the project by a certain date. For more information on condominiums, see Chapter 20.

All purchasers of pre-sale homes are given is a simplified architectural drawing of the exterior of the house (often referred to as an "artist's rendering"), and the interior floor plans. From this sheet of paper, you must visualize and project what the finished product will look like! It's really a venture into the unknown. To add to its overall impression, often the house is shown in isolation, with mature trees and landscaping sketched into the drawing. Too often the narrowness of the lot makes extensive landscaping impractical. With a model home, a purchaser can easily see exactly how the completed home will look despite the decor. With a pre-sale home, it's imagine, speculate and, too often, guess. No wonder buying a "new" home has become so considerably more difficult today. To many buyers, what builders are marketing are plans or "architectural impressions," and a choice of color selections!

As part of their sales brochure, builders include a detailed list of 30, 50 or even 100 features or "appointments" that are included in the purchase price of a pre-sale home. The list is attached to the offer to purchase as Schedule A. Some of these items are basic requirements, while others are mandatory under the local building code. Longer lists of appointments give buyers the impression of getting more value for their money.

Carefully review a builder's list of appointments before signing an offer, as it describes the basic features accompanying the house. Purchasers can compare different builders' lists to determine what is included and — more importantly — what's *excluded* from the purchase price. Like most buyers, George and Rochelle did not fully understand what different builders included and excluded in the list of appointments. George and Rochelle were very afraid of overlooking something, perhaps only a subtlety in wording, that would cost them money in the long run.

To resolve this uncertainty, George and Rochelle put another HOBS idea to work before they bought their pre-sale home. Besides visiting a number of new home sales centers in their price range, they also picked up a list of appointments for slightly more expensive homes. Then they prepared a chart of items each builder included in the purchase price. With all the facts laid out before them, George and Rochelle could readily compare the features offered by the various builders. The few higher-priced homes on the chart also were a valuable yardstick. By comparing what each builder offered, George and Rochelle could tell if one builder in their price range offered good value for the money by including features normally only found in higher-priced homes.

Several basic questions should be addressed at this stage, about houses in general and particular builders' products. What modern features should buyers be looking for in a property? Why is one house more suitable *for you* than the home offered by another builder? What features distinguish one house from another? It's extremely important to carefully consider these points when buying a newly-built home, simply because at this stage the house does not yet exist. Here are some of the questions to consider about features in a house:

Rooms

How many rooms are in the house? What are their types and sizes (bedrooms, bathrooms, kitchen, living room, dining room, family room or den, and laundry room)? Is there an en suite bathroom in the master bedroom? Are any of the rooms located over the garage? If so, how much insulation will be installed? Insufficient insulation for a room over a garage can be like living in an ice box. What is the overall layout of the house and the rooms? Does it suit your lifestyle? Is the house a center hall plan? Will traffic flow easily from room to room? Is the kitchen also a hallway? Is the dining room near the kitchen? Do the dining room and living room adjoin? Is the kitchen at the rear of the house? Is the laundry room on the main floor or in the basement?

Other Interior Features

How many levels of stairs are there? Is there adequate counter space in the kitchen? Is there sufficient space for a fridge, stove and dishwasher? Will the vanities and medicine chests have mirrors? Is the door chime included? Will the handrail and pickets be made of wood, or just the rail? Is there a kitchen hood fan? Is it ducted to the outside? What type of floor coverings will be provided — vinyl, carpeting (how thick an underpad) or hardwood floors? How high is the basement? Is there a fireplace? (a "must" in new homes today despite their energy inefficiency.) Are any appliances included in the purchase price (fridge, stove, washer, dryer, dishwasher)? Are light fixtures included in the purchase price? Is there a sliding door to a outdoor patio?

Storage

Everyone seems to need a lot of storage space in a house. Is there ample closest space? Where it is located? Is there a linen closet? A broom closet, where cleaning materials and a vacuum cleaner can be stored? Is there a pantry in the kitchen? Sufficient cupboards in the kitchen? Will the front closet be large enough to hold winter outerwear?

Heating and Cooling

Most new homes today are heated by natural gas, currently the cheapest method of heating a home. How is the home heated? Will it be air-conditioned? Will a humidifier be attached to the furnace to keep the air moist over the long winter? Will the furnace have an electronic air cleaner?

Plumbing and Electrical

How many outside hose bibs will be installed? Will the plumbing be roughed in for a dishwasher? Will the necessary ductwork be installed for a central vacuum system? Is the house pre-wired for an electronic security system or intercom? Fuse box or circuit breakers? What is the amperage? (100 amps is standard.) Copper wiring? Will there be sufficient electrical outlets in "high volume" rooms such as bedrooms and kitchen? How many outside electrical outlets will be installed, and where? Will a heavy duty plug be installed for a stove and dryer?

Exterior Features

Is the garage wide enough and long enough for two cars? Is the driveway paved or gravelled? Will the garage door pull out or roll up? Will the windows be single paned or thermopane? Will all windows have screens on them? Will the doors have deadbolts? How large is the backyard? Is there enough room for children to play? Will there be a patio? How large?

Abbreviated versions of three builders' lists of appointments appear below, followed by commentary. The three homes listed are a three-bedroom house of 1,300 square feet built by Archie Homes; a 2,200-square-foot four-bedroom house contructed by Bonzo Homes; and a five-bedroom house with over 3,000 square feet, built by Casha Homes.

EXTERIOR FEATURES

	Archie Homes	Bonzo Homes	Casha Homes
Exterior construction	brick and aluminum	all brick	all brick
Driveway	crushed stone	crushed stone	paved

Garage	single car	double car	double car
Can buyers select —exterior bricks —and colors	no	no	brick yes, color no

INTERIOR FEATURES

Railings	oak hand rail and railing	oak pickets and railing	oak pickets
Door chimes	wiring only	yes	yes

KITCHEN FEATURES

Hood fan	yes	yes	yes
Ducted	no	ducted to exterior	ducted to exterior

BATHROOM FEATURES

Medicine cabinet with mirror	yes no	yes no	yes yes
Tub tile enclosure	to four feet	to ceiling	tiled on walls and ceiling
Colored plumbing fixtures	white	yes	yes

FLOORS

Carpeting – weight – underpad	yes not specified not specified	yes 30-ounce 7/16 inch	yes 35-ounce 1/2 inch
Kitchen	vinyl asbestos	vinyl asbestos	ceramic
Vestibule	vinyl asbestos	ceramic	ceramic
Main floor	vinyl asbestos	carpeting	ceramic

Living room	carpeting	carpeting	parquet
Dining room	carpeting	carpeting	parquet
Family room	carpeting	carpeting	parquet
Stairs	carpeting	carpeting	parquet
Bedrooms	carpeting	carpeting	carpeting
Baths	vinyl asbestos	ceramic	ceramic
Laundry room	vinyl asbestos	vinyl asbestos	ceramic

DOORS AND WINDOWS

Windows	double-glazed with sliders	double-glazed with sliders	casement windows (thermo-pane)
Screens	on opening windows only	on opening windows only	on opening windows only
Garage door	pullout	wood rollup	wood rollup
Trimmed doorways	no	yes	yes

ELECTRICAL AND LIGHTING

Outside outlets	one	one	one external and one in garage
Amps	100	100	200
Circuit breaker	no	yes	yes

PLUMBING AND HEATING

Air Conditioner	no	yes	yes
Furnace	gas	gas with humidifier	gas with humidifier and electronic air cleaner

Fireplace	one	one	one plus rough-in in basement
Laundry tub	single fiberglass	single fiberglass	single enamel steel
Exterior hose faucets	one	two	two
Rough-in for dishwasher	yes	yes	yes

Exterior construction

In a solid brick home, popular with many Canadians, brick is an essential part of its actual structure. But most homes built today have a wood-frame construction over which is applied an external veneer. Find out if the external veneer will be wood, aluminum or brick. If brick, (known as "brick front"), will it be clay, the preferred type, or calcite? As many older homes have solid brick construction, the use of the brick as an external veneer to convey the impression of being a "brick" home remains very popular.

Walls

Determine whether the foundation of the house will be concrete block, the traditional foundation material, or poured concrete. Poured concrete foundations can be constructed faster, an important consideration to builders. So too with the types of materials used for internal walls. Lath and plaster walls are much stronger and more solid, but are rare in new homes today. Instead, drywall or plasterboard is used almost universally in newly-built homes.

Driveway

Will the builder pave the driveway in asphalt? If so, at whose expense? Paving a driveway could cost upwards of a thousand dollars.

Color Selection

Can you select your own colors for bricks, aluminum siding, paint and shingles? Not too often. Many builders have architecturally controlled exterior color selections. Within the subdivision, no choices or changes of exterior colors is permitted. This prevents a monotony of exterior colors and unplanned color combinations.

Certain lots are pre-selected to have dark brown bricks and light trim, with others to have light brown bricks and dark trim. Still others will be built with reddish brown bricks with cream trim, and so on. Choosing a particular lot takes on added importance if the external color scheme is predetermined. If this is the case, at least learn what color combination applies to the lot you are selecting. Make sure the offer states what color scheme will apply, so it can't be changed without your approval. Inquire now to avoid surprises later.

Railings

Many new home purchasers have been disappointed to learn that only the *handrail* of their staircase is wooden. The vertical *pickets* are made of steel. The Bonzo Home features both wood pickets *and* railing, just as in the more expensive Casha Home.

Kitchen Hood Fan

A ducted kitchen hood fan will remove cooking odors from the stove area to outside the home. An unducted fan does little more than swirl the air around the kitchen. Again, only by comparing the three lists did George and Rochelle learn that the Bonzo Home included this feature.

Bathroom and Tub Enclosure

How high above the tub will tiles be laid in the bathtub enclosure? In a Bonzo Home, the walls are tiled to the ceiling, and in a Casha Home the ceiling itself is tiled. A nice touch, if it's available.

Floor Coverings

No-wax vinyl flooring is very popular today in high-traffic areas of new homes. Ceramic tiles add to the appearance of floors, but are more expensive to install. When considering carpeting, remember the greater the weight of the carpet, the better its quality. Thick underpadding is recommended by carpet experts. Parquet flooring is a luxury appointment that's often available only as an extra. Carefully check the type and quality of floor covering to be applied in each area of the house. Most builders offer upgraded and different types of floor coverings as an extra.

Windows

Sealed double-pane windows insulate a home better than double-glazed windows. Many people prefer the look of casement windows to sliding glass or double-hung windows.

Garage Door

Wood sectional roll-up garage doors are generally preferred over metal pull-out garage doors because of shorter driveways.

Electrical

A 200-amp service can carry a greater electrical load than the standard 100-amp service. Circuit breakers are preferred over fuse boxes as well, for reasons of safety and convenience.

Get the Complete Plans

A complete set of plans for the house will show the layout, dimensions and location of all rooms, doors and windows, fireplaces, staircases, washrooms, closets, kitchen (including areas for fridge and stove), plus laundry room and garage. Don't rely on the small sketch of the house given to everyone who visits the sales office. Instead, ask the sales agent for the detailed plans and drawings of the house. If they are not in the sales trailer, though they should be, then ask the agent to have the plans available the next day. Remember that you have to visualize, imagine and often speculate as to what the final house will look like. This is made much easier with the proper drawings, rather than an oversimplified "artist's rendering or impression."

Find out if the square footage of the house includes the garage. Surprisingly, some builders include the garage in the square footage to make the house appear larger.

As part of your comparative shopping process, you should compare the information in the sales literature against the actual list of appointments appearing in Schedule A to the offer. If an item in the sales brochure is omitted from Schedule A, as occasionally happens, then it won't be included in the purchase price. Don't expect your lawyer to analyze Schedule A that carefully. The lawyer's role is to examine the legalities of the transaction, not how high the tile will extend in the bathtub enclosure.

Whether or not you have any say in selecting the external house colors, most buyers are given some options in choosing interior colors, materials and decor. Usually samples of the materials and colors that will be used in the house are on display in the sales office. Areas where buyers can select from builders' samples include paint (see how may different color selections are allowed; whether the entire home must be painted one color; how many coats of paint will be applied — two coats of paint, where one of them is primer, is really only one coat); ceramic tiles; carpeting; vinyl flooring; kitchen cabinets; countertops; range hoods; bathroom fixtures; bathroom tiles; and bathroom accessories (towel bar, soap dish and toilet paper dispenser). Usually the color selection cannot be changed once submitted. Keep a copy of your color list and features just in case anything supplied is wrong. Also see what the electric light fixtures look like.

Besides the essential features of a house, a detailed inventory of extras and upgrades is always available for those who want to pay more. Sixty to eighty possible extras and upgrades are not uncommon, among them extra basement windows, wall plugs, light fixtures, and insulation; better quality laundry tubs, doors, taps, windows, carpeting, floor coverings and air conditioning. And the list goes on.

Factory-installed extras on a used car may bring the seller a higher-than-average price for the vehicle. But rarely does the increase cover the full cost for those extras. It's the same with homes. Rarely will a subsequent purchaser pay considerably more for a house, simply because top quality carpeting, additional electrical plugs and better quality windows were originally installed. That is why we often hear people say, "We won't get the money out of the house that we put into it." The reverse, though, is usually true for a premium lot — one that is wider, deeper or in a prime location. Remember that upgrades and extras should only be installed when they suit *your* lifestyle and plans for the house.

Considerable premiums are tacked onto some extras and upgrades, compared to their normal cost in the marketplace. Installing extras and upgrades can cause monumental headaches for builders, as they are a further step towards constucting custom-built homes. During sellers' markets, when the demand for newly-built homes outstrips the supply, builders try to avoid customizing a house. Instead of mass-producing each home exactly the same, with identical features and appointments, the builder must take extra time to build one house differently from the others. When builders already have difficulty meeting closing deadlines, the slow delivery of upgraded materials could hold up closing even further.

Of course, it is the builder who ends up bearing the extra cost. When the market is strong, builders often don't need or want the aggravation of customizing a house. By charging inflated prices, builders hope to discourage purchasers from selecting extras and upgrades.

Still, many buyers are prepared to pay a premium to have the builder take care of these extras and upgrades. This way, special features can be installed and suitably finished by the builder while the house is being constructed.

Whenever the proposed extra or upgrade will replace a feature normally provided by the builder, find out how large a credit will be given. Quite often what builders are prepared to pay purchasers for *not* installing standard grade materials is small indeed. Originally, Gary and Judy wanted all the floors left bare so they could install their own high-quality floor coverings after closing. But the builder offered a very nominal credit for not laying the standard grade carpets and floors, not nearly what those items were worth. Eventually Gary and Judy decided to forget about upgrading the floors, and accepted what the builder included in the purchase price.

Of course, the reverse is true during a slow buyers' market. To make a sale, builders are more prepared to customize a house. Reasonable prices will be charged for upgrades and extras, and good-sized credits will be given for items not installed. With strong bargaining, some features might even be included in the basic cost of the house. All the more reason why buyers, as part of their part of their HOBS, must have a firm grasp of the state of the market before ever making any commitment to purchase.

Always look at the cost of upgrades and extras very carefully. Often it will be considerably cheaper to buy them from a building supply retailer and have them installed by independent tradesmen after closing. But keep in mind the size of the offsetting credit. If it's too small, you may have no choice but to order the extra or upgrade through the builder — or to forget about it completely.

Tips and Pointers

When buying a pre-sale home from plans, always do the following as part of your home-buying strategy:

1. Study the drawings and floor plans carefully. Never make any decisions based on first impressions alone. Review every inch of those plans to establish the location of walls, stairs and rooms.

Measure room sizes and compare them to your present home to ensure they satisfy your requirements. Measure and draw scale models of your furniture, and rearrange it on the plans to see if it will fit into various rooms. Draw sketches and imagine how the various areas of the house will look on completion.

2. View any houses that are occupied and completed, if possible, or that are nearly completed. This will help you to determine how the interior of your house will look.

3. Get a second opinion about your impressions from a friend or family member who is knowledgeable about homes or familiar with blueprints. Take your advisor to the sales office as well, to review the actual plans for the property. It never hurts to get an unbiased, reliable and objective opinion. If possible, speak to someone who recently bought a home from plans (preferably from the same builder) to see how the actual house compared with the home owner's mental impressions.

4. Don't be afraid to question the sales agent about the layout of the house, especially if you have any doubts about the floor plans. A sincere sales representative will understand the difficulty you may have in translating words and drawings into mental pictures of what the completed home will look like. Any sales agent who will not devote the time to the buyer reflects badly on the builder. To get an agent's undivided attention, arrange a private appointment for an off-peak time after hours or on a weekday. Then the agent will have plenty of time to discuss and review the plans with you.

5. Inspect any model homes that are built, especially if it's the model you may buy. Learn exactly what is included in the purchase price and what is optional. Remember that what you see is not necessarily what you get. Most model homes are very tastefully and lavishly decorated, and equipped with luxurious furnishings and accessories, woodwork, trim and mouldings, mirrors, window and wall coverings, light fixtures, appliances and exterior landscaping. But don't let the cosmetics of the model home sway you. Many of these extras and upgrades are for display purposes only. *Too often these extras, options, features and upgrades are not included in the purchase price of the stripped-down house,* although they may not be clearly marked that way. Check carefully what is standard with the house and what is not, to avoid any misunderstandings and disappointments later. Be absolutely certain that any model home feature included in the purchase price appears in the of-

fer. Even add to Schedule A the words "as per model home" to clarify what you intend to get on closing. Don't be afraid to ask the sales agent exactly where it is listed in Schedule A. Remember, if it's not in the offer, it's not part of the deal.

6. Building today's mass-produced homes resembles the assembly-line construction of a car. Aside from the finishings, every home of a particular style is built according to the same plans. Some purchasers, though, want to customize the layout of the house. This could involve adding, moving or removing a wall (assuming it is not load-bearing); hanging a door in a different location; redesigning a room, or other changes to the architectural plans. Provided no structural changes are involved, these plan alterations can easily be made before construction begins. Remember that in a seller's market, builders are understandably reluctant to make any changes to the plans, so anticipate this. If one buyer does not want the home "as is," someone soon will appear who does. When the market is soft, the chance to customize your home is one of the first features builders will offer.

7. Remember to constantly refer back to your shopping lists of needs and wants. Part of the home hunting process at this stage is to see how many items on those lists are satisfied by each particular home. Where appropriate, shift items from one list to another, and reassess their priority. This is the only way to ensure the house you buy satisfies all your needs and as many wants as possible.

8. Refer to the list of various builders' appointments outlined earlier in this chapter. Highlight those items that provide good value. Keep the list handy for future reference.

9. In the space below, record special features and overall impressions of interesting properties immediately after seeing the homes. Otherwise you'll start to confuse what different builders are offering. Attach any sales brochures or data sheets that highlight the homes. While they're still fresh in your mind, rank the various properties on how well they satisfy your unique needs and wants.

	<u>House 1</u>	<u>House 2</u>	<u>House 3</u>

Builder
Address
Price
Mortgage Arrangements
Type of House
Style of House
Size of House
Lot Size
Parking
Municipal Easements
Party Walls
Zero Lot Line
Corner Lot
Side of Street
Zoning By-Laws
State of Development
— subdivision registered
— land serviced
— permit issued

Rooms
  bedrooms
  bathroom
  kitchen
  living room
  dining room
  family room
  laundry room
  basement

Other Interior
  Features
Storage
Heating and Cooling
Plumbing and Electrical
Exterior Features

At this stage, you should be narrowing down the choices and gaining valuable experience about buying a house. Still, it's much too premature to make any commitment to purchase. How will you pay for that house? Financial considerations are next on your HOBS agenda.

10

Your Financial Picture

Buying a home, whether resale or newly-built, involves not one but *two* major long-term financial commitments. The first commitment is the money paid to close the purchase — money that's invested in the home, and in yourself. That money is tied up, with no cash dividends, until the property is either sold or remortgaged. Besides this lump-sum investment, home ownership also involves an ongoing financial commitment to the property — mortgage, taxes, utilities, insurance, maintenance, repairs, and so on. Knowing how much it will cost to purchase a newly-built home and to carry it each month are key components of every HOBS.

Because of the major financial commitments associated with home ownership, purchasers have to be both practical and realistic. The first few months of home ownership always are the hardest, as you adjust to the larger demands on your income. With less disposable income available, some changes in lifestyle are inevitable. What is wrong with entertaining in that beautiful new home instead of going out to restaurants and lounges? Before long, home owners become accustomed to their new financial arrangements, and life returns to normal.

A commonly heard expression is that purchasers "pushed themselves to the limit" in buying a house. This is a dangerous practice, especially when buying a home from a builder, since there are so many additional costs to be faced in the weeks and months after closing. It's prudent to leave yourself a cushion and not spend your last dollar on the house, just in case.

Too often, purchasers are asked how much they want to spend on a house. Purchasers must realize that squeezing as much house as possible into a fixed, predetermined purchase price does not look at what they need to buy — what that home should provide for them. The right question to consider and *honestly answer* as part of your home-buying strategy is "What can I afford to buy?" This way your financial ability to *pay* for a house becomes the primary consideration, and not price.

Simply budgeting and calculating the *maximum price* you can afford to pay for a house is not enough. Buyers should also calculate a realistic *maximum price range* (discussed later in this chapter), and stick to it. Setting a maximum price *range* is more important than simply establishing an upper price limit, since the inevitable additional and unanticipated costs could push you into the monetary danger zone. Going in over your head makes poor financial sense, since every month will become a struggle just to keep afloat. That struggle could jeopardize your continued ownership of the property, not to mention your personal happiness. Over-extending yourself financially is the quickest way to destroy that initial passion and excitement of owning a new house.

Don't put too much stock in the so-called rules of thumb that are supposed to tell you the most expensive house you can afford. Besides their inconsistency, ranging from 2.5 times to 3.5 times your gross income, they do not inadequately consider *your* unique financial circumstances — net income earned and the amount you have for a downpayment, plus current mortgage interest rates. For example, with an annual income of $40,000 the 2.5 times rule means an affordable house would be $100,000. It assumes your downpayment is only 10 percent of the purchase price or $10,000, that the monthly taxes are $100, and that current interest rates are 12 percent. Obviously it is too simplistic to be accurate.

Another rule of thumb says 3 percent of the purchase price of a home will be spent "running it" — paying for heating, utilities, telephone and the like. Some people include fire insurance or monthly condominium maintenance fees in this figure, while others exclude it. Again, it's only a rough guideline.

There are only two ways to pay for a house — with your own money, or with someone else's money *(a mortgage)*. Mortgages cover the difference between the purchase price and what you can afford to pay from your own resources. Interest paid on mortgages booked to finance the purchase of a home is not deductible against other income in Canada. This is one reason why mortgages are very expensive loans, regardless of the interest rate charged.

To hold down the high interest cost associated with home ownership, purchasers should put down as much of their own money as possible. As Norrie and Annabelle realized, the more of their own money used on the purchase, the smaller the mortgage and the mortgage payments become, regardless of the interest rate. A larger downpayment would also enable them to buy a larger home, while keeping the same sized mortgage. In other words, determining what you can afford to buy clearly hinges on both your downpayment and size of mortgage you can arrange.

Mortgages are examined in greater detail in Chapter 15, but several preliminary comments are necessary at this time. Lenders examine both the value of a property and the borrower's income before they grant a mortgage loan. This is true whether you will be assuming a "builder's mortgage," the loan arranged by the builder for the home, or applying for your own mortgage to finance the purchase. Mortgages that exceed 75 percent of the appraised value of a property (the upper limit for a conventional mortgage) are even more expensive, as borrowers face extra costs in this "high-ratio" situation. Most lenders will not grant mortgages for more than 90 percent of the total purchase price, which means purchasers must have a minimum 10 percent downpayment.

A new idea that is all the rage today is the "pre-approved" or "pre-arranged" mortgage. In the past, where no builder's mortgage existed, the question of arranging a mortgage too often wasn't even considered until after an offer was signed. In other words, this key component was treated as a virtual afterthought! When a builder's mortgage could be assumed by the buyer, few people even thought about mortgages in the pre-contract stage, although the buyer's offer clearly was conditional on being approved to assume that mortgage. No wonder some purchasers have been upset that their deal was cancelled, learning only after they had signed the offer that they did not qualify for the mortgage.

With pre-approved mortgages, the mortgage is arranged *before* the home purchase. Purchasers know how large a mortgage can be arranged and their house price range, before any offer is signed. With a pre-approved mortgage, once the right house has been found, purchasers can act with confidence.

Shopping for a mortgage by comparing different lenders' packages, and knowing that you qualify for a mortgage well in advance of signing any offer, is a key element of your home-buying strategy. It eliminates much of the pressure buyers face, and enables them to negotiate the best possible mortgage deal. Despite their apparent attractiveness, pre-approved mortgages are not the best way to shop for a mortgage in the pre-contract stage. Because they are so convenient to arrange, too often purchasers are discouraged from thoroughly comparing different lenders' packages and features. The same holds true when assuming the builder's mortgage. How do you know if the overall package offered by either the pre-approved mortgage or the builder's mortgage is most appropriate *for you,* unless you first consider what is available from other lenders?

To resolve the dilemma, purchasers should first informally *pre-qualify* themselves for a mortgage, without dealing with a lender. Purchasers who do this will know both how large a mortgage they qualify for, plus how expensive a home they can afford to buy. This preliminary self-qualification also enables them to negotiate both the offer to purchase and the mortgage from a position of strength, since they already know what they can afford to buy and borrow. Once the necessary mortgage shopping has been completed, buyers then can seek formal pre-approval from the lender offering the best overall mortgage terms.

To pre-qualify yourself for a mortgage and determine your maximum price range, simply follow this practical, three-step guide:

1. Calculate your available downpayment. A small portion of the downpayment is paid as a deposit when you sign the offer, while the rest is paid on closing. To book a conventional mortgage, at least 25 percent of the purchase price must come from your own resources. Just because a purchaser lacks a full 25 percent downpayment does not mean he or she cannot buy a house. To make a deal, the buyer might arrange a high-ratio mortgage, or book a "conventional" first mortgage for 75 percent of the purchase price, plus a second mortgage for the remainder. Remember to set aside enough money for the many hidden closing costs that accompany every transaction.

   To see how expensive a home you can buy with a conventional mortgage, simply multiply the available downpayment by four. With $20,000 available as a downpayment, Elliott and Mandy could afford to pay $80,000 for a home with a conventional mortgage of $60,000. A more expensive home would require a high-ratio mortgage.

2. Carefully examine what it will cost to "carry" a house or pay its operating costs each month. These expenses fall into two categories: the first consists of items such as water, electricity,

heating, insurance, maintenance and repairs. To get information about these costs, speak to friends, the utilities involved, your insurance agent and other home owners. You should be able to get a reasonable estimate of what these items will cost each month.

Then explore the second category of operating expenses — the debt service costs for the mortgage (principal and interest), realty taxes and condominium maintenance (if applicable). Information on the last two components should be available at the sales office.

For a conventional mortgage, no more than 30 percent of your gross income can be applied towards payment of the mortgage, realty taxes and any condominium maintenance. Many lenders will take into account both a husband's and wife's gross incomes, if both have stable jobs. The relationship between the size of a mortgage and the borrower's gross income invites the same question phrased in two different ways. How large a mortgage can be arranged, based on the borrower's gross income? How large must the borrower's gross income be to arrange a certain-sized mortgage? The first approach is examined here while the second is discussed in the chapter dealing with mortgage financing.

Elliott and Mandy have gross incomes totalling $36,000 and they are buying a house, not a condominium. To calculate how much of their income can be applied toward payment of the mortgage and taxes, all they have to do is divide their gross income by 40. That means Elliott and Mandy could afford to pay up to $900 per month ($36,000 divided by 40) to the principal, interest and taxes on a conventional mortgage. If more money is needed to carry the mortgage and taxes each month, a high-ratio mortgage would be needed.

If the tax component was $125 monthly, Elliott and Mandy would still have $775 for the basic mortgage payment each month. What size of conventional mortgage they can arrange for $775 monthly depends on the interest rate. The following chart shows the monthly cost of a loan for each $1,000 borrowed, amortized over 25 years:

Monthly Mortgage Payment at Various Interest Rates

Interest Rate (%)	Interest cost per $1,000	Interest Rate %	Interest cost per $1,000
8.5	7.95	14.5	12.10
9	8.28	15	12.46
9.5	8.61	15.5	12.83
10	8.95	16	13.19
10.5	9.28	16.5	13.56
11	9.63	17	13.93
11.5	9.97	17.5	14.29
12	10.32	18	14.66
12.5	10.67	18.5	15.03
13	11.02	19	15.41
13.5	11.38	19.5	15.78
14	11.74	20	16.15

By dividing the amount available for the basic monthly mortgage payment by the figure for any given interest rate, Elliott and Mandy can readily see how large a mortgage they can afford to carry at various interest rates. For example, if the current rate was 12%, dividing $775 by 10.32 means they could arrange and carry a conventional mortgage of about $75,100. At interest rates of 10.5% and 13.5%, mortgages of approximately $83,500 and $68,100 respectively could be booked. No wonder lower interest rates bring more and more purchasers into the market, because they enable buyers to arrange larger mortgages as well!

With $20,000 available for a downpayment, Elliott and Mandy's combined incomes of $36,000 would easily allow them to arrange a conventional mortgage of $60,000 on a home purchase of $80,000. If they decided to buy a larger home and arrange a high-ratio mortgage, the size of mortgage (and therefore purchase price) would depend on the current interest rate. At 10.5%, they could afford to buy a house for $103,500 ($20,000 downpayment plus $83,500 mortgage); with a 12% mortgage the largest house they could afford to buy would be $95,100 ($20,000 plus $75,100); while that figure would drop to $88,100 if mortgage rates were 13.5% ($20,000 plus $68,100).

3. After calculating your downpayment and mortgage, reduce the maximum price by at least 5 percent to establish the "maximum

price range." The absolute maximum price previously established becomes the upper end of the range, while this "adjusted"
figure becomes the lower end and target price. With a price
range instead of one set figure, purchasers of newly-built homes
can accommodate some extras, upgrades, closing costs and the
like, while still remaining within budget.

To purchase a newly-built home with a conventional mortgage, Elliott and Mandy would look at the lower end of the
range, about $76,000 ($80,000 less 5 percent). If they saw a
home priced at $79,000 that satisfied their needs and wants,
they could buy it knowing that the price is within budget and
that they would qualify for a conventional mortgage. Depending on the interest rate, Elliott and Mandy also know that they
can exceed the $80,000 threshold *and still qualify for a high-
ratio mortgage.* This advance planning, a key element in their
home-buying strategy, helped Elliott and Mandy determine how
large a mortgage they could arrange. More importantly it
showed them how much they could afford to pay for a house.

Using the form below as a guide, calculate the maximum
mortgage you can afford to carry each month at various interest rates. Use Elliott and Mandy's chart as an example in
completing your calculations.

What Can Elliott and Mandy Afford to Buy?

STEP 1   Maximum Downpayment Available: $20,000

STEP 2   *Determine the upper end of the range*

          Gross income divided by 40 = Gross monthly
                                        payment

          $36,000 divided by 40   = $900

          Less: 1/12th of annual taxes   ($125)

          Maximum monthly amount
          available for principal
          and interest payments $775

Divide this figure by the interest factor on page 74 to calculate the Maximum Mortgage available at various rates, in thousands (i.e., $775 divided by 9.97 = $77,700).

At x %, Maximum Mortgage is $ _____ + Maximum Downpayment = Maximum Purchase Price (upper end of range)

at 10%, $775 ÷ 8.95 produces
$86,600 + $20,000 = $106,600
at 11%, $775 ÷ 9.63 produces
$80,500 + $20,000 = $100,500
at 12%, $775 ÷ 10.32 produces
$75,100 + $20,000 = $95,100
at 13%, $775 ÷ 11.02 produces
$70,300 + $20,000 = $90,300

STEP 3   *To determine the lower end of the range (the target sale price), reduce the Maximum Purchase Price for any given interest rate by 5%.*

Interest Rate	Top of Range	Bottom of Range
10%	$106,600	$101,270
11%	$100,500	$95,475
12%	$95,100	$90,345
13%	$90,300	$85,785

What Can You Afford To Buy?

STEP 1   Maximum Downpayment Available: $ _____

STEP 2   *Determine the upper end of the range*
Gross income divided by 40 = Gross monthly payment

$ ÷ 40   = $ _____

Less: 1/12th of annual taxes   ($_____)

Maximum monthly amount
available for principal
and interest payments $_____

Divide this figure by the interest factor on page 74
to calculate the Maximum Mortgage available at
various rates, in thousands (i.e., $775 divided by
9.97 = $77,700).

At x%, Maximum Mortgage is $ _____ +
Maximum Downpayment = Maximum Purchase
                        Price (upper end of
                        range)

at 10% $ _____ + $ _____ = $ _____
at 11% $ _____ + $ _____ = $ _____
at 12% $ _____ + $ _____ = $ _____
at 13% $ _____ + $ _____ = $ _____

STEP 3   *To determine the lower end of the range (the target
price), reduce the Maximum Purchase Price for any
given interest rate by 5%.*

Interest Rate	Top of Range	Bottom of Range
10% $ _____	$ _____	
11% $ _____	$ _____	
12% $ _____	$ _____	
13% $ _____	$ _____	

By now, purchasers with a home-buying strategy will be very
anxious to start seriously looking for a newly-built house. Ready
to seriously look — yes; ready to buy — no. Not quite yet. Their
home-buying strategy must still be applied in several more areas,
before they make any commitments to purchase. These include
selecting a builder, choosing a lawyer and, next on the agenda, how to manage without your own real estate agent.

Tips and Pointers

- Put as much money down as possible; it makes carrying a mortgage that much easier.
- Pre-qualify yourself for a mortgage before going house-hunting; it will help you determine how much you can afford to borrow and buy.
- Calculate the maximum price range for a house, using the lower end of the range as your target price.

11

Don't Go It Alone When Buying a Newly-built Home

While buying a home can be one of the happiest events of your life, it can also prove to be one of the most anxious, aggravating and frustrating of times. So much needs to be done and so many potential pitfalls await the unwary, that the initial excitement can fade away as the pressures begin to mount. One of the reasons for having a home-buying strategy is to anticipate and prepare for problems that might be faced, to help keep the level of tension to a minimum.

A key component of HOBS for a resale home is to associate yourself with three real estate professionals — a qualified home inspector, a knowledgeable real estate lawyer, and a trustworthy real estate agent. Without these specialists, purchasers of resale homes run the risk of buying someone else's headaches, or facing problems (usually financial) that often could have been resolved before any firm commitments were made.

But what about the newly-built home scenario? Many people like Chris say, "Sure we need a lawyer, and we'll get one, eventually. The lawyer will process the purchase after the offer is signed, and make sure that the title is properly transferred on closing. But the builder won't allow any changes to the offer, anyway. So why get a lawyer before we've bought?"

What about a home inspector? "Not for a newly-built home," Chris argues. "His job is to examine old homes for mechanical and structural soundness. Newly-built homes don't have problems like that. Nobody has a new home privately inspected."

As for a real estate agent, Chris's question is, "What agent are you talking about? It's a known fact that buyers of new homes never have a separate real estate agent to represent their interests. The person in the sales trailer is the only agent involved in the transaction, and works for the builder. So, finding the right house rests totally on my shoulders."

For these reasons, buying a new home would appear to be totally different than buying a resale home. The general consensus seems to be that you go it alone buying a newly-built home! But that's not the way it has to be. Just because purchasers like Chris lack their own real estate agent when buying from a builder does not mean they are isolated, helpless and friendless.

In considering whether new home purchasers like Chris are on their own when they buy from a builder, several key points must be kept in mind. First, although buyers of newly-built homes lack their own real estate agent, not all resale purchases use a separate real estate agent either. Although a new home sales agent technically represents the builder, the key role they can and should play to assist purchasers should never be overlooked or downplayed. But it's even more important to recognize and understand the agent's limitations and restrictions to learn just how far they can go to help new home purchasers. Situations will arise where agents could find themselves in a conflict of interest, meaning purchasers must rely on substitute players for information and advice. Who should plug the holes and protect a purchaser's interests? None other than a qualified real estate lawyer and a home inspector!

Purchasing any home involves three steps: choosing the house to buy, drawing the offer to purchase, and negotiating the final terms of the contract. Resale real estate agents are matchmakers who bring buyers, sellers and homes together. Since resale home buyers rely heavily on a real estate agent's judgment and expertise, finding the right agent is almost as important as finding the right property. Once a suitable resale home is located, the agent prepares the offer to purchase. Then follows the toughest role of all, where the agent helps the buyer haggle and dicker with the seller until a deal is struck.

Of course, not all people use their own agent when they buy a resale home. Very often, the seller's agent also acts for the purchaser. So much for the idea of separate representation in all resale transactions. Also, in private sales no agent is involved at all. Who finds the house being privately offered for sale? The buyer, Eric. Who prepares the offer? Eric's lawyer. Who does the negotiating? Eric, directly with the seller. Purchasers like Eric often do quite well when they buy a resale home privately. So in many ways buying a newly-built home parallels the private resale transaction. Just like Eric, Wayne does not have his own real estate agent when he buys from a builder. And just like Eric, it's also up to Wayne to locate the house that is right for him.

Even when a real estate agent is involved, how can buyers go looking at houses until they carefully look at themselves first, and know what they need and want in a house? How can an agent know what a potential buyer needs from a house if the buyer himself doesn't know first? Where no agent is involved, whether in a resale or new home situation, having a home-buying strategy is absolutely crucial. To find the right property, purchasers must rely even more on their HOBS. Wayne's home-buying strategy will help him decide what he needs, what he wants, what he can afford, and what features he should look for in a community, a neighborhood, a home site and dwelling. With a HOBS, purchasers never need to "go it alone."

At this stage, the similarity ends between private resale and newly-built home purchases. In contrast to the private sale, in which the buyer's lawyer prepares the offer, builders have their own Offer to Purchase form which buyers like Wayne must sign. Some buyers get the feeling they are standing alone against the builder at this point, because most offers are very one-sided or pro-builder. For his own peace of mind, Wayne should take the offer to his lawyer *before it is signed.* He or she will review, comment on and revise it, if possible. Most importantly, Wayne's lawyer will also make sure Wayne understands the contents of the offer before it's etched in stone. This way it's no longer Wayne by himself against the builder. (Selecting a lawyer is reviewed in Chapter 13, while builders' offers are examined in Chapter 18.) It is important to emphasize at this stage that you should never sign an offer before your lawyer has had a chance to review it. Putting pen to paper prematurely could prove costly.

Some negotiations for private sales collapse at the very last moment because the parties deal directly with each other. Perhaps a seemingly innocent statement may be taken out of context by either the buyer or the seller during their face-to-face meetings. This lack of an intermediary can lead to heated emotions, regrettable comments, and a breakdown in negotiations.

Seldom does this occur with new home transactions, because buyer and builder don't deal directly. Acting as go-between is the sales agent. Besides this, there is seldom much room to haggle and dicker anyway. Quite often (depending especially on the state of the real estate market) the seller's position is that this is our first, last and only package. Whatever limited maneuvering is possible is usually conducted in a professional manner through the new home sales agent.

Buyers often overlook the fact that new home sales agents lead double (but not necessarily romantic) lives in acting for both the buyer and builder. On the one hand, they are paid by and represent the builder. Their job, plain and simple, is to sell the builder's homes. But to do this effectively, a good sales agent must thoroughly understand the builder's product and be prepared to answer every inquiry a purchaser has about the builder, the community and the neighborhood.

A sales agent with only a few details about the homes they are selling is not going to be able to properly assist prospective purchasers. Agents selling new homes must know every square inch of each house type offered, *plus* every square inch of the builder's contract. This includes clauses dealing with a builder's mortgage (if available) and details about early termination of the transaction. New home sales agents must be fully aware of what is standard in a house, where the purchaser can make optional selections, and what items are extras and upgrades. They must also fully understand the planning, construction and sales process, especially if pre-sale or pre-registration pre-sale homes are being marketed. An uninformed agent reflects badly on the builder.

Successful new home sales agents gain the confidence of buyers by acting as friend, listener and nursemaid before the offer is signed. Just as in a resale purchase, you should spend some time with the agent reviewing your HOBS — your needs, wants, personal tastes and financial position. A good agent would much rather sell you a different model of home than the one you first considered, than have you buy elsewhere. But without these preliminary discussions, how can the sales agent know what you are looking for and what you can afford to buy? It never hurts either, to indicate how much you are relying on the agent's experience and expertise. Most agents will respond by being warm and helpful. To ensure you can have the agent's attention for an extended period of time, arrange an appointment at off-peak hours, on a weekday or after hours. Avoid the busiest time of all — weekends.

Those new home sales agents who really have buyers' interest at heart will *encourage* them to take their offer to a lawyer before they sign it. But too often, the reverse is true. Prospective purchasers like Jerry and Cheryl were urged to sign the offer right in the sales pavilion, without having the opportunity to have their lawyer review it. Why agents do this is obvious: they fear the lawyer will talk Jerry and Cheryl out of the deal for some reason and cost them a potential sale. Agents trying to get the offer signed right then and there will use phrases like these: "It's the builder's standard form offer, the one everybody signs;" "No changes to the offer are permitted, even if it is reviewed by a lawyer;" "A price increase can be avoided, if the offer is signed today;" and "Another purchaser is interested in the property, so you'd better submit the offer now."

By insisting on a commitment this way, agents really have no way of knowing whether purchasers fully understand what they are signing. But an offer submitted after review and comment by a qualified real estate lawyer actually benefits everyone. Buyers like Jerry and Cheryl have an opportunity to get an independent expert opinion about issues that concern them. In turn, the agent will be free from any allegations by the buyer of distorting the facts or misrepresenting the terms of the offer. Both sides can be more confident that the purchaser appreciates what the offer says, before it is signed.

Some cooperative sales agents will even have the builder put a short-term "hold" on the house for several days, during which the builder will not sell the home Jerry and Cheryl are interested in to anyone else. This "freeze" gives Jerry and Cheryl the time they need to have their lawyer check over the offer and answer their questions. When talking with a sales agent, see if this arrangement can be made.

Purchasers are always concerned about who else will be moving into new subdivisions. With two pre-school children of their own, John and Carrie wanted to buy in an area where other young children lived. This would be easy to determine in a resale transaction. Driving through a neighborhood and seeing tricycles on the sidewalk would likely give John and Carrie all the information they needed. It's not so easy in a new home subdivision. To feel reassured that young families were buying in the area, John and Carrie were shown the list of other purchasers from their builder. Then they telephoned several of the names and confirmed that other families with young children had bought in the area. In fact, one of the other buyers was a friend of Carrie's from her high school days. To know more about other purchasers, you should do as John and Carrie did as part of their home-buying strategy. Ask the sales agent to see this list of purchasers. Any reluctance on the agent's part to produce it could cost the builder a sale.

A good salesman in any field must convince people that their needs are being satisfied. To sell Ron and Iris a house, the sales agent must do more than just sell them on a particular home. Because the community and neighborhood are developing, the new home sales agent must also provide them with whatever information is available about future shopping, schools, transportation services and the like. It's up to Ron and Iris, though, to independently verify what they are told.

The new home sales agent also must sell Ron and Iris on the builder, and more importantly on himself. Although the builder constructs the home, Ron and Iris will have very little direct contact with the builder. To Ron and Iris and most buyers of newly-built homes, the sales agent *is* the builder, someone in whom the buyer must have complete confidence.

Once the offer is signed, it is important that the lines of communication with the agent be strong. Even though only one agent may be involved in the transaction, buyers should never hesitate to contact him or her for a status report or an update on the latest developments. When you need to know "what's happening" prior to closing, who better to turn to first than the sales agent? Who else can obtain accurate, timely information from the builder, if not the builder's agent?

As the builder's representative, buyers expect their sales agents to be candid, frank, open, and most of all, honest. After all, this is what buyers expect from builders themselves. Sales agents are expected to disclose fully and completely on behalf of the builder exactly what is happening and why, especially if problems have arisen. Anything less than this is unacceptable. A buyer should never hear news first through the grapevine, and second from the agent.

Any sales agent's job is only finished when the deal has closed and you have taken possession of your home. Unfortunately, some new home sales agents think their job is done once the ink is dry on the contract. During the extended period of time between acceptance and closing, a lot of information must still pass between buyer and agent. So much so, in fact, that the work of a new home sales agent really begins only when the offer is signed! This is why it is so important to establish a good rapport with the sales agent before the offer is signed.

This is especially true when problems arise with the transaction, such as a delayed closing. If this happens, the new home sales agent really is on the hot seat. On the one hand he is used by the builder as a go-between, conveying information to and from the purchaser.

Yet the sales agent also is the builder's first line of defence, shielding the builder from direct contact with the purchaser. And the sales agent is also the first person a purchaser like Doreen will look to when she has problems with the builder! With no support from the agent, Doreen will lose confidence in him and ultimately in the builder. Consequently, new home sales agents must be both diplomat and advocate, ally and referee, confidante and mediator. Talk about difficult situations! No wonder new home sales agents walk a very delicate line between standing up for the builder and taking the side of the buyer, while also remaining impartial.

No matter how good a rapport and relationship you have with a sales agent, never put your complete and blind trust in him. Although sales agents can provide considerable assistance and information during the purchase of a newly-built home, there are restrictions on how far they can go to help buyers. Since their first loyalty is to the builder, new home sales agents cannot jeopardize the builder's interest in the transaction. In the pre-contract stage, sales agents are not likely to volunteer unfavorable information, especially if they believe it will encourage purchasers to buy elsewhere. Even after the offer is signed, agents cannot take the purchaser's point of view if it will prejudice the builder. In such a classic conflict-of-interest situation, the new home sales agent will always side with the builder.

There are often times when buyers of newly-built homes cannot afford to accept outright what they are told. Simply being careful is not enough. New home buyers must also be super-cautious, inquiring at all times, asking for proof of what they are told and then checking it out. Being skeptical and doubting may not be your style. But what is the alternative, especially if the information given to you turns out to be incorrect? Who can provide impartial and factual information to you? How can purchasers adequately protect themselves?

A good real estate lawyer can help. Hiring a lawyer means more than just retaining someone to search title for closing. A qualified real estate lawyer can provide you with much of the independent verification you need about the wording of the contract and the other issues that can arise during the transaction. Consulting a lawyer before you sign an offer is a key component of a HOBS, since purchasers can confirm what they are told by the sales agent before they make any final commitments. The advice of your lawyer in the period between acceptance and closing is an equally important part of your home-buying strategy. Your lawyer can ensure you are made totally aware of all developments that occur during that time. If you cannot get a satisfactory answer from the sales agent, chances are the lawyer can. Look to your lawyer for information, guidance and support. Here are a few examples of how a lawyer can help a buyer:

- When Murray was told that the interest rate on his new mortgage was "capped," or guaranteed not to exceed a certain percentage, he insisted that his lawyer highlight that clause in the offer.
- Lou had been told that a vacant tract of land adjacent to his new home was to be developed with single-family homes. After getting names and phone numbers from his lawyer, Lou contacted the local municipality to confirm what the agent had said. After all, Lou didn't want to find a high-rise apartment or a plaza in his backyard in two years' time.
- Mary's offer contained a clause that freed the builder and the sales agent from responsibility for any promises, statements or commitments that did not appear explicitly in the offer. With this in mind, Mary called on her lawyer a number of times between acceptance and closing to make sure various statements made by the agent really did appear in the offer.

Another expert needed by purchasers of newly-built homes to protect their interests in the interval between acceptance and closing is the private home inspector. Few people have the technical expertise to fully understand how a new house is built and how it works. If buyers "go it alone" buying a newly-built home, how can they ever expect to be fully satisfied with what they receive?

Too often purchasers are overwhelmed by the entire new home scenario, and unintentionally ignore defects, deficiencies and uncompleted work. Or seeing defects, buyers feel they're in a "me against him" position, buyer against builder, with the builder holding all the cards. The advantage will remain with the builder, unless the purchaser hires a home inspector to examine the house *before* turning over any money on closing. By matching the builder's level of expertise now, new home buyers gain much needed confidence for future dealings with the builder. (Hiring a home inspector is reviewed in Chapter 27.)

The argument that "purchasers go it alone buying a newly-built home" is far from the truth. Try to work as closely as possible with the sales agent, while keeping in mind where his or her legal loyalty lies. Additional help from your real estate lawyer and home inspector will give you the necessary protection you need when dealing with your builder. Just as people are different, so too are builders. Some are more accommodating than others. Knowing more about your builder is one of the most important safeguards purchasers have to minimize the problems they could face in the future.

Remember too the importance of your home-buying strategy. Properly established and applied, it offers purchasers of newly-built homes much needed security, information and guidance.

Tips and Pointers
- New home sales agents can be very helpful. But understand just how far they can go to assist you.
- See if a "hold" can be put on a house you want to purchase until your lawyer has had a chance to review the offer.
- To avoid "going it alone," rely on your home-buying strategy, your lawyer, and your home inspector.

12

Be Sold on a Builder before You Buy

Any employer who hires new personnel asks for references before making any final decision. The same is true with companies that issue credit cards. In both cases, it makes good business sense to get references and check them out, and to rely on on people's previous dealings with the applicant. When you buy a house and apply for a mortgage, your background will be extensively reviewed, as the lender wants to ensure you are a credit-worthy person. Why shouldn't new home buyers also check out builders' reputations? In fact, shopping for a builder is just as important as shopping for that newly-built house. Before buying a house, buyers must be sold on a builder. Besides buying his product, buyers are also buying a builder's reputation. Purchasing a house without knowing as much as possible about the builder is like driving a car with a blindfold on. It's dangerous. A song from the movie *The King and I* says it all: "Getting to know you, getting to know all about you." Then and only then are you ready to buy one of his homes.

Irv and Lillian are considering the purchase of a home from a builder. Like most purchasers, there are questions that immediately come to mind: Which builder should they choose? How do they choose a builder? How can they learn more about a builder? What do they have to know about a builder? Having a home-buying strategy for a newly-built home is the best way to answer these questions.

Since purchasers like Irv and Lillian are the ones who decide which builder gets their business, doesn't it make sense for them to get builder's references first? Doesn't it make sense for Irv and Lillian to do their homework, to thoroughly investigate what the builder has done in the past, and to find out what his previous customers think of him? Isn't this the best precaution available so purchasers can protect their own interests? Checking out a builder is one of the most useful preliminary steps purchasers can take as part of their HOBS. Unfortunately few purchasers actually investigate builders this way, as it has not been the "accepted" way of doing things. Until now.

When buying a pre-sale or newly-built house, the most important consideration is the reputation of the builder. Builders do not establish track records by running roughshod over buyers. Their reputations are carefully nurtured over time and are the result of showing a genuine, sincere interest in previous purchasers. New players on the scene can gain a good reputation in a community only by treating their buyers with respect and dignity. Despite the full-page ads and the weekend sections of newspapers devoted just to newly-built homes, word-of-mouth advertising is still the most single sought-after form of publicity. Referral business is still the cornerstone to a successful project. A good, solid reputation is still the most important asset a builder has to market.

Knowing more about your builder is essential because of the way new homes are constructed today. A builder really is an umbrella, a co-ordinator for up to twenty different trades who do the actual construction. Few builders employ their own bricklayers, carpenters and painters. Yet even though the builder may do little direct work on the house, he's the one who is responsible to the purchaser, not the tradesmen whom the builder hired. Because of this arrangement, builders can side with purchasers if problems arise, challenging the inferior work done by these hired tradesmen. Learning how far a builder will "go to bat" for people who buy his homes becomes very important.

Occasionally a builder goes bankrupt after the offer is signed and the deposit is paid. What then for the purchaser? Losing the house and any increase in its value is bad enough. But if the necessary precautions haven't been taken to protect the deposit (by dealing with a builder registered with the New Home Warranty Program or by paying it to the builder's lawyer in trust), the deposit will be lost too. All the more reason to deal with a reputable builder, one with an established track record. While it's not an absolute guarantee, past performance does provide important reassurances to new-home buyers.

How can buyers learn more about different builders? First of all, ask the builder or his sales agent for more detail about his home-building background and experience. In what other areas has he built, especially in the last few years? How long has he been in the business? Just because a builder is new is not necessarily a black mark against him. With years of construction experience working as a tradesman for other builders, he may have only recently decided to set up his own firm. Or the builder may have just moved to a community, although he has been building homes for years elsewhere.

Next, independently verify what you have been told. Contact the local home builders' or real estate association. What information do they have on the builder? Have there been any serious complaints from previous purchasers? What information is available about his financial stability? That's an important question when work remains unfinished on closing. Has your lawyer heard of the builder or dealt with him in the past? What experiences, good and bad, have other clients had? Ask the same thing of friends, relatives, neighbors and co-workers. Is the builder registered with the New Home Warranty Program (which is mandatory in Ontario, and voluntary elsewhere)?

Get to know who's actually behind the builder's trade name, as these people are really the ones you are dealing with. Consider the case of a builder like Mac Mack, who antagonized and offended many of his purchasers and developed a tarnished reputation under the name of Barkokba Homes. It is not difficult for Mack to set up a new company called Karbobka Homes and immediately start selling homes again. It's still the infamous Mac Mack building the homes, but now he's masking his true identity behind a new corporate cloak. In the pre-contract stage, the buyer must find out if a wolf lurks behind that sheep's clothing.

Remember too that good builders with proud names and reputations at stake do not change business names like Mac Mack did. These builders advertise and promote their names heavily, as the public identifies them with a certain type of home, quality of construction, and a high regard for their purchasers. A good reputation in the public's eye is one of their most valuable assets. The buyer can feel reassured in dealing with these builders.

Another aspect in selecting a builder is knowing how the builder treated other purchasers, both before closing and through his customer service department after closing. To do this, you must go on site, and visit and talk to purchasers of homes in other projects developed by the same builder you are considering. This can be especially helpful if some homes in the subdivision that interest you are now built, sold and occupied. Don't be shy or afraid to bang on doors in trying to learn what people think about their builders. Ask if you can step inside a house to see the quality of workmanship. What you learn first-hand this way could determine what builder you decide to buy from.

Ask these purchasers if they are pleased with the finished product. Has the builder been reputable, straightforward, honest and reliable? Did he deny buyers access to their house while work was progressing? Was the house fully completed (or at least the interior) when the deal closed? Were all the proper color selections included in the house? Was the pre-delivery inspection (see Chaper 26) meaningful or just a quick run-through? Was the house well constructed?

How were complaints from buyers handled? Was unfinished work completed promptly? As we'll see in Chapter 14, this is extremely important, considering how little assurance purchasers have that the work will indeed be done. Were defects and deficiencies rectified in short order? Has the purchaser faced any serious problems that remain unresolved? Were there any emergencies? How were they handled? Did the builder offer to conduct a one-year inspection just before warranty coverage expired? What about a six-month inspection?

Did the builder's after-sales service department respond quickly when repair work was needed? Or did it take repeated requests, demands and even threats? Did the builder convey the impression that any remedial work was being done as a favor, rather than as a contractual obligation? Did anyone have to take the builder to court because of defects, deficiencies or uncompleted work? What was the builder's attitude towards his purchasers? Did he belittle them or make them feel important? In short, how did the builder treat his buyers?

Did the builder meet his deadlines? If not, did he provide ample notice? If closing was delayed for any reason, did the builder offer any temporary alternative accommodations or compensation? Were there any last-minute surprises, financial or otherwise?

Good communication between builder and buyer is essential in a newly-built home transaction. Find out if the builder communicated well with his purchasers, especially if problems arose with the transaction. If a purchaser learns that one problem has been concealed, he will inevitably begin to doubt the builder and wonder what else the builder is hiding.

Ultimately, the selection of a builder depends on your own instinct and common sense. Remember that no builder is perfect,

and no builder builds a perfect home. In many respects it is a judgment call, depending to a large extent on a builder's reputation.
Previous buyers who speak highly of their builder are an indication that the builder has met their expectations. A builder constantly criticized and condemned by his purchasers is a builder to
avoid. A disreputable builder with a new corporate identity is still
a disreputable builder. While there are no certainties and
guarantees when you buy a home from a builder, past performance
is a very good way to chart future prospects.

Buying a newly-built home can be like buying hair shampoo.
Putting aside all the adverising and slick marketing tools, only one
important question remains: What does the public think about
the product? If the word is good, you will want to buy it. But
shampoo that doesn't meet with your approval can be easily thrown
out. That's not so with a house. *Now* is the time to do your
homework. *Now* is the time to check out different builders. *Now*
is the time, before you make any commitments whatsoever to buy.
The time you invest checking out builders may be some of the most
valuable time you will spend putting your home-buying strategy
to work.

Choosing the right real estate lawyer is another of those all-
important decisions buyers must make. Now is the time to select
a lawyer, to prepare yourself for the moment when you will sign
an offer to purchase.

Tips and Pointers

- Three important factors when buying a newly-built home are
  builder, builder, builder. Check out his reputation and track
  record carefully.
- Speak to other people who have bought from the same builder.
  They will give you a valuable insight into a builder and his dealings with the public.
- Remember "Getting to know you, getting to know all about
  you." A prerequisite to buying a builder's home.

13

Looking at Lawyers

The importance of choosing a qualified real estate lawyer well before any offer to purchase is signed cannot be overemphasized. Offers to purchase newly-built homes can be a buyer's nightmare, chock full of onerous responsibilities and hidden financial charges for the buyer to bear and concealed escape hatches for the builder. Only by establishing a close working relationship with a lawyer in the pre-contract stage can purchasers both confidently sign and plan for the interval while the house is being built.

Look at the lawyer's position. How can a lawyer provide any guidance or advice to a purchaser if the offer already has been signed and accepted? How can a buyer confirm that the statements made by the sales agent are properly written into the offer? Once the commitment is made, the lawyer must then deal with the offer as a *fait accompli*. One of the prime opportunities lawyers have to provide invaluable information and assistance about buying a newly-built house, a particular builder, and new home offers is gone forever. What's more, having to select a lawyer once a contract is signed puts added pressure on buyers, who likely are already nervous and anxious. So be fair to yourself. *As part of your home-buying strategy, choose a lawyer to represent you early on, before you sign any offers to purchase.* Never leave it until the contract is signed and accepted.

Many people often postpone choosing a lawyer because they're intimidated by the legal profession, especially if they have never needed the services of a lawyer before. Perhaps many years have passed since current home owners last used a lawyer. Len and Gail may be afraid to contact a lawyer because they don't know who to choose and what to expect. Unfortunately, the longer Len and Gail put off choosing a lawyer, the more they actually prejudice their own interests.

Never lose sight of the fact the lawyer you select is on your side! He or she is your ally in dealing with the builder. Your lawyer's experience, knowledge and expertise is there to help you. So select a lawyer, the sooner the better.

How should newly-built home buyers decide on a lawyer to represent them? Keep in mind the legal profession is a service industry, one that's heavily dependent on word-of-mouth advertising. Satisfied clients and the referral business they generate are the cornerstones of a successful legal practice, despite the liberalized advertising rules lawyers now operate under.

When selecting any professional, experience and expertise is paramount, followed closely by how that professional treats clients. Like doctors, lawyers must be able to reassure their clients, and make them feel comfortable and relaxed. Home buyers should be looking for a lawyer who demonstrates a genuine interest in clients during this exciting time in their lives.

The role of the lawyer is part advisor, part devil's advocate, part confidant and part nursemaid. Whatever questions however routine, are put to the lawyer must be answered directly and completely. Educating clients is an important part of a lawyer's function as well. Clients must clearly understand what the offer says so they can make an informed decision about buying the house that interests them before they sign. All stages of the transaction between acceptance and closing must also be clearly explained, especially if problems arise along the way.

The best way to find an *experienced and qualified* real estate lawyer is to compile a list of prospects based on personal recommendations from family, friends, co-workers and neighbors. Ask these people about their dealings with the lawyer, about how well the lawyer handled their affairs. Other people to ask for recommendations and opinions are bank managers, insurance brokers, accountants — even your doctor. Make sure your list contains the names of at least three or four different lawyers from which to choose. One or two lawyers may be referred to several times from different sources, which can be a good indication. Remember to make your inquiries early, well before any deal is struck.

If necessary, contact the provincial law society — it operates a lawyer referral service. For a nominal charge you can arrange a preliminary meeting with a lawyer, at which time you can ask questions and learn about his or her qualifications and experience.

Then start checking out each lawyer's reputation, both in the legal community and in the community at large. Some provincial law societies dislike the term "specialist," but it is a fact that some lawyers are more experienced and better qualified than others in the real estate and mortgage field. When you select a lawyer, look for one who practices extensively on behalf of new home or condominium purchasers. It makes no sense to retain a lawyer who does not often process these complex residential real estate transactions. Remember "getting to know you, getting to know all about you." Selecting a lawyer is a lot like choosing a builder, since reputation and track record could be the determining factors in your decision.

Now, pick up the phone and call the names that appear on your prospect list. Spend a couple of minutes discussing the proposed transaction with them and review what they will charge if you retain them. Most lawyers are very sensitive when it comes to discussing their fees. Some are prepared to give price quotes over the telephone, while others won't. Other lawyers have printed price lists they will give to prospective clients.

But a purchaser faces more than just legal fees before closing. A good lawyer will tell you about the "overall closing costs" you will incur buying a newly-built house, not just what his or her legal fees will be. These overall costs include disbursements, provincial taxes, cost associated with the mortgage, and numerous price adjustments in favor of the builder. (Further information about the so-called "hidden costs" appears in Chapter 17).

These "hidden costs" usually are revealed to purchasers just days before closing. Too often they are an unpleasant last-minute surprise. To properly plan for a closing, buyers must know before they sign an offer what it *really* will cost to close the purchase. Hidden costs can be expensive. Imagine the problems you would face if you did not have enough money set aside for closing! Followers of the HOBS approach to buying a newly-built home will know all about these overall closing costs before they ever put pen to paper.

Experienced real estate lawyers should be able to calculate with reasonable accuracy the true cost of closing, even at this early stage. Unfortunately, not enough lawyers provide information about closing costs to prospective clients when initially contacted. So any lawyer who volunteers information about closing costs when asked about his fees should be seriously considered as your choice for that reason alone. This is the type of person you want to deal with — one who is honest and candid, one who has your best interests at heart.

The lawyer David and Jan chose was the only one who was prepared to discuss fees and overall closing costs over the phone. After reviewing the offer with their lawyer before they signed, David and Jan were able to budget properly for closing. This meant they were able to arrange just the right size of mortgage. More importantly, David and Jan were able to avoid the last-minute financial crisis Syd and Jackie faced, people who knew nothing about hidden closing costs until closing time.

These additional closing costs are fixed and nonnegotiable, no matter which lawyer you choose. The only variable item is the lawyer's own fee. Any lawyer who quotes a "lowball" figure for closing costs is simply baiting the hook, telling you what you want to hear, and saving the bad news until later. Don't discredit a lawyer who is straightforward with you about fees and closing costs. You will only be hurting yourself if you do.

In contrast to courtroom lawyers who charge for their time on an hourly basis, fixed "block fees" are the norm for real estate lawyers. As the fee charged reflects the work to be done, a lawyer will need more information about the proposed transaction before quoting his fee and estimating how much money will be needed to close. Typical questions a lawyer will ask include: Who is the builder (different builders have different hidden costs)? What is the purchase price? How is the transaction being financed? When is it closing?

Processing a purchase with no mortgage is easier than a deal with one mortgage. In turn, a transaction with one mortgage involves less work and is cheaper than a purchase where two mortgages are arranged. Vendor-take-back mortgages, where the seller offers the buyer a new mortgage on closing, are easier to process than new mortgages arranged with an outside lender. A transaction in which a purchaser assumes the builder's mortgage is even easier to complete. A lawyer's fee estimate should be structured this way, so the buyer knows how much he is being charged for each component of the transaction. It makes comparison shopping for lawyers' fees that much easier. Of course, unusual or unexpected problems in the transaction will require an adjustment on the quoted fee.

The sale price for a property should not be the determining factor in setting a lawyer's fee, although it is certainly considered. As far as the actual work is concerned, all purchase transactions with one new mortgage are virtually the same whether the purchase price is $75,000 financed by a $50,000 mortgage or $750,000 with a $500,000 mortgage. But the more expensive the property, the greater is the potential liability assumed by the lawyer. This accounts for the higher fee quoted on the more expensive property.

Today, many purchasers of newly-built homes pay cash to the builder and arrange their own mortgage. Where the same lawyer acts for both the purchaser of the property and the mortgage lender, as is usually the case, it would be unfair for the laywer to charge twice the purchase fee quoted. Certainly, the lawyer must spend additional time processing the mortgage for the lender. But much of the work from the purchase side applies to the mortgage transaction as well. Therefore, the additional fee payable for work on the newly-arranged mortgage should take this into account.

Legal fees in real estate transactions are negotiable in most areas of Canada, although suggested fee schedules or "tariffs" are published by local law associations. Often the fee quoted will be less than tariff, as the legal profession is a very competitive business. Out-of-pocket disbursements always are an extra charge to the quoted fee.

While prudent purchasers will shop around and carefully compare price quotations for legal fees, remember that what you are shopping for is a service, not a product. Keep in mind that quality is the key and not cost when dealing with professional services. This means there is more to choosing a lawyer than just the price. Purchasers will get what they pay for. *Never let price alone be the deciding factor in choosing a lawyer.*

Like any other professional in his field, a lawyer who specializes in real estate work will charge a premium for his services. But it's often worth the extra expense. Since most closing costs are fixed anyway, the only monetary savings comes from shaving down the lawyer's fee. But to save $25 or $50 and reject a highly recommended lawyer, when tens and even hundreds of thousands of dollars are at stake, just does not make sense. Why choose the cheapest lawyer over an acknowledged expert when the savings may represent less than one-tenth of one percent of the total price for the house? That's being penny-wise and pound-foolish. When you're making that sizeable a financial commitment, consider the extra fee as money well spent, a form of insurance that you are getting the best possible legal representation.

Once you have chosen a lawyer, arrange a meeting even if you do not yet have an offer ready for consideration. This way, your lawyer can become familiar with you and your plans and will be available, "on standby." Once you've found a suitable home and you are ready to submit an offer to purchase you can contact your lawyer on short notice to review and comment on the offer.

During the introductory meeting, you should finalize both the fee being charged and the payment schedule. A lawyer's fee is usually paid in full on closing, although alternative arrangements are possible, if settled early. Be prepared for your lawyer to ask for a retainer of several hundred dollars once the offer is accepted to cover the cost of initial expenses.

It's always a good idea to understand how your lawyer's office operates. Delegation of responsibility is essential for any business, including a law office, to function properly. Find out which secretary will assist the lawyer with your file. The secretary can answer most of the routine questions, but make sure the lawyer will be available to deal with your important concerns. Some law offices are like real estate "factories," where lawyer/client contact is virtually nonexistent. Yet the ultimate responsibility in a real estate purchase rests with the lawyer, not a secretary, clerk, assistant or para-legal. As a purchaser, you hire a lawyer. You have the right to see and talk to him or her whenever necessary.

Some purchasers believe it is better to use the builder's lawyer when they buy a newly-built home. They argue that the builder's lawyer is familar with the state of the title; that he can cut through red tape faster in dealing with the builder; and that it will save purchasers time and money, since the builder's lawyer is already doing paperwork for the property. But nothing could be further from the truth. It does make sense for a buyer and lender to be represented by the same lawyer in a purchase transaction, since their interests are compatible. But to represent the buyer and the builder puts the lawyer in a conflict-of-interest situation. If a problem arises, the lawyer would be unable to represent either client, which could cost the lawyer a very valuable client — the builder. In a newly-built home transaction, each side should have separate legal representation. Chapter 18 will examine how your lawyer can assist you by reviewing an offer to purchase before it is signed.

*   *   *

Look how far you have progressed so far. First, you've developed that all-important home-buying strategy. After giving careful consideration to your needs, wants and ability to pay, when to buy and what to buy, you began putting your unique HOBS to work. You have considered community, neighborhood, specific site factors as well as the problems associated with buying a home from plans. Items have been shifted back and forth between the "needs list" and the "wants list" and their order of priority changed. Over time you gained valuable practical experience on how to buy a newly-built home. You've also had preliminary discussions with a lawyer, one of the key role players needed to ensure you are not alone in this transaction. Finally, you realized how important it is to be sold on a builder, since buying a newly-built house also means buying the builder's reputation.

At this stage, you are ready to concentrate on finding that "dream home." Yet it is still premature to sign any offer to purchase. A whole host of other concerns must be addressed that will affect both your purchase as well as your ownership of a newly-built home. These will be examined in more detail in Part Three: Key Concerns Before You Sign.

Tips And Pointers

- Shop around for a qualified real estate lawyer before you sign an offer to purchase.
- Why reinvent the wheel? If you do not have a lawyer to act on your behalf, get references from friends and family.
- Make sure you find out about overall closing costs when you ask a lawyer for a price quotation.

Part Three

KEY CONCERNS BEFORE YOU SIGN

14

Warranties for Newly-built Homes

Would anyone today buy a new car without a manufacturer's warranty — not for 12 months, 20,000 kilometers, nothing? Very, very unlikely. In fact, the terms of a new car warranty are an important selling feature. People are also concerned about warranties when they buy a television set, VCR or even a coffee maker. Yet for some reason, this isn't the case when people buy a newly-built home. Day in and day out, Canadians will spend perhaps ten times the cost of a new car to buy a newly-built house, and not get any type of new home warranty from the builder! It doesn't make any sense, but that's what happens.

Yet there are some warranty programs on the books. In the middle 1970s, a developers' group called the Housing and Urban Development Association of Canada (HUDAC), introduced a voluntary warranty protection scheme for buyers of newly-constructed homes. Ontario is the only province to date — and one of the few jurisdictions in North America — that has passed legislation converting this New Home Warranty Plan (NHWP) into a mandatory program. In Ontario, all builders of new homes must be registered with the NHWP, and all newly-built homes must be enrolled. In other provinces, participation is totally voluntary. While some features of the NHWP may differ from province to province, the principles discussed in this chapter apply right across the country, if the builder is registered under the plan. Although the program is properly known as the New Home Warranty Plan, many people still refer to it by its old name, the HUDAC warranty, and the final inspection before closing the HUDAC inspection. This pre-delivery examination of a newly-built home is discussed in Chapter 26.

One of the very first questions a newly-built home buyer should ask is whether the builder participates in the New Home Warranty Plan. Outside Ontario, builders can offer some alternative types of warranty, but these are rare. Considering the amount of money involved, the potential for problems to develop and the lack of protection for your investment, *do not buy a newly-built home from a builder who is not registered with the New Home Warranty Plan.* Discovering that a builder is unregistered should be reason enough to leave the sales office and never return. If the builder claims to participate in the NHWP, get his registration number plus the enrollment number for the house that interests you, and confirm the information with the NHWP.

Although the NHWP has a number of serious shortcomings (which will be examined later on), it does offer purchasers of newly-built homes considerable protection compared to the alternative — "caveat emptor" or "buyer beware." Under that principle of law, buyers are truly on their own, left to assume most of the risks if problems arise after closing. Whatever protection a purchaser has against defects, deficiencies and uncompleted work is a matter of negotiation between the builder and the buyer, to be spelled out in the contract. Otherwise, purchasers must rely on the good faith of the builder to rectify or complete any defective or unfinished work — a very weak form of protection indeed! Problems that cannot be straightened out amicably must be resolved in court, a costly and time-consuming process.

Where the NHWP applies, it protects detached and semi-detached single-family dwellings as well as duplexes. Two types of coverage are provided for condominium purchases: one for the residential unit, and the other for the common elements of the condominium. Seasonal homes like cottages and renovated properties are excluded from the NHWP. High-rise condominiums are excluded in Manitoba. In Ontario, where all builders and all new homes must be covered, the cost of enrolling a newly-built home presently is $50 plus $2 for every $1,000 of the sale price. Many purchasers there pay this fee as an adjustment on closing, although the cost of the warranty is included in the purchase price of the new home in other provinces.

Since it's the house and not the buyer that is enrolled in the NHWP, any warranty coverage that remains is transferrable to a subsequent purchaser of the property. As a consumer protection measure, buyers of newly-built homes in Ontario cannot waive their right to NHWP coverage in any offer they sign. NHWP protection is in addition to, and does not take away from, any other rights or warranties the buyer may have, despite the wording of many builders' offers.

While the NHWP mainly covers post-closing problems, it also contains an important safeguard that protects purchasers before the deal closes. What happens to the deposit paid by purchasers like Guy and Anne if the builder goes bankrupt before the house is completed? The loss of a deposit is a serious concern, as deposits in new home transactions normally are paid directly to the builder and not to a real estate agent or other third party "in trust."

Deposits of up to $20,000 in Ontario (less in other provinces) are protected by the NHWP. If the builder is unable or unwilling to return that money to Guy and Anne after the transaction has been cancelled, the NHWP will repay it from a guarantee fund. Nowadays, builders ask for deposits up to $20,000 so that they can reassure purchasers that the full amount of the deposit is protected by the NHWP. *Never pay more than this protected amount as a deposit to a builder* unless other satisfactory security such as excess insurance coverage from the Mortgage Insurance Company of Canada or a letter of credit from a chartered bank is provided. If you're in doubt how large a deposit is protected, check with your lawyer.

There is serious limitation to this coverage where a condominium unit is being purchased. In Ontario, the maximum amount the NHWP will guarantee for any one condominium project is $1 million ($2.5 million in Alberta). Purchasers in a project containing over 50 units could be prejudiced by this restriction. As one of a hundred buyers in a condominium complex, the maximum deposit guarantee Michael and Susan could recover from the NHWP is $10,000. In fact, Michael and Susan assume a greater risk than Joey and Julie, who have purchased one of the 100 homes constructed by a builder in a subdivision. To better protect themselves, new condominium purchasers like Michael and Susan must make sure that *all* of their deposit is fully insured, either by the NHWP or an outside insurer.

Aside from protecting the deposit, the NHWP does little to assist buyers in the interval between acceptance and closing. In Bernie and Hilary's purchase, closing was delayed for several months, yet the NHWP was powerless to help the couple get compensation for the delay, or even to force the builder to complete the home as quickly as possible. The same was true when Rutzeer Homes decided to cancel Wayne and Lavern's offer, as it was not satisfied with the "economic feasibility and viability" of the project. In both cases, the NHWP felt that these were contractual matters to be resolved between builder and buyer in the offer to purchase. No wonder many purchasers question the effectiveness of the NHWP.

Most of the NHWP's power only apply when the deal has closed and the purchaser is in possession of the house. The basic warranty on the house, known as the builder's warranty, protects purchasers against defective materials and substandard workmanship (like parts and labor on a car) for one year from the date of possession. In addition, the NHWP offers protection against major structural defects for *only* five years from the date of possession. Let's take a closer look at the details of NHWP protection:

a)Protection against defects in workmanship and materials

According to the NHWP, every builder warrants that the house is free from defects in workmanship and materials, that it is fit for habitation, and that it was built according to provincial building code standards. During the first year after possession, it is the builder's responsibility to correct *at his own expense* any defects that are noticed and properly reported. If the builder goes out of business during this one-year period, the NHWP will honor the warranty. Complaints or warranty claims must be reported *in writing* to both the builder and the NHWP within the first year of occupancy, to extend beyond one year the builder's obligation to correct defects in the basic coverage. After the first year of occupancy, the builder has no further responsibilities to the purchaser under the plan.

There are limits to the extent of coverage provided by the NHWP's one-year warranty. First, the maximum liability coverage per unit is limited to $20,000 per home ($30,000 in Alberta). The limit may be lower for individual units in large condominium projects. In addition, the NHWP does not provide blanket warranty coverage. Only defects that could be considered the builder's fault are protected, which excludes items like normal wear and tear; normal shrinkage of materials such as caulking and grouting caused by drying after construction (a favorite exception builders use to deny liability); cosmetic damage such as minor nail pops and peeling paint; damage resulting from improper ventilation and maintenance (another favorite exemption builders use); damage caused by the homeowner's negligence; alterations and changes made by the purchaser; settlement of soil around the perimeter of the building (an unfortunate exclusion, as major settling of earth could affect the drainage of water around the building, causing flooding in the basement); surface defects that the buyer agreed to accept in writing prior to possession; plus secondary damage (personal injury or damage to personal possessions inside the house caused by a defect in workmanship and materials). In Barry and Marla's house an improperly secured light fixture crashed to the floor, cracking the ceramic tiles. The light, being a defect in workmanship, was replaced but the cracked tiles were not, being secondary damage. Despite these limitations, some builders do repair nail pops and settlement cracks in the drywall after one year, if the wall has not been repainted or wallpapered. Before you sign an offer, ask the sales agent whether the builder you plan to deal with provides this feature. If so, get this commitment written into the offer to purchase.

The NHWP also requires that construction comply with the minimum provincial building code standards. Specialty items over and above code requirements, which are often the features that turn a house into a home, are not protected. Included are upgrades, options and extras, special finishes, special materials and color choices. The proper installation and completion of these items, without any defects in workmanship and materials, is a contractual matter strictly between builder and buyer. Even with the NHWP, it's still "caveat emptor" here. Also excluded are appliances bought from the builder such as a fridge, stove, washer, dryer and dishwasher, all of which should have their own manufacturers' warranties.

The extent of warranty coverage provided by the NHWP is actually quite limited and much more restricted than most buyers at first believe. During the first year after possession, the NHWP offers protection only against defective workmanship and materials. *It does not provide that uncompleted items, deficiencies or unfinished work will be done, and it will not reimburse buyers to have these matters completed.* Imagine how shocked newly-built home buyers like Aaron and Sharon were to learn the NHWP offered absolutely no protection against unfinished or uncompleted work. Most purchasers like Aaron and Sharon incorrectly assume that the enrollment fee for the NHWP will protect them if the builder goes bankrupt and leaves work — any work — that is not satisfactory.

This exclusion of uncompleted work is the plan's greatest shortcoming by denying new home buyers coverage in the area they expect it most. When it comes to unfinished work, the NHWP again is basically saying "caveat emptor" to buyers. Ensuring the house has been completed before you take possession or having unfinished work completed after closing are strictly considered as contractual matters between builder and buyer.

Compounding this serious exclusion from the NHWP are two very important facts: i) builders' offers insist that closing take place and all money change hands when the *interior* only of the home is substantially (not fully) completed; and ii)purchasers are not allowed to hold back any money on closing to ensure any uncompleted work will be finished. Practically speaking, while buyers receive a house that is not 100 percent completed, builders receive 100 percent of the buyer's money on closing. The only guarantee the buyer has that the uncompleted work (especially on the exterior of the house) will be finished as planned is the builder's word! If the work is not done, or if the builder goes bankrupt before the work is completed, the buyer has no recourse through the NHWP, the one independent source that could protect buyers in these circumstances.

Ted and Gwen and many of their neighbors discovered the limitations of the NHWP the hard way several years ago. Their builder, Guniff Homes, went bankrupt shortly after closing. The NHWP would not install the air-conditioning system, pave the driveway or have their concrete garage floors poured, things that Ted and Gwen had already paid for. Ted and Gwen ended up paying twice to have these items completed. The homes Dean and Gene bought demonstrated an interesting distinction between defects and uncompleted work. Guniff Homes failed to install a toilet in Gene's house, and the NHWP would not deal with this unfinished item. In Dean's home, the toilet installed did not work properly. Following the builder's bankruptcy, the NHWP removed the unrepairable toilet and replaced it with a new one. In both cases work was "outstanding." In both cases the purchasers lacked what they bargained for. Dean was protected because his toilet was defective. Gene was not protected because his was considered to be uncompleted work.

Remember that the NHWP is concerned only with defective materials and workmanship. *The NHWP offers no protection against uncompleted or unfinished work.*

b)Protection against major structural defects

Many buyers like Stuart and Lily believe the NHWP offers the same level of protection during years two through five as they received in the first year of ownership. Not so. After the one-year warranty expires, all that is covered for a further four years are major structural defects.

Major structural defects are narrowly defined by the NHWP as defects in workmanship and materials that cause a load-bearing portion of the building to fail, or that materially or adversely affect the intended use of the building. Load-bearing areas include roof trusses, ceiling joists, load-bearing walls and columns, floor joists, foundation walls and footings. Significant damage due to soil movement is also included as are *major* cracks in basement walls (but not the ever-present hairline cracks).

By the NHWP's definitions then, damage to drywall and plaster, roofing materials, exterior siding, brick and stone veneer and basement and garage floors as well as dampness and damage to finishes are all excluded from protection after the first year. In other words, NHWP coverage after the first year is limited indeed. For the plan to take effect, a wall must topple over, a floor has to cave in or a roof must collapse.

Probably the biggest complaint people have about newly-built homes is leaky basements. *Minor* cracks in basement walls are not protected by the NHWP after the first year, even if water seeps through the cracks. To protect yourself, make sure you report in writing any cracks in the basement to the builder and the warranty program as soon as you detect them, and certainly *before* the basic one-year warranty runs out. After the first year, the NHWP takes a very hard line on leaky basements, considering cracks that may leak but do not threaten the structural soundness of the house to be minor. This means that despite the new home warranty, many cracks in basement walls are not covered by the plan. Many purchasers rightly feel that these cracks should be protected, as it is a problem not always noticeable until a house has had at least a year, and four full seasons, to settle.

The voluntary programs in Alberta and British Columbia will pay up to $3,000 ($2,000 in Saskatchewan) in additional living expenses and/or moving expenses, if a home must be vacated due to defects in workmanship and material which the builder or the NHWP is obligated to repair.

Pre-Closing Procedure

Whether or not the NHWP applies, all buyers of newly-constructed homes should conduct their pre-delivery inspection, or PDI, with the builder's representative several days before closing (never after).

This inspection is essential to validate coverage under the NHWP. During the inspection, make a note of both defects and un-completed items so that you have a complete record of what work is outstanding. If the house will be covered by the NHWP's war-ranty, list these items on the plan's Certificate of Completion and Possession. Consider having a home inspector accompany you on your PDI.(See Chapter 27).

Although uncompleted work is not covered by the NHWP, On-tario legislation requires that defective workmanship and materials *plus* unfinished work must be listed. This requirement is misleading to buyers, to say the least. No wonder purchasers wrongly assume that *all* items listed on the Certificate of Completion and Posses-sion, both defects and uncompleted work, are covered by the plan.

Once the PDI is completed, both the buyer and the builder sign the Certificate of Completion and Possession. The buyer retains one copy, while the another is filed with the NHWP. Several weeks later the NHWP forwards a "Warranty Certificate" to the pur-chaser. If your new home was built under the NHWP, make sure you get this Warranty Certificate. Call the NHWP if you haven't received it. If the builder has not submitted the Certificate to the plan, have your lawyer follow up on this immediately.

A detachable sticker containing the enrollment number for the house is attached to the Warranty Certificate. Place it in an acces-sible location, near the fusebox or circuit-breaker. Store the actual certificate (a copy of the Warranty Certificate issued to homeowners in Ontario appears opposite)in a safe location with your title papers and reporting letter. In condominium projects, a separate War-ranty Certificate covering the common elements is sent to the con-dominium corporation. It takes effect the day the condominium is registered.

Post-Closing Procedure

Homes are like cars. They need some time to be broken in. Obviously not all defects will become apparent when the PDI is conducted. What about defects you notice for the first time after closing but within one year of possession? By signing the Certificate before closing, will coverage on these items be denied to purchasers like Jack and Elaine? No. The NHWP warranty covers *all* defec-tive materials and workmanship, whether or not they are listed on the Certificate. Still it's prudent to be as thorough as possible on the PDI. Conducting your PDI before closing also prevents the

Warranty Certificate

(Ontario New Home Warranties Plan)

ONTARIO NEW HOME WARRANTY PROGRAM

ONTARIO NEW HOME WARRANTY PROGRAM (the "Corporation") hereby confirms that the home identified below has the benefit of the warranties set forth in The Ontario New Home Warranties Plan Act, 1976.

WARRANTY No. R _____ H _____

ADDRESS OF HOME _____

DESCRIPTION OF PROPERTY   Lot/Block _____ Plan _____

TYPE OF HOME (If Condominium, Unit No. and Plan No.) _____

DATE OF POSSESSION _____

VENDOR _____

DATE _____

ONTARIO NEW HOME WARRANTY PROGRAM

by:

_____
Registrar

_____
Chairman

WARRANTY

A The Vendor warrants to the Owner.

(a) that the home (i) is constructed in a workmanlike manner, and is free from defects in material, (ii) is fit for habitation, and (iii) is constructed in accordance with the Ontario Building Code.

(b) that the home if free of major structural defects; and

(c) that any items which have been specifically identified in the Certificate of Completion and Possession executed by the Owner and the Vendor on or about the date of possession will be constructed in accordance with the appliable provisions of the Ontario Building Code as soon as is reasonably practicable.

The foregoing warranties take effect from the date of possession specified above and expire one year after the date of possession.

B Where, pursuant to section 14 of the Act,

(a) the Owner has a cause of action in damages against the Vendor for financial loss resulting from a breach of any of the foregoing warranties and the claim is made by written notice to the Corporation within one year after the date of possession, or

(b) the Owner suffers damage because of a major structural defect and the claim is made by written notice to the Corporation after expiration of the foregoing warranties and by the fifth anniversary of the date of possession.

the Owner is entitled to be paid out of the guarantee fund for all such damages, the amount required to rectify any breach of warranty or major structural defect to a maximum aggregate limit of $20,000.

builder from claiming that defects occurred after closing, which makes them the buyer's responsibility.

If problems with the house are noticed or occur during the first year, Jack and Elaine should advise the builder's service department by telephone. If the problem remains uncorrected after a reasonable period of time, taking into account weather conditions and the availability of trades and suppliers, Jack and Elaine should send a letter to the builder stating the home's enrollment number and the builder's registration number plus the legal description for the property. The nature of the problem should be explained in detail together with all attempts the couple made to get the builder out to the house. Finally, they should ask that the necessary corrective work be done immediately. Besides keeping a copy for themselves, Jack and Elaine should send a copy of the letter to their lawyer. Many people send a copy of the letter to the NHWP as well, to notify the plan of problems with the builder. This ensures that the plan knows about the problem within that all-important first year, when the basic warranty coverage is in effect.

Notifying the NHWP is a wise move for another reason. Keep in mind that the ultimate penalty a builder can face from the NHWP is the loss of registration as a builder! The builder might act to rectify the problem at this stage, without having to involve the NHWP further.

But not all problems will be corrected to the purchaser's satisfaction. As a goal of the NHWP is to keep as many disputes as possible out of the courts, it provides a conciliation procedure for buyers and builders. At any time before the warranty expires, Jack and Elaine can request that the problem be considered by the NHWP, upon paying a conciliation fee presently set at $50. The builder must also pay a conciliation fee, based on the number of homes or units sold and the number of conciliations requested. Following an on-site investigation of the problem, the NHWP must provide a written report within 14 days, indicating what corrective work might be needed to settle the dispute. If the NHWP report says that Jack and Elaine's request for conciliation is justified, their fee will be refunded. If the necessary remedial work is left undone, the NHWP has the power to fix the defect and charge the builder for cost of repairs.

To ensure that going to court is the last resort, all offers to purchase newly-built homes in Ontario are deemed to contain a clause in which both buyer and builder agree to submit any disputes to arbitration first. No lawsuit can be commenced until 15 days after the NHWP has had this final opportunity to try and resolve the dispute. Only serious differences should ever wind up in litigation.

Since the NHWP's basic coverage lasts for only one year, some builders conduct a "one-year inspection" immediately before the warranty lapses. Some even conduct an inspection after six months, so items will not be left outstanding for up to a year. Similar to a PDI but done much more quickly, the builder and the buyer again go through the house and list outstanding items. Be sure this is done *before* the first year is up. Otherwise you will have lost your legal rights to have the builder correct the problems. If the builder will not conduct the one-year inspection with you, do it yourself. If you did not retain a home inspector for the PDI, now is your last chance to get an independent expert to examine the house for defects. Remember that to ensure NHWP coverage still applies more than one year after possession, you must send a list of outstanding defects to the NHWP *before* the first anniversary date of your occupancy has passed.

Major structural defects that occur in the second through fifth years should be reported in writing *directly* to the NHWP. Many home owners also send a copy of the letter to their builder, although the NHWP is responsible for making the repairs.

Protecting purchasers against defective workmanship and materials is a step in the right direction, but it is not enough. The exclusion of warranty coverage for uncompleted work, especially in view of the inequality of bargaining position between builder and buyer, is unfair to say the least. Whether an item is defective or incomplete, the buyer feels the house he has bought is just not right, and that work is outstanding. The comprehensive protection buyers need and expect from the NHWP just doesn't exist. It is small wonder that the NHWP is viewed in the public's eye as somewhat toothless!

Still, it's far better to have this limited type of coverage than none at all. At least it provides a mechanism to partially protect purchasers of newly-built homes and to arbitrate disputes about defective work and materials at a nominal cost.

To offer the protection Canadians expect of it, the New Home Warranty Program should be revised in the following ways:

- require that all home builders in Canada be registered and that all new homes be enrolled under the plan.
- extend NHWP coverage to uncompleted work and not just defective work.

- extend the monetary limits on condominium units so that NHWP protection is not limited against purchasers in large-scale projects.
- extend the mandate of the NHWP over leaky basements, the number-one concern of most new home buyers.
- increase the monetary protection limits for dwellings, as they were set a decade ago. House prices, values and costs have increased substantially since that time.
- extend the basic NHWP coverage from one year to a minimum of two years, so that buyers will have more than 12 months to discover any problems. It is ironic that the warranty period on the services installed by a land developer on municipal property up to the lot line is usually three or four years. Yet the basic warranty period on the house built on the other side of the lot line is only one year. In cases where the developer and the builder are the same company, the municipality obtains a longer and better warranty than the home buyer.
- offer extended warranty coverage as an option. If new car manufacturers can do this, why can't builders of new homes offer better warranties for buyers who invest five to ten times more money? A further five-year major structural defect warranty is currently available as an option in Alberta.

Tips and Pointers

- Never buy a newly-built home from a builder who does not offer NHWP coverage.
- Remember that the NHWP protects against defects in workmanship and material only, and not against uncompleted work.
- Clearly understand the limited protection offered by the NHWP before you buy a newly-built house.

* * *

NOTE:
Several changes have been announced to the New Home Warranty Program in Ontario. At the time of printing, they had not yet become law. The first-year coverage for warranted repairs will be increased from $20,000 to $50,000 (no mention was made of increasing the upper limit of coverage for condominiums). Up to $5,000 worth of incomplete work on an occupied house will be

finished if a builder goes bankrupt. Unfortunately, it does little for purchasers whose builders are on shaky financial ground but don't go bankrupt. It also does nothing to help purchasers whose builders simply refuse to complete unfinished work. Coverage for "leaky foundations" will be extended from one year to two years. Much will depend on how "leaky foundation" is defined. Continuing the past narrow interpretation of leaky basements will do little to help home owners. As an incentive, builders who meet certain standards will benefit from a reduction in enrollment fees. This is somewhat of a non-issue, since buyers and not builders pay the enrollment fee. Finally, a list of builders who achieve "a high level of performance" will be published, followed by "merit awards." Brownie points and gold stars for builders? While it will be nice to know who is doing a good job, it would be more useful to know which builders to avoid. And who will set the criteria? A novel approach, since few other industries or professions are rated and ranked this way!

15

Mortgage Matters

Just because many people today pay "all cash" for a house, it doesn't mean they are wealthy enough not to need a mortgage! Instead, it means they plan to arrange their own financing for closing. Even where the builder offers a mortgage for the buyer to assume, or if the builder is prepared to hold the mortgage, it's still important to shop around as carefully for a mortgage as you would for the house itself.

Mortgage packages vary greatly from lender to lender. With so many different features in the marketplace, choosing the right mortgage is no easy task. New home purchasers like Steve and Nancy can get their mortgage financing in three different ways:

a) have the vendor/builder take back a mortgage for the unpaid balance of the purchase price (VTB mortgage);
b) arrange their own "outside" financing; or
c) assume the builder's mortgage, an option that is not available to resale purchasers.

This chapter will examine the basics of arranging a mortgage to finance the purchase of a newly-built home. More detailed information on the strategy of mortgages — what they are, how to arrange the best possible mortgage, how to pay it off quickly and what to do once that is done — is available in my Canadian bestseller *Hidden Profits in Your Mortgage*.

As part of your home-buying strategy, you should go mortgage shopping well before the offer is submitted. Never leave it to the very end. Canvass a number of lenders to learn more about the different packages available in the marketplace. The goal is to help you decide what mortgage offer, including the builder's mortgage, is right for you.

If you do this early on, you can eliminate the pressure and anxiety most purchasers needlessly inflict on themselves as they wait to "get word" about mortgage approval. Pre-qualify yourself well in advance, even before you go out house-hunting. You can hold informal discussions on mortgage financing with different lenders well before you sign an offer, and then formally apply for the best possible mortgage as soon as the offer is accepted. If you and your home pre-qualify for a mortgage, the question is no longer whether a mortgage will be available to you; instead it's a question of *who* will grant you the loan on the best possible terms. Properly applied, a home-buying strategy means little will need to be done after the offer is signed than to submit the mortgage papers and await formal approval.

What is meant by a "builder's mortgage?" To help sell his product, Nebbish Homes makes special arrangements with an institutional lender for mortgages that purchasers can assume on closing. Nebbish Homes can then offer the mortgage as a selling feature of the house, much the same as home size, amenities and color selection are selling features. On closing, buyers take over this mortgage and agree to make all payments directly to the lender. It is called a builder's mortgage even though the builder — Nebbish Homes — steps out of the picture after arranging it. A builder's mortgage, then, is one arranged but not financed by the builder of the house. The actual mortgage lender is a financial institution.

Many resale offers to purchase are made conditional on buyers arranging their own financing within a very short time after acceptance. Offers to purchase newly-built homes work somewhat differently. If Norm and Ellen want to book their own mortgage, that's fine with the builder. But the builder will rarely allow the offer to be made *conditional* on Norm and Ellen arranging their mortgage, especially if a builder's mortgage or a vendor-take-back mortgage is available. This is one reason why preliminary discussions with different lenders and pre-qualifying yourself for a loan are so important when buying a newly-built home.

If you are planning to arrange your own financing, take the unsigned mortgage commitment to your lawyer for review and comment before you sign it, just as you would your offer to purchase. Again it's a form of insurance, so purchasers know the mortgage commitment says nothing more or less than what it's supposed to say. The cost to the purchaser is nominal, since it shouldn't take an experienced real estate lawyer long to consider the contents of the mortgage commitment.

All home owners should be familiar with some basic terms about mortgages:

Equity — The owner's interest in the property. To calculate equity, deduct all outstanding mortgages from the fair market value of the house. If Don and Lyn own a house worth $100,000 and owe $63,000 on their mortgage, their equity is $37,000.

Term — The life of the mortgage, anywhere from six months to ten years. Do not confuse it with amortization.

Amortization — The length of time it will take to pay off the mortgage in full, assuming no late payments and no prepayments. At the end of the amortization period, the loan is totally paid off. Shorter amortizations mean higher mortgage payments, but lower overall interest costs. A typical mortgage could have a three year term and a 25 year amortization. This means it matures in three years, with payments calculated as if it will take 25 years to totally repay the loan.

Blended payments — Each payment a borrower makes is comprised of a principal portion and an interest portion. While each payment is the same during the mortgage term, with each payment the principal component increases while the interest portion decreases.

However Steve and Nancy finance their purchase, they must understand a number of common characteristics about mortgages before they can make an informed decision. Lenders consider both the property and the borrower in deciding whether to grant a mortgage and, if so, what amount. Institutional lenders will insist that the property be appraised to determine its value, even though the sale price should give a good indication what it is worth. The cost to the purchaser for the appraisal is $150 to $200. Private lenders will often waive the need for a appraisal. An appraisal is not necessary with a VTB mortgage, or where the builder's mortgage is being assumed.

All lenders use a simple "loan-to-value" ratio to determine if the property qualifies for a mortgage. "Conventional" mortgages cannot exceed 75 percent of the appraised value of the home. This means that on a $100,000 purchase, a conventional first mortgage cannot exceed $75,000. But purchasers like Rodney and Miriam who have less than a 25 percent downpayment still can buy a home and book a mortgage — at additional cost.

One alternative is to arrange a conventional first mortgage, plus a small second mortgage at a higher interest rate for the shortfall. Another alternative is to book what is called a "high-ratio" mortgage for this high-risk loan. While the interest rate charged would be the conventional mortgage rate, Rodney and Miriam would arrange mortgage payment insurance (examined in Chapter 24) on the entire amount of the mortgage. Applicable to both outside financing and builder's mortgages, this insurance protects the lender if Rodney and Miriam default on their payments. The insurance fee is quite expensive, as high as 2.5 percent of the total amount borrowed, and usually is tacked right on to the mortgage. When George and Gracie borrowed $80,000 on a high-ratio mortgage, the $1,200 insurance fee added to the mortgage meant that it was registered for $81,200. This means George and Gracie owed more on the mortgage than they actually borrowed! Up to 95 percent of the appraised value of a home can be borrowed in some cases, although most lenders insist that at least 10 percent of the purchase price be paid with the buyer's own money.

Calculating how large a conventional mortgage can be booked within the property requirement is very simple. Assuming the purchase price equals the appraised value, just multiply by three the amount of money you have as a downpayment. A $25,000 downpayment will permit a conventional mortgage of $75,000. If the mortgage you need to purchase the home is less than or equal to this figure, you've passed the property value test. If you need a larger mortgage, a high-ratio or second mortgage will be necessary.

In addition to property values, lenders will also carefully examine a purchaser's gross income, to assess the borrower's financial ability to repay the loan. Before they decide if the income requirement is satisfied, lenders will need detailed information about your financial resources. The combined gross incomes of both spouses is usually taken into account if both have stable jobs, with a strong likelihood of continued employment.

Two income tests are rigidly applied to qualify borrowers for a mortgage. According to the key Gross Debt Service (GDS) test, the mortgage payment (principal and interest), taxes and maintenance for a condominium mortgage should not exceed 30 percent of the borrower's gross income before deductions. In addition, lenders examine how much of a borrower's gross annual income is needed to finance *all* debt payments, such as house, car loan, personal loan, credit card payments and the like. Using this second test, the Total Debt Service or TDS ratio, lenders figure that total debt payments should not exceed 37 to 40 percent of a borrower's gross income.

Figuring out if the cost of carrying a home will exceed 30 percent of your gross income is a complex formula. An easier way to see if you earn enough money is simply to add together the monthly mortgage payment (principal and interest) amortized over 25 years; one-twelfth of the estimated annual taxes; and the monthly condominium maintenance payment, if applicable. Then multiply this figure by 40 and you'll have your answer. If your gross income exceeds this threshold figure, you've met the important GDS requirement. Now you know that you earn sufficient money to qualify for a conventional mortgage.

John and Dianne found this a handy way to assess their financial situation, so they could negotiate the best possible mortgage from a position of strength. To finance their house purchase, John and Dianne calculated that the monthly payment would be $610. With annual taxes of $90 a month, (to find out what property taxes will be, ask your sales agent or contact the local municipality) the gross income they needed to qualify for this mortgage would be $610 + $90 = $700 x 40, or $28,000.

Your biggest problem, though, may be to determine the size of the monthly mortgage payment. To do this, refer back to the chart in Chapter 10 which lists the monthly payment per $1,000 of mortgage loan at different interest rates, amortized over 25 years. Earlier in this book we used the chart to calculate how large a mortgage could be booked, depending on the borrower's gross income. Now you can use it to figure out how much you must earn to carry a particular mortgage. After you choose a likely interest rate, multiply the figure by the size of mortgage needed to finance the purchase, in thousands of dollars. What appears in your calculator is the approximate monthly mortgage payment. For instance, John and Dianne needed a $63,000 mortgage and the current interest rate was 11 percent. By multiplying 9.63 (the monthly interest cost per $1000 according to the chart for an 11 percent monthly mortgage) by 63 and rounding the result upwards, they soon learned that their monthly mortgage payment would be about $610.

Keep in mind that different lenders offer different mortgage packages, and that there is more to a mortgage than just interest rates. The rate should be the first, but never the last, factor you consider in a mortgage. But what else should you take into account when making this all-important decision? The factors outlined below apply to the three different ways of financing your new home purchase: VTB mortgage, outside financing and builder's mortgage.

a) Interest Rate

Interest rates are closely associated with the term of a mortgage. Long-term mortgages carry higher interest rates, since borrowers pay a premium for the security of a long, fixed-rate commitment from the lender. Short-term mortgages (six months or a year) carry lower interest rates, but they also subject borrowers to the volatile interest rate market that much more frequently. The rate charged for similar terms is usually identical.

But don't expect an outside lender to fix a maximum rate or cap for the loan, as is often the case with a VTB or builder's mortgage. Where a rate cap applies, make sure there isn't a gap in the cap which could lead to a higher-than-anticipated rate being charged. More information on interest rate caps appears below.

b) Term

Ask yourself how long you expect this house will satisfy your needs and wants. Are you looking at living in the home just for a couple of years, or a long time? The point is, the mortgage term should never exceed your anticipated period of ownership. This is difficult to answer, considering you haven't even bought the house yet! When in doubt, round the term down and not up. Booking a five-year mortgage makes little sense if you plan to sell in two or three years. Besides a higher interest rate and a large monthly payment, you might also face a sizeable prepayment penalty if you sell the house before the mortgage matures.

c) Frequency of Interest Calculations

The more often a mortgage is *calculated,* the more expensive the loan becomes for the borrower. This has nothing to do with how often the *payments* are made: weekly, bi-weekly, semi-monthly, or monthly. A mortgage calculated semi-annually (the standard way of doing it in Canada) is cheaper than a mortgage calculated monthly.

Canadian mortgages are payable "not in advance." Payment is made at the end of the month, unlike rent which is paid "in advance" at the beginning of the month. While rent for July is payable July 1, the mortgage payment for July is paid August 1. Borrowers benefit as they, and not the lender, get the use of the money for the entire month.

d) Realty Tax Account
Many lenders collect one-twelfth of the estimated annual realty taxes with each monthly mortgage payment. As the tax bills are issued, they are paid from this tax fund the lender maintains. Rarely is the rate of interest on savings accounts paid on the funds held in this account. Besides this, lenders insist that up to six months' taxes be prepaid into the account before they come due, to ensure enough money is available when the next bill arrives. As part of your home-buying strategy, negotiate with your lender to pay your own taxes. It's one of the few areas where loan officers do have some flexibility.

e) Assumability
Canadian mortgages may be automatically assumed by any buyer of a home without the lender's consent, unless a restriction appears right in the mortgage. Today, most mortgages contain a "due on sale" restriction, which allows the lender to decide if an existing mortgage can be assumed when the property is sold.

f) Portability
Portability can be considered as "the new kid on the block." Suppose existing homeowners like Nick and Maria decide to "trade up," to buy a larger house with a larger mortgage. If the person who buys from them does not want to assume their existing mortgage, Nick and Maria might face a sizeable prepayment penalty to pay off this loan. Yet they still need a new, larger mortgage to finance their next purchase.

With portability, Nick and Maria can take their old mortgage to their new house, like their furniture, and eliminate the prepayment penalty. If they need a larger mortgage, the "old" money (the portion of the mortgage from the existing mortgage) is blended with the "new" money (the extra money being lent to finance the purchase) in setting the interest rate. Of course, the lender's income and property criteria must continue to be met.

g) Prepayment (The "Open" Privilege)

Interest paid on mortgages in Canada is generally not deductible against other income (as is the case in the United States). So most Canadians try to pay off their home mortgages as soon as possible. By doing so, borrowers like Bill save interest *plus* income tax on earnings needed to finance that prepayment. In Bill's case, a prepayment of $500 saved him $6,000 in interest over the amortized life of the mortgage. But as a taxpayer in the 33 1/3% marginal tax bracket, Bill needed to earn $9,000 income and pay tax of $3,000 to be left with that $6,000. In other words, the $500 prepayment effectively saved Bill $9,000 in income.

For a mortgage with a 25-year amortization, the lender assumes the same payment will be made every month for those 25 years. Any additional money paid before it is due, called a prepayment, can significantly reduce the interest cost for the loan. The four different ways of Paying Off your Principal Sooner — the POPS Principle examined in much greater detail in *Hidden Profits in Your Mortgage* — are reducing the amortization; increasing the mortgage payment; making a lump-sum prepayment; and fast-pay mortgages (paid weekly and bi-weekly).

Carefully note the prepayment privileges in your mortgage, and make sure they appear right in the mortgage document. This is important, as a mortgage is closed (it has no rights of prepayment) unless it contains a prepayment clause. To get rid of this non-deductible expense, it is first necessary to book a mortgage with the most liberal prepayment privileges. Otherwise, you could find yourself saddled with a financial albatross for many years to come.

Now let's examine in more detail the three methods by which buyers of newly-built homes can finance their purchase.

1. Vendor-take-back (VTB) Mortgage

VTB mortgages are really nothing more than a deferred payment of part of the purchase price. Instead of receiving all its money on closing, Buildo Builders took back a mortgage from Denis and Marie to help them buy the home. The mortgage, which ran for several years, represented the unpaid portion of the purchase price.

Most offers in which the builder will hold a VTB mortgage are made conditional on the standard credit check, so the builder can be sure that the purchaser earns sufficient income to carry the mortgage. Unlike resale transactions, a VTB mortgage for a new home is not automatically booked and committed just by signing the offer.

The terms of the VTB mortgage appear right in the offer to purchase. Points to consider include the size of the mortgage; the interest rate; the amount of the payment (or the amortization period); and the mortgage term. Additional clauses dealing with prepayment privileges and assumability on sale also must appear right in the offer.

Since most VTB mortgages are for very short terms — one to three years at best — they should never be considered as permanent financing. Although Buildo Builders agrees to wait several years to receive this deferred payment of the purchase price, it is unlikely that Buildo will renew the VTB mortgage on maturity. This means Denis and Marie will incur refinancing costs in the near future. They could have avoided these costs if a long-term institutional mortgage had been arranged at the outset.

In cases where the builder is prepared to accept a VTB mortgage, watch for the following clauses in the offer to purchase. If you are in doubt about any of these clauses, have your lawyer check them out and explain them to you *before the offer is signed.* Remember that the terms of the vendor-take-back mortgage are dictated by the terms of the offer. If it's not in the offer, it's not in the mortgage.

a) Can the quoted interest rate be altered? If interest rates fall, will the rate on the mortgage drop? If rates rise, will you have to pay any increase?

b) Can you add to the downpayment and reduce the size of the VTB mortgage? Are there any administrative fees for this?

c) Do you have to pay any charges associated with the VTB mortgage, such as the fee charged by the builder's lawyer for processing the mortgage?

VTB mortgages are rare when a newly-built home is sold. In resale transactions, home owners who are anxious to sell may offer to hold mortgages on their former homes. But few builders want to tie up valuable capital this way for a number of years, especially when the demand for newly-built homes is strong. When the market is somewhat slower, Essare Homes might be more willing to take back a mortgage from Ron and Paula in the hope of getting that sale. Essare Homes might even lower the interest rate to slightly below the "ongoing" rate, again with a view to making the sale, or possibly take back a small second mortgage to finalize the deal.

When a builder like Essare Homes takes back a mortgage, that mortgage is often sold to another lender. It makes no difference to Ron and Paula who owns the mortgage, since its terms won't change. However, it makes a world of difference to Essare Homes as the builder can make the sale, liquidate the mortgage for cash, and use the proceeds to build other homes.

2. Arranging Your Own New Mortgage

This is the most common scenario today. A newly-built home is sold for cash, and the purchaser arranges his or her own mortgage for closing. At that time the mortgage proceeds, coupled with the purchaser's own funds, are paid to the builder.

Where are mortgages available? Traditional sources include institutional lenders like banks, trust companies, insurance companies and credit unions. If you hire a mortgage broker to help you find a mortgage, know what they charge before you use their services. Many lawyers and accountants also have clients who invest in mortgages. To stay competitive, private lenders usually offer more liberal prepayment privileges, or interest rates slightly lower than those charged by institutional lenders.

Determine from the lender what the rate is; for how long it is guaranteed; whether the size of the mortgage can be reduced before the loan is actually advanced; and if so, at what cost. When you arrange your own mortgage most (but not all) lenders will allow you to reduce the size of the mortgage at nominal or no cost. Also find out about the closing costs associated with this new mortgage (examined in detail later in this chapter).

3. Assuming the Builder's Mortgage

On closing, Steve and Kerry can assume the mortgage previously arranged by their builder with a financial institution. To calculate how much money they must pay on closing, Steve and Kerry deduct the amount of this mortgage from the purchase price. If the purchase price is $100,000 and the mortgage to be assumed is $70,000, Steve and Kerry pay "cash to the mortgage," or $30,000 to the builder on closing.

Just like the VTB mortgage, the offer to purchase is conditional on Steve and Kerry applying to assume the builder's mortgage; providing all the necessary financial information to the lender who holds the mortgage; and on the lender approving them for the loan. In other words, Steve and Kerry really haven't bought that newly-built home until the lender is satisfied they qualify for the mortgage. If you sign this type of offer, make sure the deposit is refundable if the lender doesn't approve you for the mortgage. Believe it or not, some offers say that the builder can keep the deposit!

By assuming the builder's mortgage, Steve and Kerry assume all the builder's rights and obligations under the mortgage. To protect their interests, lenders insist that purchasers sign a formal mortgage assumption agreement before closing, to create a direct contractual link between the lender and the buyer.

For a number of reasons, many purchasers choose to assume the builder's mortgage on closing. Sometimes it is the best mortgage package available to satisfy their unique needs and wants. Others choose it for convenience, since there's no need to shop around for a mortgage. All the buyer has to do is apply for the mortgage and wait to hear that they have been appoved. Unfortunately, the ease and convenience of assuming a builder's mortgage could end up costing you money.

Never choose a builder's mortgage simply because it is available. Choose a builder's mortgage strictly on its merits. It should be the last mortgage you look at — never the first. Just because a builder's mortgage is available does not eliminate the need to go mortgage shopping, comparing the packages different lenders have to offer. How else will you know if it would be better to pay all cash to the builder or arrange your own financing elsewhere? Unless you shop before selecting, you will never know if the builder's mortgage package contains the most appropriate features *for you.*

Newly-built home buyers like Owen and Melodye must understand what the offer says about the builder's mortgage *before they sign the offer.* A number of blank spaces appear on most new home offers where details about the mortgage — the principal, interest rate, term and payment or amortization — can be inserted. When filling in the blanks, new home sales agents highlight these features as being the terms of the mortgage to be assumed. But that isn't necessarily so!

Owen and Melodye should be on the lookout for hidden clauses that appear in their new home offer dealing with the builder's mortgage. These printed form offers are laden with unexpected provisions that can dramatically alter the character of the builder's mortgage being assumed. Many sales agents themselves aren't familiar with these clauses buried in fine print. It's absolutely essential that Owen and Melodye fully understand what these clauses say, as they could affect the decision whether to apply for the builder's mortgage.

Ask the sales agent pointed questions about the terms of the loan (see below), but never accept what you are told at face value. Have your lawyer confirm what the offer says about the builder's mortgage, while reviewing the unsigned offer. Learning more about the builder's mortgage and any hidden clauses in the offer is another important application of HOBS.

a) *What is the interest rate on the builder's mortgage?*

How firm is the rate? — One of the first paragraphs in the offer contains the particulars of the builder's mortgage. But in many offers, in clauses that otherwise have nothing to do with mortgage financing, you may find statements like this: "If the vendor is unable to obtain the mortgage on the terms as stated, the purchaser agrees to assume a mortgage containing those terms and at such interest rate as the vendor is able to arrange."

Other similar clauses may quote an interest rate for the mortgage, "or such rate of interest generally prevailing amongst institutional mortgage lenders 30 days before the actual closing date." In other words, despite the sales agent's assurances, the interest rate quoted may not be the interest rate you pay on the mortgage! When interest rates sky-rocketed in 1981 and 1982, many builders arbitrarily invoked these clauses. This meant some buyers who had previously been approved for a mortgage no longer qualified and lost their house. Others were saddled with interest rates far higher than anticipated.

When quoted a "firm" interest rate, make sure it really is firm. Find out how long that fixed rate is guaranteed.

Is there a "cap" on the interest rate? — Some builders now offer "capped rates," a guaranteed maximum interest rate payable on the builder's mortgage. This is an acceptable alternative if no firm rate is available. But don't go breathing a sigh of relief until you learn more about the cap and how the rate will be set. No matter what the sales agent tells you, the definition of a rate cap can vary from offer to offer.

Generally speaking, there are two different types of caps: i) a stated maximum rate for the mortgage (the preferable choice); and ii) a surcharge over a rate *that has not yet been determined*. The first type is straightforward. Under no circumstances will the rate exceed a certain amount. Find out when the interest rate will be fixed. Will it be 30, 60 or 90 days before closing, or somewhere in between? And what happens if rates drop between the date of fixing and the day the deal closes? Will you get the benefit of the reduction in rates? Some lenders allow this and others don't.

Purchasers must be cautious, where rate caps are in the second category. Find out when the rate will be set to which the cap is applied. If the base rate is to be fixed just 30 days before closing, a rate cap of 1/2% will only protect purchasers against a rate increase for the last month before closing. Any increase in interest rates until then is totally ignored. When Sam and Roz signed their offer, the interest rate was 11%. Thirty days before closing, mortgage rates had climbed to 13%. All the rate cap did was guarantee that the interest rate would not exceed 13.5% on closing, a far cry from the rate in effect when Sam and Roz signed the offer.

Be wary of interest rate caps that are really interest rate "floors." Henry's offer said the rate would be "not less than 11%." After a moment's thought, he realized the rate would be *no lower* than 11%. But how high could it go? The sky's the limit!

How long is the capped rate guaranteed? — However the rate cap is calculated, be sure the cap really is a cap. Other clauses in the offer could give the builder or the lender an escape hatch that could cost money. Determine how long the rate cap will apply. This is extremely important, since closing may be a long way off.

Lenders will argue that they can't be expected to hold a rate forever. Yet purchasers of newly-built homes could face a real dilemma. For example, if the guaranteed period for the interest rate is six months after acceptance, what happens if the deal is not scheduled to close for another nine months? In that case, the capped rate really isn't a cap at all, purchasers having no assurance the capped rate will still be available on closing. With the worthless cap in place, on closing the buyer could be forced to take whatever interest rate the builder can arrange, if he can arrange any mortgage at all.

Knowing the duration of the guaranteed rate cap is also crucial if closing is delayed for any reason. Make sure the guaranteed period extends past the original scheduled closing date. Otherwise, in addition to the expense and aggravation caused by the delayed closing, you also might be open to the vagaries in the interest rate market immediately before closing. If closing is delayed, a substantial interest rate increase could even jeopardize your mortgage approval and threaten the entire transaction.

Some mortgage lenders will approve you for a mortgage without making any commitment on the rate. This is especially true for condominium units bought before construction even starts. The lender may wait until 90, 60 or just 30 days before closing to set the actual interest rate. As no capped or guaranteed interest rate is offered, purchasers who are unsure when the house will be ready for occupancy also face the uncertainties of the interest rate market.

Be absolutely certain the clause dealing with interest rates reads exactly as the sales agent described it. Too often, purchasers without a home-buying strategy are unaware until just before closing that the rate charged can be higher than they anticipated. If you are quoted a fixed interest rate or a fixed rate cap without variation, make sure the offer says so in plain English. If necessary, let your lawyer revise it. If the builder is sincere about the interest rate then the proposed changes should be acceptable. If the builder rejects the amendments, be thankful you did not sign the offer first. Think how close you came to being hoodwinked! Obviously the builder was not prepared to put his money where his mouth was.

One way to avoid all these problems is to pay cash to the builder and arrange outside financing. Yet this strategy also leaves you open to changes in the interest rates for some time. Obviously, there is no easy or right answer to the question of interest rate caps.

b) How long is the mortgage term?

Many offers state that the mortgage has an "original term" of, say, two years. But if the mortgage was registered 10 months ago, it actually has only 14 more months to run. Therefore, whenever this expression appears, make sure the word "original" is deleted.

In another part of the same clause, or buried elsewhere in the offer, the buyer may agree to assume the builder's mortgage with such term, payments or amortization as the lender may establish. This means an anticipated five-year mortgage could end up having just a one-year term. With a clause like this, the lender (and not the purchaser) has the final say on the mortgage's term. If a fixed term is quoted, make sure the offer does not contain this type of variation clause, or have your lawyer change it before you sign.

c) Other mortgage clauses

Are second mortgages allowed? — Kevin and Sheri have only a 15 percent downpayment. To avoid the sizeable CMHC insurance fee, they would like to assume the builder's first mortgage and arrange a small second mortgage from Kevin's Uncle Fred for the balance. Unfortunately, most offers prohibit buyers from registering any second mortgages until the full amount of the first mortgage has been advanced to the builder, which is usually not done until well *after* closing. This prohibition on second mortgages ensures that the builder's mortgage maintains complete priority over the second mortgage. Purchasers who arrange their own first mortgage do not face this problem.

As for Kevin and Sheri, they are left with several options. One is to pay the CMHC fee on the builder's mortgage, something they really do not want to do. Another option is to hold off registering the second mortgage until the first mortgage is fully advanced. But few second mortgage lenders will allow this, since the security for their loan does not exist until well after the money for the second mortgage is advanced.

To resolve the issue, Uncle Fred registered the second mortgage with the consent of the first mortgagee, the bank. When the bank's final mortgage advance is made to the builder, Uncle Fred must agree to postpone his second mortgage to the first mortgage. This cumbersome arrangement, called a postponement, will cost Kevin and Sheri more money because of extra legal documents that must be prepared and registered. Keep this complication in mind if you need a small second mortgage and are planning to assume the builder's first mortgage on closing.

Can the offer be cancelled if the mortgage is unavailable? — Many people buy newly-built homes on the strength of the builder's mortgage. Yet most new home offers also contain some type of escape clause that allows the builder to cancel the deal "if the vendor is unable, for any reason whatsoever, to arrange first mortgage financing." This clause, which usually appears in the section of the offer dealing with interest rates, aims to protect the builder in the event that a mortgage cannot be arranged at the stated interest rate. Without making it explicit, this clause makes the offer conditional on the builder's being able to arrange the mortgage loan as stated in the offer.

This may be fine for the builder, but it isn't very reassuring for purchasers! First of all, how many people are even aware this clause exists? How many people know that the deal is off if interest rates rise between acceptance and closing and the builder cannot arrange the mortgage?

And even if Ron and Dora were prepared to seek outside financing and pay a higher rate of interest than they were originally quoted for the builder's mortgage, the builder is under no obligation to let them do so once the offer is signed! The clause effectively gives the builder unlimited freedom to cancel the offer, at his whim and discretion, if he encounters any problems whatsoever booking the mortgage. Open-ended clauses like these, which invite abuse by unscrupulous builders, should be eliminated.

Before any offer is signed, find out whether the mortgage terms are fixed, or if the builder's mortgage has yet to be arranged. The answer will tell you much about a builder, his honesty and integrity.

i) If the builder's mortgage has not been arranged, then obviously the cancellation clause cannot be deleted. This means the stated terms of the mortgage are meaningless and cannot be relied on. Also, the builder still can call off the deal. Since the mortgage has not been arranged, then the builder should not be selling buyers on the fixed terms and capped rate of the mortgage; to do so is touching on misrepresentation.

ii) If the builder's mortgage has been arranged, obviously there's no need for the cancellation clause and it should be deleted. After all, the terms of the mortgage are fixed, and the purchaser can be assured it will be available on closing. An amendment to the offer deleting this escape route should be easy to obtain. If the builder refuses to amend the offer, you really have to wonder why, and what he is trying to hide. The builder's refusal to change the offer in these circumstances is reason enough to say thanks, but no thanks, to the builder.

If the sales agent assures you that a mortgage can definitely be arranged on the stated terms, ask the builder to give you that commitment in writing. Have the builder agree to take back a mortgage on the exact same terms as the builder's mortgage in the event he encounters any problem arranging the mortgage described in the offer. Don't agree to a deal where the entire transaction remains conditional on the builder booking that loan.

Can the lender force a change in the closing date? — Consider this statement found in some builder's printed form offers: "Should the vendor be required by the first mortgagee to move up the closing date by no more than 30 days, the purchaser agrees to close on such advanced closing date even though the dwelling may not be substantially completed or ready for occupancy." In other words, the lender can force both the builder and the buyer to reschedule closing to a date earlier than anticipated, even though the house is not ready for occupancy. Astounding!

When this point is raised by the buyer, most sales agent verbally insist that the clause will never be invoked. Yet as long as it stays in the offer, it certainly can be used if the circumstances warrant it. So be firm. If the builder says the clause is not needed, then strike it out. If the builder insists that it remain in the contract, either walk away from the deal or proceed with caution. Clauses like these are a concealed trap for the unwary — all the more reason to take the builder's standard printed form offer to your lawyer for review before you sign it.

When must you apply to assume the builder's mortgage? — Most offers give purchasers very little time after acceptance to apply for mortgage approval, often 21 days, even though closing is in the distant future. Non-compliance with this time limitation could allow the builder to cancel the contract. To avoid this situation, be sure to make your mortgage application promptly.

Despite the wording in the offer, many builders will not even hand over the mortgage application within this time period. If this is the case, get a letter from the builder specifying that the mortgage papers do not have to be filed until a certain date, or confirm this deadline in a letter to the builder. Then the builder (and not you) will be responsible if the mortgage application is not filed on time. Otherwise, if the builder is looking for a loophole to help him terminate the deal, he has the ideal route.

Does an interest buy-down benefit me? — Don't be fooled by low interest rates on a builder's mortgage. To induce buyers to purchase their homes, some new home builders offer lower-than-market interest rates, through a procedure called an "interest rate buy-down." In reality, it's just a modern application of an old adage — "you can pay me now, or you can pay me later." Remember that lenders and builders do not bear the cost of discounting the interest rate. You can be sure that the full cost is paid by you, the purchaser. If the interest rate of the builder's mortgage is substantially below current interest rates, the builder has probably bought down the interest rate and added the cost to the sale price of the house.

Schloof Homes is selling newly-built homes at a time when the current five-year first mortgage rate from most lenders is 11.5%. But Thornhill Trust is offering builder's mortgages to Schloof Home buyers at 9%. On a $50,000 mortgage, the 2.5% interest rate differential for five years will cost Schloof Homes $4,442.20 per house, a cost it will pass on to its purchasers. Thornhill Trust still receives exactly 11.5% over the five years: the 9% on the mortgage, with the difference made up from the lump-sum payment of $4,442.20 plus the interest it generates over that five-year period. By offering its homes at lower-than-market interest rates, Schloof Homes has a much more marketable product.

Eyer Homes offers a different type of interest rate buy-down, a one-year interest-free $10,000 second mortgage. With current interest rates at 11.5%, the cost to Eyer Homes is only $1,057.91, a cost passed on to the purchaser anyway. What a great marketing tool!

Despite their initial appeal, interest buy-downs do have their drawbacks. To finance the $4,500 the builder tacks on to the purchase price to cover the buy-down, purchasers like Harry and Gina effectively must add it to the mortgage they arrange or assume for closing. Having a larger mortgage could be a problem when it comes up for renewal in the future and the interest rate charged returns to normal.

If the interest rate on the builder's mortgage is substantially below current rates, see if the builder will accept a lower purchase price and allow you to pay all cash for the house, if you arrange outside financing. In Harry and Gina's case, the discount off the purchase price should equal $4,500, the cost of the buydown. The builder receives exactly the same amount of money either way. But Harry and Gina end up paying less for the house and carry a smaller mortgage even though they are paying the current interest rate. Of course, Harry and Gina must be sure the reduction in the purchase price matches the additional cost they face to finance their own mortgage. There are computer software programs and mortgage discount books that can provide this information in minutes.

Other mortgage terms — Rarely does the offer spell out what privileges the builder's mortgage contains such as assumability, portability, prepayment privileges, and so on. Usually the purchaser agrees to accept "such terms and conditions as the mortgagee deems advisable." But if certain mortgage privileges are important to your home-buying plans, make sure the offer states that the builder's mortgage will contain those clauses. If this can't be done, consider getting outside financing.

4. Hidden Costs in Mortgage Transactions

Home buyers are often amazed to learn what concealed charges they may face, either in arranging a mortgage loan to finance a purchase or assuming the builder's mortgage, or occasionally when the builder agrees to accept a VTB mortgage. Unfortunately for purchasers, these items are never laid out neatly in one section of most builders' offers to purchase. More often they appear throughout the document, phrased in expressions the average buyer does not understand.

Most of these charges are non-negotiable "cash" costs, payable up front on closing as an adjustment to the builder. You don't get your deed unless they are paid. When you meet with your lawyer before signing the offer, ask him which of the following hidden mortgage costs apply and what the approximate charge for each will be. These charges will all be revealed to you sooner or later. But it's better to learn this information sooner so that you can plan and budget for them. Otherwise, these hidden mortgage costs could be a cash flow killer on closing. Here's some of the more common charges:

i) Arranging/Cancellation/Reduction Fee
Most builders charge buyers for their cost of arranging a builder's mortgage. These include all appraisal costs, initiation and administrative charges, legal fees and disbursements. These unexpected costs to the purchaser could be as high as $300. Most builders used to absorb the cost of arranging a builder's mortgage, but those days of "no-cost financing" are gone. Purchasers who arrange outside financing pay similar charges plus a mortgage appraisal and application fee of $150 to $200.

When a builder arranges financing for a project, the lender commits and sets aside a certain sum of money for builder's mortgages. As some buyers pay all cash or arrange their own mortgages, the builder uses less of these committed funds. But lenders usually charge builders a pre-determined administrative fee or penalty for tying up those funds. Some builders now pass on this cost, about $150, to their purchasers. In other words, some buyers end up paying the builder's costs when they assume a builder's mortgage, and others end up paying the builder's costs when they don't assume it! Talk about hidden costs! They're charged if they borrow and charged if they don't!

After reviewing an unsigned offer to purchase with their lawyer, Carey and Sharon added a clause which proved extremely helpful.

As they were unsure of how large a mortgage they needed for closing, Carey and Sharon asked the builder for a larger-than-expected mortgage. They also wanted the flexibility to shop the mortgage market, to see if a better mortgage deal would be available shortly before closing.

The clause added to the offer let Carey and Sharon ride two horses at the same time. At no cost to them, it allowed Carey and Sharon to reduce the size of the builder's mortgage or eliminate it completely if they wanted to arrange outside financing. All Carey and Sharon had to do was to notify the builder of the amount of the builder's mortgage to be assumed (if any) on closing, at least 30 days before closing.

Many agents in the sales pavillions will tell you that the builder's mortgage can be reduced in size or totally eliminated at no cost to you. But don't take that statement at face value. Many offers today include buried clauses that charge purchasers an administrative fee in these circumstances. Unless you check it out before you put pen to paper, you could end up paying an unexpected fee if you decide to cancel or reduce the size of the builder's mortgage.

ii) Interest on the Unadvanced Portion of the Mortgage

When a builder's mortgage is assumed on closing, the offer requires that purchasers pay a sizeable credit to the builder as an adjustment for something called "interest on the unadvanced portion of the mortgage." This charge is necessary because few builder's mortgages are fully advanced by lenders on closing. Lenders retain funds, often 15 percent or more of the mortgage principal, until work on the property is fully completed, including laying the sod and paving the driveway. This holdback of funds protects purchasers who assume builders' mortgages by ensuring that funds are available to complete any unfinished work if the builder goes bankrupt. This type of protection is not available to buyers who arrange outside financing.

Without doubt, this non-negotiable cost is one of the most confusing conditions of a new home offer. Effectively, it forces purchasers to pay interest on the full amount of the mortgage, even if that mortgage is not fully advanced on closing!

Rick bought a newly-built home from Adanac Homes and closed the deal on December 2. On closing he assumed a $60,000 mortgage Adanac had arranged with Gelt Trust at 12%. Rick also had to pay $600 to Adanac Homes as a closing adjustment for "interest on the unadvanced portion of the mortgage." Since Rick had not taken the offer to his lawyer before signing it, he still needed an explanation of why he had to pay the charge and how much would be refunded and when.

Unknown to Rick, only $51,000 of the $60,000 mortgage was advanced by Gelt Trust to Adanac Homes at the date of closing. The remaining $9,000 was to be advanced when all work on the house was completed. In effect, Adanac Homes was financing $9,000, or 15% of Rick's $60,000 mortgage with Gelt Trust on a short-term basis, until the mortgage was fully advanced.

In his offer, Rick agreed to make the full monthly payment to Gelt Trust in the normal fashion, as if Adanac had already received the full $60,000 from Gelt Trust, even though that mortgage was not yet fully advanced. Obviously Gelt Trust was being paid more than it was entitled to receive. On the other hand, Adanac Homes was receiving nothing, even though it was financing 15% of the mortgage. This is where the $600 Rick paid on closing to Adanac Homes comes into the picture. It represents a non-interest bearing fund from which the interest owing to Adanac on its "loan," the $9,000 unadvanced portion of the mortgage, is paid. As in Rick's case, this charge often is at least one percent of the principal amount of the mortgage.

Rick's mortgage was fully advanced to Adanac five months after closing, on May 2. Since Adanac financed $9,000 of the total mortgage for those five months, it was entitled to receive $540 ($9,000 times one percent per month for five months) as the interest owing on its "loan." After the final mortgage advance was made, Rick was entitled to a refund from Adanac of the remaining $60. By May 2, Adanac had received everything it was entitled to: the final mortgage advance plus interest owing to it on its "loan," the unadvanced portion of the mortgage.

And what about Gelt Trust? Since it advanced only $51,000 on the mortgage on closing, it was entitled to receive interest only on that amount of money for five months. Yet it had been getting monthly payments from Rick as if $60,000 had already been advanced. By paying interest on the full $60,000 mortgage, Rick has been paying Gelt Trust $90 more a month than it was owed. Does this add up to a windfall for Gelt Trust?

No. To balance the books, this extra $90 paid each month is credited as a prepayment of funds to reduce Rick's outstanding indebtedness. The $540 Adanac Homes retained from the $600 fund should equal the amount prepaid by Rick to Gelt Trust over those same five months. When all is said and done, both Adanac and Gelt Trust get what they are entitled to. Once the final mortgage advance takes place, the net cost to Rick should be nil. He may have even gained by prepaying his mortgage as well.

Yet Rick does incur an indirect cost, namely the unanticipated $600 charge he paid as a closing adjustment to Adanac Homes according to the contract. No mention was made of this adjustment in his discussions with the sales agent. Not having a HOBS, imagine how agitated Rick was to learn for the first time about this unanticipated expense just days before closing. It devastated his carefully planned cash projections.

Several other comments about "interest on the unadvanced portion of the mortgage" are worth mentioning. To secure the $9,000 in unadvanced mortgage funds until it was paid, Adanac Homes registered a "vendor's lien" on closing against the title to Rick's property. Once the final mortgage advance was made, Adanac offered Rick a release of this lien, provided he paid the cost to prepare and register it. This is yet another minor buried cost Rick could have anticipated with a HOBS.

To make sure you get back the unused "interest on the unadvanced portion of the mortgage," review the offer to see how the refund will be returned. In most offers, the obligation to request a refund rests with the purchaser. Once all the work is completed on your house, including all exterior work, check with your lender to confirm that the final mortgage advance has taken place. Then write a letter to the builder, asking him for an accounting of how the fund was applied plus a refund of any money remaining in the fund. Remember to do this! It's money rightfully owing to you.

When you review the offer with your lawyer, determine how much money is needed to establish this fund. Too often, all the offer indicates is an estimated or "reasonable" amount. Try to get a specific sum inserted right in the offer, since what is reasonable to you may not be reasonable to the builder. In any event, expect that between 1% and 1.5% of the total amount borrowed will be credited to the builder for this purpose.

When you call your lender to confirm that the mortgage has been fully advanced, ask also how much is outstanding on the mortgage, and when the next payment is due. Because of the unexpected prepayment arising from this delayed mortgage advance, the existing amortization schedule will be out-of-date. A new one must be ordered at nominal cost. Armed with the revised outstanding balance from the lender, you can compare the amount owing after the prepayment against what should have been outstanding, as shown in the original amortization schedule. This allows you to verify that the net sum used for "interest on the unadvanced portion of the mortgage" was actually prepaid against your mortgage, as intended.

iii) Interest to the Interest Adjustment Date (IAD)

The IAD is one of the legitimate but hidden costs involved in financing the purchase of the newly-built home. Simply put, it means buyers/borrowers who close their deals in mid-month pay interest on the loan earlier than normal for the month in which they close. Again, if buyers do not realize this charge exists, interest to the IAD could raise havoc with their cash flow on closing.

Harvey and Donna assumed a $50,000 mortgage at 11% when they closed their new home purchase on June 20. Their lender wants them to make monthly payments on the first of the month. As Canadian mortgages are paid "not in advance," (in arrears at the end of the payment period) their first regular mortgage payment will be due on August 1. It will cover the month of July, the first full month they own the property. July 1 is considered by the lender to be the "interest adjustment date" — the date the mortgage effectively begins to run.

What about the 11 days in June, the so-called "broken" month? Obviously, Harvey and Donna are responsible for interest on the mortgage during that time. But how is this interest paid to the IAD, and when? Here is the one time that interest on a mortgage might be payable "in advance," and calculated daily.

When a builder's mortgage is assumed, the lender will deduct interest for the broken month from the money paid to the builder. In turn, the builder demands a similar credit from Harvey and Donna on the closing adjustments. In other words, Harvey and Donna pay $165.75 up front to the builder on closing, and the builder pays it to the lender. So Harvey and Donna end up paying 11 days early the interest due on July 1 for the broken month of June. One consolation is that no mortgage payment is due for almost a month and a half, until August 1. When outside financing is arranged, a similar amount is deducted by the lender at source from the mortgage advance made to the purchaser.

Closing earlier in the month would compound the situation even further, since a larger amount would be deducted on closing for interest to the IAD. Yet closing later in the month is not an appropriate answer, since closings late in the month have problems of their own (see Chapter 28).

Interest to the IAD is one of those hidden closing costs that can be easily and accurately calculated, and planned for. Simply multiply the amount of money being borrowed by its interest rate, and divide the total by 365. Then multiply that figure by the number of days remaining in the broken month. In Harvey and Donna's case the figures looked like this: $50,000 x 11% = $5,500; divided by 365 = $15.0684; multiplying that figure by 11 days = $165.75.

iv) Establishing a Realty Tax Account

As noted earlier, many institutional lenders collect one-twelfth of the estimated annual taxes from borrowers with each monthly payment. These funds are kept for the buyer in a tax account from which tax bills are paid. For Joe and Kay's new home purchase, closing in late September, the annual taxes were estimated to be $1,440. All current year's taxes were paid prior to closing. Added to each monthly mortgage payment after closing is $125, which is paid into this tax account.

Between closing and mid-February, when the interim tax bill for half the year's taxes will be issued, four mortgage payments will be made. This will put $500 into the tax account. But the interim tax bill will be approximately $720, creating a shortfall of $220. To make sure sufficient funds are on deposit when the first tax bill is issued, the lender demanded a credit from Joe and Kay of $220 when they closed their purchase. Just as in the case with interest to the IAD, the lender charged this sum to the builder who in turn charged it to Joe and Kay as a closing adjustment. Where outside financing is arranged, the lender deducts the appropriate amount for this purpose at source from the mortgage advance.

Not all lenders operate tax accounts. If Joe and Kay could pay their realty taxes directly rather than through the mortgage lender, they could eliminate this lump-sum tax account contribution, an expense levied at the worst possible time, right before closing. Find out if this tax account expense will be a hidden cost in your purchase, and if so, how much is involved. Avoid cash flow problems by asking the right questions now.

v) CHMC/MICC Payment Insurance Fees

Where more than 75% of the purchase price is borrowed on a first mortgage, insurance is needed to protect the lender and ensure that the mortgage is paid promptly. Insurance on these high-ratio mortgages is charged on an escalating scale. If the mortgage does not exceed 80% of the appraised value of a newly-built home, the insurance is 1.75% of the total amount borrowed; 2.5% up to 85%; and 3% up to 90% of the appraised value. Newly-constructed condominiums are subject to a further one percent surcharge. Protection for the lender is very expensive for borrowers. Normally this charge is added right on to the amount borrowed, rather than being paid on closing.

vi) Other Insurance
Life insurance and rate insurance premiums may be payable as well, at the purchaser's option. For further details, see Chapter 24.

Whether you are assuming the builder's mortgage or arranging outside financing, take a copy of the accepted offer to the lender. If you are selling one home and buying another, take copies of both offers to the lender plus details of any outstanding mortgages. This is necessary so the lender can establish the equity on your existing home. An "equity" letter is usually also required from your bank to confirm that you have sufficient money on deposit to pay the remainder of the balance due on closing. Expect the lender to request a letter from your employer, certifying how much salary you earn. And then wait, patiently. Approval takes some time, especially when a builder's mortgage is involved. That's all the more reason why it is so important to informally pre-approve yourself for a mortgage. It makes the wait much easier to take.

Amortization schedules are invaluable aids for home buyers; they show how each mortgage payment is allocated between principal and interest, plus the balance outstanding after each payment. Inexpensive to obtain ($5 to $10), they often provide the incentive Canadians need to start paying off their principal sooner. For more details on how to order and read a schedule, and how to use the information it contains to save thousands of after-tax dollars, see my book *Hidden Profits in Your Mortgage*.

One of the biggest problems existing home owners face is closing both the sale and the purchase the same day. Normally the sale is closed first, followed by the purchase. To happen the other way around, you'll have to arrange bridge financing, our topic in the next chapter.

Tips and Pointers

- Never assume the builder's mortgage without going mortgage shopping first. Have comparisons at hand.
- Pre-qualify yourself for a mortgage early. Be sure to determine that you can satisfy the income and property criteria.
- Carefully review the part of the offer dealing with mortgage financing with your lawyer. Be on the lookout for hidden clauses and hidden costs.

16

Bridge Financing

One of the biggest problems existing home owners face is closing two transactions — the sale of your present home plus the purchase of your newly-built home — on the same day. Unless special arrangements are made with the builder for early possession, the sale must be closed first. Only then can the net proceeds from the sale be used to close the new home purchase. Assuming no major problems occur, it could be well into the afternoon or early evening before you are able to move into your new home.

One solution to the problem of back-to-back deals is to arrange bridge financing and close the purchase days or weeks *before* the sale. To close the purchase, you borrow money from the bank on a short-term basis equal to the net proceeds from the sale. When the sale is completed, the borrowed funds are returned to the bank, with interest. Bridge financing (also called interim financing) is often cheaper in the long run, and a lot less aggravating than closing both deals the same day. When developing a home-buying strategy, existing home owners should consider closing the two transactions on two different days, using bridge financing to close the gap.

Marshall and Shelly are typical home owners. Closings for both their Queen Street sale and their King Drive purchase are scheduled for July 31. The deals had to close in that order, since the proceeds from the old home are needed for the purchase. Closing the sale first thing in the morning is out of the question as Ian and Marie, the purchasers of the Queen Street property, have arranged a new mortgage to finance their purchase. Those funds will not be released until 10:00 a.m., the day of closing. Not until then can things start to happen, and a lot has to happen that day!

First, that money has to be delivered to Ian and Marie's lawyer, deposited in his bank account to be withdrawn for delivery in the Queen Street transaction. Only then can Marshall and Shelly's lawyer use it to close their King Drive purchase. Luckily Ian and Marie are moving from an apartment. Otherwise, Ian and Marie's purchase would also depend on them completing the sale of their existing home, which would delay matters even more.

As events turned out, the closing of Marshall and Shelly's King Drive purchase was unavoidably delayed until 4:00 p.m. for two reasons: waiting for the Queen Street sale to close plus the sheer volume of business in the registry office that day, the busiest day of the month. Back on Queen Street, the movers had loaded up the truck by noon. Now they were waiting and waiting and waiting, at Marshall and Shelly's expense, to get access to the new house on King Drive. Even after that deal closed, it took over an hour before keys for the new house were released to Marshall and Shelly, and they actually took possession of the new house. More than five hours were wasted which cost Marshall and Shelly over $300 in extra moving charges.

Bobby and Pam had heard of the problems and costly delays people faced closing back-to-back transactions the same day. As part of their home-buying strategy, they also scheduled their South Road sale to close on July 31. With closing of their new home purchase on Kent Crescent set for July 27, four days earlier, bridge financing was necessary.

How much bridge financing did Bobby and Pam need to arrange? Like most people, they initially thought it was necessary to bridge finance the entire new home purchase price. Not so. All they had to bridge finance was the net equity in their existing home on South Road. All other funds needed to complete the Kent Crescent purchase would be available regardless which deal closed first.

Bobby and Pam bought the new home on Kent Crescent for $125,000. They assumed a $90,000 builder's mortgage and paid $35,000 cash. Of the cash amount, $25,000 was coming from the South Road sale as their net equity in that property, and $10,000 from their savings. No matter when the Kent Crescent purchase closed — July 27, July 31, or any day before, after or in between — everything except the $25,000 net equity in their old home would be ready for closing. All they would have to bridge finance is that net equity of $25,000.

On July 27, Bobby and Pam used that $25,000 to finance their Kent Crescent purchase. Although it was closing day, July 27 was not a moving day. Excited as any new home purchasers would be, Bobby and Pam did not go to work. Instead they spent the day finishing up packing, and buying a few items for the new house. Once they received the keys later that afternoon, Bobby and Pam moved some fragile items to Kent Crescent, and spent part of the evening giving the new house a good cleaning.

Right on schedule, the movers came the next morning to their old house, loaded up the truck, drove to Kent Crescent and immediately began unloading the truck. No need to wait for keys; Bobby and Pam had received them the previous day! By 3:00 p.m. the move was over. The couple spent the next two days unpacking, and converting that new house into their home. A few items that Bobby and Pam wanted to move themselves were brought to the new home each night. Then it was time for one last trip to South Road to clean up the old house, look back on the good times it had given them, and bid a fond farewell.

The morning of July 31, Bobby and Pam continued to unpack their belongings and put everything in its place. Immediately after the South Road sale closed, $25,000 plus interest was sent to the bank by their lawyer to retire the bridge financing. By the end of that day, Bobby and Pam no longer owned two houses, and they no longer owed any bridge financing.

As Marshall and Shelly learned the hard way, money can often be saved by arranging bridge financing, compared to the additional costs of closing two deals the same day. The total cost to Bobby and Pam's for the bridge financing was $200, which was $100 less than what Marshall and Shelly paid as waiting time to the movers.

Bobby and Pam learned the easy way that many of the important benefits of bridge financing are non-monetary. Staggering the two closings allowed them to move without the pressures, anxiety and aggravation most purchasers face with double-ended transactions. With bridge financing, life could return to normal quickly after closing.

As a very short-term unsecured loan, bridge financing is not cheap, but it is not as expensive as many people fear. Many financial institutions charge a basic administrative fee in the $150 range plus interest. Very often the interest charged is a floating rate of prime plus 2%. Because fees vary from lender to lender, it's wise to shop around and compare costs.

Beware that most financial institutions are very reluctant to grant an unsecured bridge financing loan unless the borrower is a well-known and established customer. The best source of funds may well be the bank or trust company you normally deal with.

Another likely source for bridge financing is the lending institution providing the financing for the purchase. The better the package, the more likely bridge financing can be included in it. When Keith and Rena met with their bank manager, they discussed both bridge financing and the mortgage to finance the purchase. Both loans were granted.

Before he approves any bridge financing, the lender will want copies of firm (not conditional) offers on both houses. He also needs to know how much you owe on your existing mortgage, and how large a new mortgage you require. All this is needed, of course, to verify your net equity in your old home, which is the maximum amount that will be bridge financed. While the deals are being processed, the lender may also want written assurance from your lawyer that everything is proceeding normally, and that no problems are anticipated in either transaction.

Since the loan is unsecured, the lender needs to be sure he will not have to chase after the borrower for payment once the sale closes. To ensure prompt payment after closing, lenders insist that purchasers like Bobby and Pam sign a "Letter of Direction" which authorizes their lawyer to forward to the lender the amount borrowed plus accrued interest and administrative charges from the sale proceeds. This is paid right off the top, *before* any money is paid to Bobby and Pam. The lawyer must also acknowledge in writing that he will honor the terms of the Letter of Direction immediately after the sale closes. Only with this assurance will the lender release the bridge financing funds. If you are thinking about bridge financing, make sure your lawyer will agree to sign this acknowledgment.

Some lenders today ask for different types of security for bridge financing. When you're shopping for bridge financing, don't just ask about the lender's charges; ask if the lender will want any security for the loan besides the Letter of Direction. If so, you will have to provide that security at your expense. Different additional forms of security may include a subsearch of title to your current home, verifying the information you have given about outstanding mortgages (inexpensive); a mortgage registered against either or both your old and new homes (very costly indeed); and a written undertaking to have the bridge financing registered immediately against either or both properties, if the purchase closed but the sale did not for any reason (no cost, if loan not registered on title).

Bridge financing poses a "chicken and egg" dilemma for buyers, since no commitment will be given by the lender until both transactions are firm. Yet a buyer like Alex cannot make both transactions firm and have two different closing dates, until he knows he can arrange bridge financing. Once both offers are signed and both deals are scheduled to close the same day, it's very hard to reschedule one transaction and then arrange bridge financing. This is why Alex should make preliminary inquiries and seek informal assurance about bridge financing, before he signs the second offer and fixes its closing date. Any snags encountered this early probably would force him to close both deals the same day. If everything is acceptable, Alex can firm up both offers with staggered closing dates, knowing his bridge financing will be available when he needs it.

Learn from other people's experiences. Too often people with back-to-back deals wish at the end that they had arranged bridge financing in the beginning. As part of your home-buying strategy, seriously consider closing the purchase first, before the sale, using bridge financing. To do this, the transactions must be scheduled right at the outset to close in that order. Bridge financing could then offer one of those rare opportunities when borrowing money is the cheaper alternative!

Tips and Pointers
- You only need to bridge finance the net equity in your home. All other money will be available for closing anyway.
- Find out if the lender will want any security in addition to a Letter of Direction.
- See if bridge financing is a viable alternative now, before the offers are signed.

17

What Does It Really Cost To Close?

Years ago, when a buyer paid the purchase price stated in an offer for a newly-built home, the property was transferred to that buyer. Not so today. New home offers are chock-full of expensive closing costs submerged in fine print. In many cases these charges can easily exceed two and even three percent of the purchase price. By passing on these items to purchasers as closing adjustments, builders can appear to sell the basic house for a lower, more acceptable price.

Why do purchasers of newly-built homes have to pay these additional costs? Because the contract they sign with the builder says so. Quite often purchasers are shocked to learn that costs they expected to be included in the purchase price are not. The individual charges may be small, but collectively they can play havoc with a buyer's cash flow for closing. Some charges are ingenious methods builders use to borrow interest-free money from buyers. Others are subject to possible readjustment after closing.

Not all builders charge purchasers with all the possible additional closing costs. It's as if there's a grab-bag of potential charges and individual builders pick the ones to include in their contract. Try as you will, it's virtually impossible for the buyer to amend the builder's offer and delete these clauses. The standard builder's response is that everyone pays the charges, without exception.

Builders rarely offer information about closing costs early on. Too often purchasers without a home-buying strategy sign a contract to buy a newly-built house, and know nothing about the true amount of money needed to close. If this information is not disclosed early on, closing costs become unanticipated "hidden" costs that are sprung on purchasers at the worst possible time, just before title changes hands. Imagine the crisis you would face if you were already pressed to the financial limit!

There should never be any hidden closing costs when buying a newly-built home. Hidden costs are only hidden because they haven't been revealed yet. They won't stay concealed forever, though. So the longer you put off learning more about these closing costs, the more likely they will become eleventh-hour bombshells, causing purchasers to scurry about for funds. Last-minute surprises like these are never pleasant.

To properly budget your finances for closing, it is absolutely essential that you know early on how much you can afford to spend, how large a mortgage to arrange, and the total amount of the closing expenses. Knowing your overall closing costs *before you sign any offer* is a key ingredient of your home-buying strategy. Most of the "hidden" closing costs can be determined with reasonable accuracy even before a written commitment is made. By asking the right questions of the right people at the pre-contract stage, the dilemma of hidden costs when buying a newly-built home can be totally eliminated. You will know how much money to set aside for closing before the deal is even a deal.

Don't be surprised to find that many new home sales agents are reluctant to disclose or even discuss these additional charges. Remember that their job is to sell homes. Being too candid by telling you what it really will cost to close could scare you away.

The best person to give an accurate estimate of these overall closing charges is your lawyer. The best time is during the initial meeting when he or she reviews the unsigned offer to purchase. An experienced real estate lawyer can provide you with valuable insights into the types and amounts of hidden closing costs. In this way, you can anticipate what the closing costs will be and avoid a cash flow crunch. *Before signing any offer to purchase, determine what these hidden charges are and how much money should be set aside for closing to pay them.*

The exact charge for some of these costs is not spelled out in the offer. Instead, a "reasonable charge" determined at the builder's discretion is collected. Whenever possible, have the precise amount or at least a maximum figure for these items inserted right in the offer. If this cannot be done, ask your lawyer for an estimate of these charges based on past experience.

Closing costs fall into six categories: a) legal fees; b) disbursements; c) provincial taxes; d) mortgage expenses; e) adjustments with the builder (where many of the hidden costs are buried in new home contracts); and f) miscellaneous costs. If the figure your lawyer quotes for closing costs seems high, remember that it includes much more than just legal fees.

Here's a simple formula to calculate how much money you'll need to close. First, add together the purchase price, legal fees, disbursements, provincial taxes, adjustments and miscellaneous costs. This is the gross amount needed to close. Then deduct from it the deposit and money from other sources such as a new first mortgage (minus deductions made by the lender); a vendor-take-back or builder's mortgage; and the sale of an existing home after expenses. The figure that pops out of the calculator is the net amount of money needed to close the new home purchase.

Cliff and April are buying a $120,000 house. On signing the offer they paid a $10,000 deposit. A new $80,000 mortgage is being arranged, with $30,000 cash to be paid on closing. During the pre-contract preliminary meeting with their lawyer, Cliff and April learned about the following charges: legal fees $600; disbursements, $175; transfer tax, $925; and adjustments, $1,500. This meant the gross amount needed to close was $123,200. After deducting the net advance on the mortgage ($79,650) and the $10,000 deposit, the net amount of money needed to close was $33,550. Since Cliff and April originally expected to pay $30,000 in cash on closing, the "hidden" costs totalled $3,550.

To avoid any last-minute surprises, Cliff and April's lawyer told them to budget another $250, or a total of $3,800 for closing costs. When the final bill came in, the closing costs totalled only $3,475. Cliff and April used the $325 "found" money to buy some accessories for the new house.

Here are the closing costs that purchasers of newly-built homes must know about:

a) Legal Fees
The lawyer's "take home" pay before expenses varies greatly, depending on the province, the region, the community and the individual lawyer. More information on lawyers' fees appears in Chapter 13.

b) Disbursements
These are out-of-pocket expenses lawyers incur on behalf of their clients. The items and amounts charged for each item differ from file to file and municipality to municipality. Typical disbursements include:

i)   *Title search* — The cost of ordering deeds, mortgages and other registered instruments, which are reviewed and summarized to ensure good title to the property. This item usually costs at least $25, depending on the complexity of the state of the title.

ii)   *By-Law/zoning/work order report* — To ensure that the property complies with zoning by-laws, and that no work orders are outstanding. Typical cost: $25.

iii)   *Subdivision agreement report* — The cost of obtaining a report from the municipality stating that all the terms and conditions of any subdivision agreement have been complied with in full, and that occupancy is permitted. Normal charge is $25.

iv)   *Tax certificate* — Certifies that no property taxes are outstanding. Usual charge is $10.

v)   *Utilities certificate* — Confirms that no public utility charges are unpaid. Typical charge is $10.

vi)   *Personal Property Security Act searches* — Ascertains whether any liens exist against personal property being purchased from the builder. This item runs in the $10 range, based on a cost of $2 per name search in Ontario.

vii)   *Registration charges* — The cost of registering each deed and mortgage. In Ontario, the cost of registering a document is $16.

viii) *Execution certificate* — It indicates that there are no outstanding judgements against the purchaser, the vendor, or prior owners of the land. Depending on the number of previous owners, this cost could run to $25 or more.

ix)   *Transportation and courier charges* — Couriers are a necessity in any real estate transaction, to deliver time-sensitive documents and mortgage funds to and from a lawyer's office. Budget $30 for this, plus an additional charge if the registry office is located out-of-town.

x)   *Amortization schedule* — It shows the breakdown of each mortgage payment between principal and interest, plus the balance outstanding after each payment. Typical charge is $5 per mortgage.

xi)   *Estoppel certificate* — The certificate issued by the condominium corporation that provides information about the status of the unit plus outstanding arrears in maintenance payments. Normal cost is $25.

xii)   *Long distance telephone charges* — May run $10 and up, if applicable.

xiii) *Photocopy/miscellaneous charges* — $15 and up, depending on the nature of the cost incurred.

c) Provincial Taxes

i) *Transfer tax* — Depending on the province, a special one-time tax is assessed whenever title changes hands. Unless this tax is paid, the deed will not be registered. In Ontario, for example, Land Transfer Tax is levied against all properties — residential, commercial, industrial, agricultural or recreational. Inter-spousal transfers are exempted though. This transfer tax is levied on an escalating scale of $5 per $1,000 of purchase price on the initial $55,000, and $10 per $1,000 on the balance. A surtax of $5 per $1,000 is imposed on that part of the purchase price in excess of $250,000, where the property contains one or two single-family residences.

On a $100,000 purchase in Ontario, Land Transfer Tax would total $725, calculated as follows:

$5 per thousand x 55 = $275
$10 per thousand x 45 = $450
$725

ii) *Retail sales tax* — Retail sales tax is payable to most provincial governments when you buy personal property such as appliances. It doesn't matter if the appliances are bought from a retailer or a builder — the tax is still due. Usually the portion of the purchase price allocated to personal property appears right in the offer. Multiply that figure (say $1,500) by the rate of provincial sales tax (say 7%) to see how large this expense will be (in this case $105).

d) Deductions on the mortgage
These are the costs associated with your new mortgage. If outside financing is arranged, the cost of these items will be deducted from the mortgage advance. If a builder's mortgage is assumed, the charges will appear as credits to the builder on the Statement of Adjustments. Whether any particular item applies depends on the terms of the particular loan, and the wording of your builder's contract. As discussed in Chapter 15, these items include: arranging /cancellation/reduction fee; interest on the unadvanced portion of the mortgage; interest to the interest adjustment date (IAD); establishing a realty tax account; CMHC/MICC payment insurance fee; and other insurance fees (life and rate).

e) Adjustments

Before closing, you should carefully review the Statement of Adjustments with your lawyer. Prepared by the builder's lawyer, this document "fine-tunes" the transaction by distributing the various closing items between the builder and the buyer. Charges are calculated on a daily basis right up to the day of closing. The purchaser is responsible for the payment of all items on the day of closing, even though he does not own the house for the entire day.

The Statement of Adjustments applies to the transaction between builder and buyer only. It does not reflect any outside mortgages being arranged. When David bought a Buyit Home for $90,000 in an all cash transaction, he had to pay the builder $90,000 on closing. The fact that David financed the purchase with a $60,000 mortgage was immaterial to Buyit Homes. Whether David begged, borrowed or stole the money, all the builder wanted to see was $90,000 cash on closing.

A typical Statement of Adjustments appears opposite. In this transaction, Darryl bought a newly-built home from Elliott Homes for $120,000, with an $8,000 deposit. According to the offer, Darryl was to assume the builder's mortgage for $75,000, and the builder agreed to hold a $10,000 vendor-take-back second mortgage for one year. Darryl was to pay the remaining $27,000, the "unadjusted" balance of the purchase price, on closing, subject to the "usual" adjustments and special "contractual" adjustments described below.

The Statement of Adjustments shows how the final balance due on closing was calculated. Everything in the right-hand column is a credit to the builder, Elliott Homes, and everything in the left-hand column is a credit to Darryl as purchaser. Most adjustments are listed as credits to the builder. Both columns must add up to the same figure. Therefore the adjusted balance due on closing is a "plugged" figure, one that's inserted to make both columns match. The difference between the adjusted balance due on closing and the unadjusted balance due on closing represents the net amount of the adjustments.

Keep in mind that changing one component on the Statement of Adjustments will affect the balance due on closing. If a credit to the builder (such as taxes) increases by $100, the balance due on closing must be increased by $100 as well, so that everything will continue to balance. For the same reason, if a purchaser's credit increases by $50, then the balance due on closing must fall by $50. Changing the closing date would involve recalculating all the figures. Part of Darryl's lawyer's job is to independently verify each item on the Statement of Adjustments with written reports. Shortly before closing, Darryl was told that these closing adjustments totalled $4,051.23. To understand how this figure was calculated, let's examine the Statement of Adjustments.

STATEMENT OF ADJUSTMENTS

SELLER: ELLIOTT HOMES
PURCHASER: DARRYL
ADDRESS OF PROPERTY: 36 SHIMMIT ROAD, METROPOLIS
CLOSING DATE: JULY 20 (200 DAYS)

	Credit Purchaser	Credit Seller
Sale Price		$120,000.00
Deposit	$8,000.00	
First mortgage assumed with Supertrustco	75,000.00	
Interest to the interest adjustment date		271.23
Contribution to tax account		250.00
Interest on the unadvanced portion of the mortgage		900.00
Mortgage arranging fee		300.00
Second mortgage taken back by builder	10,000.00	
Realty taxes		
— based on land taxes only of $365.00:		
Vendor has paid $365.00		
Vendor's share 200.00		
Credit vendor 165.00	165.00	165.00
Insurance Policy		250.00
New Home Warranty Program Insurance Fee		290.00

Hydro and Water Connection
   Charges and Meters
     –water meter $250.00
     –hydro meter   400.00
     –hydro connection   250.00
     –Credit vendor   900.00   900.00

Damage to grading and
   subdivision services   500.00

Tree planting charge   225.00

Adjusted balance due on
closing $31,051.23

TOTALS $124,051.23 $124,051.23

No adjustment is made for any metered utilities — hydro, water or gas charges. The builder is responsible for any of these costs up to the date of closing, when new accounts will be set up in Darryl's name. In condominium purchases there are two possible situations. The charges can be calculated on consumption as measured by meter or there may be one meter for the whole project, with individual charges included in the maintenance fee. Either way, no adjustment is necessary.

What is the nature of all the adjustments?

i)   *Sale Price* — The starting point for the entire transaction is always credited to the seller. This assumes the price is not subject to a price escalation clause, discussed in Chapter 18.

ii)   *Deposit* — The money paid by Darryl when the offer is signed is always credited to the purchaser. If both parties agree that it should be paid, interest on the deposit could be credited to Darryl on the Statement of Adjustments. This is the usual procedure when interest is payable in a condominium purchase on the money paid at interim occupancy. In noncondominium purchases, this interest is sometimes forwarded directly to the purchaser shortly after closing.

iii) *First Mortgage Assumed* — This is the builder's mortgage Darryl assumes on closing. Taking over the builder's obligations on this mortgage is part of the "consideration" Darryl gives the builder. Therefore its outstanding principal is credited to Darryl and reduces the balance due on closing.

     Darryl is not assuming a builder's mortgage that requires

CMHC or MICC insurance. If he had, the insurance charge would normally be added onto the amount borrowed rather than being paid on closing. The mortgage then would be registered for the combined figure of $76,125 and the builder would receive a credit on the Statement of Adjustments for the insurance fee ($1,125) paid to the insurer. The net amount credited to the purchaser is $75,000, the exact-sized mortgage he agreed to assume. If $75,000 outside financing was being arranged and insured this way, the mortgage would be registered for $76,125. After deducting the insurance fee ($1,125), the net amount advanced to the purchaser would be $75,000, as anticipated.

iv) *Interest to the Interest Adjustment Date (IAD)* — As Canadian mortgages are paid at the end of the payment period, Darryl's first mortgage will fall due on September 1 for the month of August, the first full month of the mortgage. Interest to the IAD represents the interest due for the 12 days in the "broken" month of July. With an interest rate on this mortgage of 11 percent, 12 days' interest totals $271.23, a credit given to Elliott Homes, which in turn pays that amount to the lender, Supertrustco. Further details on this nonnegotiable cost appear in Chapter 15.

v) *Contribution to Tax Account* — Supertrustco wants to be sure it will have enough money in the tax account to pay all property taxes when the bill is issued. To do this, it insists on getting a lump-sum payment from Darryl on closing. Although Darryl's payment is credited to Elliott Homes, the builder pays a similar figure to Supertrustco as well. Some lenders insist that the entire estimated taxes for the balance of the year must be paid up front on closing. Find out now if your lender will insist on this type of payment at closing. For more information, see Chapter 15.

vi) *Interest on the Unadvanced Portion of the Mortgage* — As noted in Chapter 15, Elliott Homes (like most builders) collects money from purchasers like Darryl as a closing adjustment to compensate for interest lost when the mortgage is not fully advanced on closing. This adjustable deposit, which often exceeds 1 percent of the size of the mortgage, is nonnegotiable.

vii) *Mortgage Arranging Fee* — Rather than absorbing it, many builders today make purchasers pay the cost of arranging and assuming the builder's mortgage. This also applies in some cases if the builder's mortgage is not wanted by the buyer, or if the mortgage is reduced in size. Not all lenders levy a fee, and to make a deal some builders will waive the charge. See Chapter 15 for particulars.

viii)   *Second Mortgage Back* — Besides assuming the builder's first mortgage, Darryl is giving a $10,000 VTB second mortgage to Elliott Homes. Since this mortgage represents a deferred payment of the purchase price, Darryl is credited with this amount on the Statement of Adjustments. After all, if there had been no second mortgage, the adjusted balance due on closing would have been $10,000 higher.

ix)   *Realty Taxes* — Until closing, realty taxes are nominal since the property is only assessed as vacant land. After closing, a supplementary assessment for residential purposes is made which increases the taxes. Elliott Homes is responsible for taxes only until the date before closing. Darryl's responsibility begins on that day.

Concerning taxes, it's important to consider when in the year the deal closes. If the current year's taxes have not yet been determined, which is quite common when the deal closes in the first six months, taxes are adjusted on the most up-to-date figures available, last year's bill. In Darryl's case, however, this year's tax bill is available. Calculated on a daily basis, Elliott Homes is responsible for 200/365ths of the land taxes, or $200. Since it has already paid the $365 tax bill for the entire year, the builder has overpaid taxes by $165. To ensure this money is refunded to the builder, Elliott Homes receives a credit from Darryl for this amount on the Statement of Adjustments.

Builders agree in writing to recalculate the realty taxes once the final bill is issued, and to reimburse any money owing to the buyer. This is extremely important if taxes are adjusted based on last year's figures, since a refund is usually owing to the purchaser. If you close your purchase in the first half of the year, contact your lawyer about the possible readjustment of taxes by the builder to you, once the final tax bill has been issued. Make a note on your calendar to contact your lawyer during the summer. Money may be owing to you. But to receive it, you have to ask for it. Make sure you do!

Some offers (not Darryl's) force buyers to prepay an estimated amount for realty taxes for the balance of the calendar year on closing. This prepayment is often lumped in with the deposit for interest on the unadvanced portion of the mortgage. Builders estimate the taxes and collect money from purchasers as if the house had already been completed and assessed for the full year. The builder promises to readjust and fully repay the taxes when the final tax bill is issued.

In Gary and Abby's case, Brighto Homes collected as an adjustment on closing the total estimated taxes for the rest of the year. Since the deal closed June 30 and the estimated annual taxes were $2,000, in effect Brighto Homes had the use of $1,000 of Gary and Abby's money interest-free, even though it would not have to pay any of those taxes.

When the final tax bill was issued, it was sent to Gary and Abby for payment, and not to the builder. Since the couple had to pay the outstanding taxes to the municipality before Brighto Homes refunded the prepared taxes, Gary and Abby ended up paying their taxes twice, at least temporarily. Some builders insist on this arrangement when the purchaser assumes the builder's mortgage, and the lender maintains a tax account. But in Gary and Abby's case, they arranged their own mortgage financing with no tax account. Prepaying taxes this way is also inappropriate if the proper adjustment for realty taxes is already made on the Statement of Adjustments.

Be on the lookout for this nonnegotiable clause and budget accordingly. Otherwise the cash flow problems resulting from having to temporarily pay your taxes twice, and seek a refund later, could be catastrophic.

Also beware of clauses that force you to pay next year's taxes as a closing adjustment. This could involve having to lay out thousands of dollars now for obligations that are still months in the future.

x) *Insurance Policy* — As a builder's mortgage was assumed, Elliott Homes insisted that Darryl also assume the fire insurance policy it had arranged ("the builder's insurance"). This assures Supertrustco that adequate insurance coverage is in effect for closing. Even though the premium on the builder's insurance may be slightly discounted, most purchasers like Darryl still prefer to arrange their own insurance coverage. If that is the case, amend the clause in the printed offer that requires you to assume the builder's insurance on closing. Many builders will allow this as long as you produce the new insurance coverage on closing.

Darryl, though, was forced to take the builder's insurance

on closing and pay the full year's premium of $250. In the meantime, he also had arranged his own coverage to take effect on the date of closing. Now he had two insurance policies. To resolve the dilemma, Darryl cancelled the builder's insurance immediately after closing. Several weeks passed before his refund, less the usual administration or cancellation fee of 10 percent, was sent to him. Insurance policy premiums are a prime example of a refundable charge that can devastate a purchaser's cash flow for closing.

xi)   *New Home Warranty Program fee* — An optional charge that virtually all builders who participate in the plan pass on to their buyers. In Ontario the basic cost is $50 plus $2 per $1,000 of purchase price.

xii) *Hydro and water connection charges and meters* — Most builders charge purchasers with one or both of these non-negotiable items. On the average the cost of a water meter is $150 to $250, while a hydro meter can cost up to $400. These figures don't include the connection charges, either. Whether the obligation to pay these items is pointed out when the offer is signed or just before closing, newly-built home buyers are irked about this hidden cost. Buyers expect these meters and connection fees to be included in the purchase price.

xiii) *Damage to grading and subdivision services* — Until the municipality assumes responsibility for the subdivision several years after it is fully developed, the subdivider/developer is responsible for any damage caused to the services installed, including grading and drainage. Like some builders, Elliott Homes wants to be sure that money is available from Darryl and other home buyers to repair any damage they cause to the services installed, or to the master grading and drainage plan. To do this, Elliott Homes collects an arbitrary sum of money, often as high as $500, from Darryl as security, or charges him with the cost of the security deposit or letter of credit paid by Elliott Homes to the developer. Where this item appears in an offer, it is nonnegotiable.

In fact, this hidden cost really is a little more than an interest-free loan to the builder. These funds will be refunded to Darryl once the municipality assumes the subdivision, *usually on request only*. Remember to ask for a refund or else the loan will turn into an interest-free gift to the builder.

xiv) *Tree planting charge/sod fee* — These are the latest — and some of the most comical — hidden charges builders have devised. Most municipalities require that trees be planted on the boulevard between the road and the sidewalk. The developer plants the "tree" (what will be planted is little more than a twig, so perhaps this cost should be called the "twig" fee) and charges the cost to the builder, who in turn passes it onto the purchaser. The cost to Darryl for this non-negotiable expense is $225. Imagine, too, his reaction to the clause in the offer, where he "acknowledges that a tree may not necessarily be located on his lot"!

Some builders (not Elliott Homes) request cash contributions from purchasers towards the cost of laying sod in the yards. One of the more ridiculous charges passed on to new home purchasers, purchasers do not find the obligation to pay it so amusing. Average cost: $200.

xv) *Additional Obligations* — In some offers, the builder stipulates that purchasers must complete certain work on their property within a specified period of time. Where Harry and Linda bought their home, all driveways were to be paved. In their offer, Harry and Linda (and not the builder) agreed to pave the driveway within 18 months of closing. By checking out costs before they signed any offer, Harry and Linda knew the cost would be about $1,000. Yet to ensure the work was done, the builder on closing took a $750 security deposit. The deposit would be refunded when the work was completed by Harry and Linda within the 18-month time limit. But if the driveway was not paved by Harry and Linda on time, the builder would use these funds to pave the driveway, and then sue Harry and Linda for the difference. Again, the builder had an interest-free loan until the work was finished.

Buried in Ricky and Lucy's deal was a different type of clause about paving the driveway. While the builder would provide the base coat for the driveway, finishing it would be its responsibility but at Ricky and Lucy's expense ($300) — payable as a nonnegotiable closing adjustment.

Homes that back onto major thoroughfares usually have a fence in the rear and may require landscaping as well. Some builders pass on this cost to purchasers of these homes. The amount will vary from location to location.

In condominium purchases, an adjustment is made for the monthly condominium maintenance or common expense fee. Since this is normally paid in advance on the first of each month, builders get a credit from buyers for any amount overpaid to the condominium corporation for the month of closing.

In addition, many developers insist that a reserve fund be established immediately after closing for major and emergency repairs. Purchasers often pay one month's maintenance as the initial, nonnegotiable contribution to this fund.

f)   *Miscellaneous Expenses*
Four items fall into this category: bridge financing, home inspection, fire insurance, and moving costs.

i)   *Bridge financing* — If you decide to put the purchase before the sale, what will the bridge financing charges be? See Chapter 16.

ii)   *Home inspection* — If you decide to hire a home inspector for your pre-delivery inspection, what will his fee be? See Chapter 27.

iii)   *Fire insurance* — What will be the cost of the new fire insurance policy you will need for closing? See Chapter 24.

iv)   *Moving Costs* — Whether you move yourself or hire a mover, there will be some expenses. What will they be?

To assist you with your budget for closing, begin preparing both a preliminary Statement of Closing Costs as well as a preliminary Statement of Adjustments in the space below. Do it in pencil so changes can easily be made. Ask as many questions as necessary to get the answers you want. Don't be part of the crowd that complains about last-minute hidden costs. Find out about them now.

STATEMENT OF CLOSING COSTS

I	Fees	– purchase	$
		– mortgage	$_____
			$_____
II	Disbursements	– title search	$
		– by-laws/zoning/work order search	$
		– subdivision agreement report	$
		– tax certificate	$

– utilities certificate	$
– Personal Property Security Act searches	$
– registration charges	$
– execution certificate	$
– transportation and courier charges	$
– amortization schedule	$
– estoppel certificate (condominiums only)	$
– long distance telephone charges	$
– photocopy/miscellaneous charges	$_____
	$_____

III Provincial taxes – land transfer tax $
                    – retail sales tax $

IV Adjusted balance due on closing
(from Statement of Adjustments) $
TOTAL GROSS AMOUNT NEEDED TO CLOSE $_____

V   Mortgage Considerations (for an arranged and not a builder's mortgage)

Amount of new mortgage applied for	$
Less: deductions on the mortgage	
– mortgage arranging/ application fee $	
– interest to the interest adjustment date $	
– establishing realty tax account $	
– CMHC/MICC payment insurance fee $	
– life and rate insurance fee $_____	$_____
NET ADVANCE ON NEW MORTGAGE	$_____

SUMMARY:

Total Gross Amount Needed to close	$_____
LESS: net advance on the new mortgage	($_____)
DIFFERENCE: approximate net amount needed by purchaser to close transaction	$_____

The miscellaneous charges also should be added to this net amount, to learn the overall amount of money needed to close.

– bridge financing	$
– home inspection	$
– fire insurance	$
– moving charges	$
TOTAL OVERALL AMOUNT OF MONEY NEEDED TO CLOSE	$_____

STATEMENT OF ADJUSTMENTS

	Credit Purchaser	Credit Seller
Purchase Price		$
Deposit	$	
First mortgage assumed	$	
Interest to the Interest Adjustment Date	$	
Contribution to tax account		$
Interest on the unadvanced portion of the mortgage		$
Mortgage arranging fee		$
Second mortgage taken back by builder	$	
Realty taxes		$
Insurance policy		$
New Home Warranty Program fee		$
Hydro and water connection charges and meters		$
Damage to grading and subdivision services		$
Tree planting charge/sod fee		$
ADJUSTED BALANCE DUE ON CLOSING	$ _____	_____
TOTAL	$	$

Tips and Pointers

- Know what your overall closing costs will be before you sign any offer to purchase. Hidden costs are closing costs that are revealed for the first time at the last minute.
- After you have calculated your estimated closing costs, leave yourself a financial cushion in case your forecasts are slightly inaccurate.
- Remember to contact your builder after closing to request a refund of adjustable costs.

18

The Builder's Offer — A Different Kind of Contract

Before you buy a newly-built house, it's necessary to sign an Offer to Purchase, also known as an Agreement of Purchase and Sale. Before signing that piece of paper, put aside your emotions and excitement for the house momentarily and remind yourself of the commitment you are making.

No document is more important to the transaction than the written offer. It sets out your rights and obligations as well as those of the builder, and governs the relationship between the parties to the date of closing and beyond. Most offers say there is "no representation, warranty, collateral agreement or condition" affecting the property or the contract. In straightforward English, "what you see is what you get."

New home offers are a buyer's nightmare, a minefield for the unwary. Unlike the resale home market where standard form offers are used, each builder has his own Offer to Purchase form. Lengthy and much more complex than resale offers, they are usually printed in very small type, and have a number of blank spaces to be filled in. And builder's offers are full of conditions a new home buyer would never anticipate, plus clauses that obligate and commit purchasers in ways they would never imagine.

One of the fundamental principles of your home-buying strategy is to understand *before you sign* exactly what that new home offer says. Know what you're committing to before making that commitment. The builder knows what the basic contract says. It has been prepared to the builder's advantage by his lawyer, at the builder's expense. Do you know what it says? Are you aware of all the conditions that must be satisfied before the house can be built? Are you aware of all the hidden costs buried in the fine print? Are you aware of the many escape hatches that allow a builder to terminate the contract?

Purchasers who try to read the fine print in the offer inevitably become bored, begin to fall asleep, complain about their eyesight, or throw up their hands in despair. Reading the contract is one thing; understanding what it says is another. That fine print can be exasperating.

As a purchaser applying a HOBS, you will, of course, not sign any contract without taking it to your lawyer first. While you may not thoroughly read the offer, your lawyer certainly must. An experienced real estate lawyer knows what to look for in a new home offer. With tens of thousands of dollars at stake, the cost of having your lawyer carefully examine the unsigned new home offer, to help you understand what it says and avoid its hidden traps, is a pittance by comparison. *Because they are so complicated, never sign a new home offer until your lawyer has reviewed it, and until you thoroughly understand what it says. Buyers applying their home-buying strategy will not sign any documents until they read the chapter "All Systems Go."*

This chapter is not designed to present buyers with precedent clauses they can insert in new home offers. Instead, it examines issues that every new home buyer should be concerned about, and makes concrete suggestions to address these issues. By knowing what questions to ask, purchasers will find it much easier to discuss the offer and their unique concerns with their lawyer. In turn, this will enable their lawyer to best protect their particular interests and circumstances.

Never, never, never simply rely on what a new home sales agent says. Apparently some agents talk out of both sides of their mouth. Why else would most new home offers contain the following "zinger"? *"The purchaser relieves the vendor of any obligation to perform or comply with any promises or representations as may have been made by any sales representative or in any sales brochure unless the same have been reduced to writing in this offer."*

Translation: if it's not in the offer, it's not in the deal, despite what the agent (or the sales brochure) says!

Despite this clause, agents cannot say whatever they want without assuming any responsibility, because that would be misrepresentation. But because of this clause, new home buyers must be much more wary than they were in the past, and independently verify that every important verbal promise or guarantee indeed appears

in the offer. This is especially true with features that accompany
the house, the amenities listed in Schedule "A". Too often prospective purchasers are told items are included in the purchase
price, only to find that the offer makes no mention of them. All
the more reason to see your lawyer before you sign that offer, and
it becomes binding.

New home sales agents will try to reassure you that the contract
is "just the builder's standard form offer" that hundreds of other
people have signed in the past. Therefore, they reason, you really
don't need to take it to your lawyer for review, comment and possible revision before you sign. Some agents will even resist your intention to see your lawyer, offering excuses such as: taking the contract to your lawyer is a waste of time since no changes are permitted; as another party is interested in the house, the contract
must be signed now; and, a price increase takes effect tomorrow
so you'd better sign the offer tonight. Ignore the excuses and
arguments. Always take the draft offer to your lawyer first. Turn
your back and walk away if the agent refuses to give you the draft
offer. If this is any indication of how you're going to be treated,
neither the agent nor the builder are worth dealing with.

The draft offer you give to your lawyer should be fully completed, ready for signature. Too often, many buyers take a blank
form to their lawyer. But what distinguishes your deal from
everyone else's, are the terms typed into those blanks. It's much
easier for your lawyer to advise you about what the offer says, if
the complete contract can be reviewed. Don't be afraid to ask the
sales agent to complete the offer before you take it to your lawyer.
Any agent who is sincere about you as a prospective buyer will gladly
do this.

Whenever possible, leave the unsigned offer with your lawyer
so that he has an opportunity to review it privately, without the
pressures of meetings, telephone calls and clients. When you meet
a day or so later, it's right down to business. During that meeting
expect your lawyer to do the following:

a) Review the offer with you. The lawyer's job is to ensure that
   you understand what the contract says (and doesn't say) and
   the obligations arising from it, so you know what you are committing to. Don't expect the lawyer to deal with every word or
   even every paragraph. Only the highlights need to be explained
   in detail. To help your lawyer, mention the issues that concern you most, so that extra emphasis can be given to those

topics. Remember that reviewing Schedule "A," the list of features you get with the house, remains your responsibility (see Chapter 9). If you are in doubt whether any important items are included in the purchase price, ask your lawyer to check it out.

b) Comment on the offer and provide advice based on his or her experience. All the conditions in the offer and how they work should be reviewed. Your lawyer should explain every way the builder can cancel or terminate the offer, which would prevent you from getting the house. He or she should also tell you about the closing costs you will face, especially the hidden charges, and how much money will be needed to close. Mortgage financing should be considered, comparing the terms of the builder's mortgage with outside financing. Closing dates and the problems of a delayed closing should be reviewed. An experienced real estate lawyer can verify much of what the sales agent told you, and ensure that key clauses and features appear right in the offer. The unusual and unexpected "zinger" clauses outlined in Chapter 19 should be examined, too. Make sure you discuss the development process, and understand where a particular lot is in that process. Only then can your lawyer advise you when, and whether, the deal will close.

c) Consider making reasonable, but necessary, revisions to the offer once you understand what certain clauses say and their legal consequences. Only changes that offer you more protection and fairer treatment should be added. Don't expect your lawyer to totally rewrite the contract, as builders have a tendency to automatically reject offers that have been substantially amended. Any lawyer who does that could jeopardize your getting the house. Lawyers experienced with new home offers know what clauses are standard and what clauses are not; those that can be changed and those that must remain intact.

Yet few contracts for newly-built homes are totally set in concrete, even in a strong seller's market. Rarely will builders inflexibly reject reasonable changes to their offers, as long as they can live with the amendments. In fact, sometimes "throw-away" clauses are deliberately inserted into an offer (clauses that builders expect to be revised). This allows purchasers and their lawyers to feel they have made changes to the offer, when the builder never had any intention of relying on that clause anyway!

To simplify matters, some lawyers put all the proposed amendments, including changes to the plans, on a separate sheet of paper, attached to the offer as a schedule. This way the offer itself remains untouched and all the changes are easily noticeable. Remember, if it's not in the offer, it's not part of the deal.

If modifications to the offer are not allowed, then you must decide how important these changes are to you. If a clause is of great concern, you must decide whether to withdraw from the deal or go on and take your chances. Purchasers who choose to proceed further will probably rely on their lawyer's opinion and experience to help them assess the downside risk. While the lawyer's opinion is not a guarantee, it at least offers purchasers some comfort by knowing how similar situations were handled in the past.

When reviewing a new home offer, buyers and their lawyers must be on the lookout for several different categories of clauses that could lead to future problems:

1. The "standard" new home clauses, many of which are anything but standard, discussed in this chapter.
2. Mortgage financing, discussed in Chapter 15.
3. Closing costs, especially unexpected hidden costs buried in new home offers, examined in Chapter 17.
4. Ways the builder can terminate the contract (Chapter 19).
5. "Zingers" or unusual clauses and potential pitfalls that can cause serious grief for unwary buyers (Chapter 19).

All of these clauses are legal contractual agreements between the builder and the buyer. What's unfortunate, however, is that builders often fail to properly disclose these clauses to purchasers. No wonder the home-buying public gets the impression they are playing a cloak-and-dagger game with builders. If problems arise and a builder finds it necessary to invoke these clauses, the parties end up polarized. Often it's unclear what upsets purchasers more — the meaning of the clause, or the builder's failure to provide full and complete disclosure of these clauses when the offer was first presented.

Having your lawyer review and revise the offer ensures you will not face this dilemma. Not only will you know early on that these clauses exist but, more importantly, you will appreciate their significance. Then you can make an informed decision whether to buy that newly-built house, knowing fully what potential problems you might face in the future. To buy a newly-built home any other way is dangerous.

Whether any particular clause applies to your situation depends on the wording of your builder's offer. While wording may vary from builder to builder, most offers contain similar clauses. Here are the basics:

The Purchaser (Buyer)

The purchaser is the one who signs the offer and is obligated to close the deal. Don't worry if your spouse is unavailable to sign the offer. Although she signed the offer to purchase herself, Debbie can direct in writing before closing that title be registered to Debbie or to Vince, or to both Vince and Debbie. Written directions like these are very common.

The Property

Newly-built homes are described by their lot and plan, the legal description for the property. Municipal addresses are available as closing approaches. To find out what your street address will be, call the local post office and supply your lot, plan and street name. Sometimes the sales office will have this information as well.

If the subdivision is registered, the plan number should appear right on the offer to indicate that one of the major hurdles in the development process has been cleared. Of course, the subdivision must be serviced and a building permit issued before work can begin on your house. But with a registered subdivision, you can at least verify the precise dimensions of your lot.

If you are buying a pre-registration pre-sale home, you should keep several things in mind. First, the lot dimensions are subject to change. Purchasers must agree to accept any minor variations to the size, frontage and depth without getting any reduction off the purchase price. Second, the deal can close only if the draft plan is registered, and this does not always happen. In other words, the offer is conditional on the subdivision being registered, though the offer may not clearly say so. Most importantly, when a home is bought from a draft or unregistered plan of subdivision, closing is well into the future. While the offer may stipulate a closing date, it is virtually meaningless and should not be heavily relied on, since so much must happen before even the first shovel can go into the ground. For more information on the development process, see Chapter 8.

Unlike resale offers, few new home offers state whether any particular lot will be subject to a right-of-way or easement. Instead, the buyer must accept the property subject to whatever easements are needed for hydro, water, fuel, telephone, cable television, catch-basins, municipal or other services. In addition, purchasers must agree to grant whatever easements are required in the future, including a maintenance easement in favor of your neighbor. If you are particularly concerned about this, carefully review the plot plans now. Refer back to Chapter 8 for more details.

Model and Elevation

Most offers boldly state the buyer has inspected the house plans, specifications and lot plan before signing the offer. So make sure you do! Be sure the plans are accurate. No one wants to see a mirror image of his house being constructed!

Despite all the precautions, the house ultimately built for you may be totally different than the house you bought. Purchasers must acknowledge in the offer that all sizes, dimensions, measurements, locations, sketches, renderings and layouts are approximate. Builders also have the right in most offers to make such deviations, alterations, changes and modifications to the building specifications, elevation, plans, drawings and design "as it deems fit," without affecting the purchaser's rights. In some offers, the builder can even reverse the layout from what was depicted in the promotional literature. In that case, even examining the plans may not help you all that much. But imagine how much worse the situation would be if you hadn't reviewed the plans to begin with.

Some builders arbitrarily assume the right to make these variations, and give the mortgage lender the right to approve them. By signing the offer, purchasers are deemed to have approved the changes, (even if they are never told what they are), and still must close the deal! Other builders take more radical approaches. If the model or type of house as specified in the plans and specifications approved by Robert and Rosette cannot be built on the lot they have selected, some offers give the builder "in his absolute discretion" the right to switch lots! So even the location of the lot isn't guaranteed! Still other offers say that if the model or type of house bought can't be built on the lot selected, the builder can cancel the deal and return the deposit. Of course, neither the agent nor the builder are at all liable to the purchaser in the event of cancellation.

With a pre-registration pre-sale house, building a certain type or model could be a problem if the dimensions of the lot are later changed. But after the subdivision is registered, the builder should know what types of homes can be built on specific lots. An unscrupulous builder, however, may have "oversold" a lot; that is, selling a larger house than will fit on the lot to satisfy a purchaser. Then the builder must apply for a variance permitting the oversized house to be built. If he is successful, a building permit will be issued. If the variance is denied, the deal is off at nominal cost to the builder.

In effect these clauses make the offer conditional, without making it explicit. If the house sold to Robert and Rosette can't be built, then why was it sold to them in the first place? These clauses don't exactly boost the confidence of purchasers of newly-built homes. Few people realize these clauses exist in offers. Even fewer will be able to amend them.

Any changes or modifications you want to the design of the house must appear in writing in the offer; verbal promises that these will be made are not legally binding. If in doubt, put it right in the offer.

Purchase Price

The purchase price is technically the "package of consideration" paid to acquire a home. Three types of consideration in various combinations can be given to a builder on closing:

a) Cash (payment now): Here the balance due on closing — the amount of money paid by the purchaser to the builder on closing — is the entire purchase price less the deposit;
b) A vendor-take-back mortgage: a deferred payment of the purchase price (payment later). Here the balance due on closing is the purchase price less the deposit, less the amount of the mortgage;
c) The assumption of the builder's mortgage (a "cash-to-mortgage" transaction). When the buyer assumes the builder's mortgage, the balance due on closing is the same as in (b).

If a purchaser arranges outside financing, the balance due on closing between the builder and the buyer is the purchase price less the deposit. The transaction between the buyer and the builder is "all cash" (category "a"), and the mortgage proceeds paid to the builder on closing form part of that cash payment.

As a rule, larger-scale builders hold firm to their asking price, while smaller builders are more flexible. Still, it never hurts to try and negotiate a lower purchase price, especially when the market is quiet. Even if a builder is not willing to lower his price, you may be able to win other concessions. Extras or upgrades might be included at nominal or no cost. Interest might be paid on the deposit, something that's not normally done. Better terms on the builder's mortgage might be offered, although you should be wary of the buy-down mortgage, as discussed in Chapter 15.

Beware of Price Escalation Clauses!

They allow builders to increase the purchase price by up to a fixed percentage, often as much as 3 percent. Builders argue that the escalation is needed to cover increased construction costs for pre-sale and especially pre-registration pre-sale homes in the long interval between acceptance and closing. While this type of clause is legal, its inclusion in an offer should be disclosed by the builder, even before your lawyer tells you it exists.

Try to have this escalation clause deleted. If the builder keenly wants your business, he will hold to his price until closing. If you accept a price escalation clause, you should assume that the full increase will be added to the basic purchase price when you budget for closing. Otherwise, you could find yourself short several thousand dollars.

Deposits

A deposit is the money the purchaser pays when the offer is submitted. It's not the same as the downpayment, the money paid on closing. In Paul's purchase the downpayment totalled $25,000. Of that figure, the deposit was $5,000 and $20,000 was paid on closing.

Deposits serve two purposes. If the deal closes, it represents a partial payment of the purchase price. Because a deposit can be lost if the deal doesn't close, it is also a guarantee to the builder that the buyer is serious about the deal. If the purchase doesn't close, the deposit could be tied up for years in litigation.

How large a deposit should you pay? Buyers naturally want to pay the smallest deposit possible because once it leaves their hands, they may feel they have lost control of that money. Of course, builders want the largest possible deposit to deter a purchaser from simply walking away from the deal.

New home deposits are usually larger than those for resale transactions. Minimum new home deposits of $10,000 are not uncommon. In recent years, some builders have asked for a series of deposits, meaning additional money is paid in stages between acceptance and closing. These additional deposits are an inexpensive way for builders to finance part of the construction of a house, especially if the builder doesn't pay interest on the deposit.

Deposits paid to builders who participate in a new home warranty program are protected in case the builder goes bankrupt. In Ontario, the only province in which participation in the New Home Warranty Program is mandatory, deposit protection is limited to $20,000. In other provinces it's even less. Staggered deposits that add up to the insurable limit have become commonplace in recent years. The total of all deposits, whether they're in a lump sum or in stages, should not exceed this limit, unless you have additional insurance coverage from the Mortgage Insurance Company of Canada.

If the builder is not a participant in the new home warranty program, never pay the deposit directly to him. If the builder goes bankrupt, you will rank as an unsecured creditor and probably lose your deposit. To protect yourself, pay the deposit cheque to the builder's lawyer or the real estate agent *in trust,* and make sure your offer states this as well. The deposit is usually an uncertified cheque that is certified and put into the bank once the offer is accepted, and the deal is definitely on.

Any additional deposits are paid by post-dated cheques delivered to the builder when the contract is signed. Most offers say that if a cheque is returned marked "insufficient funds," the builder can cancel the contract and keep all previous deposits with no recourse for the buyer. If your offer contains this clause, either amend it or be absolutely certain your cheque will clear the bank.

Unless the offer specifically provides for interest to be paid on deposits, no interest will be paid. (One major exception is the newly-built condominium, discussed in Chapter 20.) By keeping the interest on the deposit, builders claim they are better able to hold down the purchase price. *If you want interest on the deposit, you must specifically ask for it in the offer.*

Interest earned on a deposit is taxable and must be declared on your next income tax return. Expect to receive a T5 Supplementary form sometime before February 28th in the year following the year the interest was paid.

If you are a home owner and are buying another home, make sure the deposit paid on your sale does not exceed the real estate agent's commission. Otherwise, *inadvertently* you could find yourself short of money to buy that newly-built home.

Both Moe and Larry sold their homes for $100,000, with 6% commission payable, netting each of them $94,000. The deposit in Moe's sale was $5,000, meaning on closing he would get $95,000. By paying $1,000 to the real estate agent right after closing, Moe had the full $94,000 to close his new home purchase. But Larry took an $8,000 deposit on his sale which was paid to the real estate agent. This meant that Larry received only $92,000 from the purchaser. The other $2,000 was to be forwarded to him sometime *after closing* by the real estate agent. Since that money would not be available for use on the new home purchase, Larry had to arrange a short-term $2,000 loan to close the deal.

Dates

One of the blanks to be filled in is the "irrevocable date" — the date by which the builder has to make up his mind whether or not to accept your offer. To give the builder ample time to make a decision, at the builder's request the sales agent inserts a date which is a week or two in the future. This procedure is in marked contrast to resale offers, where 24 to 48 hours is the norm. Why the delay for newly-built homes? In many cases, the principals of the builder's company may meet only once a week to review and approve offers.

According to Dave and Bonnie's offer, they were not allowed to revoke or cancel their offer from the time it was submitted until the irrevocable date. To most people, this means that the offer remains outstanding and ready for acceptance during that time. But unless a red wafer seal is also affixed next to their signature, Dave and Bonnie can still revoke the offer during this supposedly irrevocable period!

If the irrevocable date passes and Dave and Bonnie have not been told whether their offer has been accepted, then there is no deal. The offer has expired, and there is no obligation for either party to continue negotiations. If the builder misses that date and you still want the house, you can waive his tardiness and keep the deal alive. But if you decide you don't want to sign a waiver to continue the deal, you don't have to.

Another blank to be filled in on the builder's new home offer is the closing date, also referred to as the completion date. This is the date the deal closes, the date the builder gets his money and the buyer becomes the owner of the house.

After consulting with the builder, the sales agent inserts the scheduled closing date. Unlike the resale market, there is very little room to negotiate here. Usually the builder decides when the deal closes, since the builder wants to get paid as soon as the house is ready for occupancy. Make sure the house does not close on a weekend or holiday. If closing is inadvertently set for a weekend or holiday, it takes place the last business day *before* the original scheduled closing date, and not the first business day afterwards.

Whenever possible, avoid closings on Fridays, the last few days of the month, and especially the last Friday of the month. Transactions can close just as easily, and probably faster on a Tuesday than on a Friday, or on the 10th or the 20th of the month than on the 30th. High-volume days at the registry office mean lengthy line-ups and delays just to register instruments. In turn, this can mean you'll receive the keys to that newly-built home late in the day, and possibly waste time having the movers sit around, waiting to get into the new house — all at your expense!

Despite what sales agents say, end-of-the-month closings are not more convenient. Adjustments are made on a daily basis anyway, so buyers don't save money by closing at the end of the month. Getting mortgage money is not a problem either, since lenders advance funds every day of the month. But movers charge a premium of 10 percent or more at the beginning and the end of the month. Rental trucks are also in heavy demand on weekends and at month's end. For a number of reasons, avoid closing the deal at these peak periods.

Whether you are a tenant or own a home, you should try to close your purchase transaction at least a week before you move from your old premises. This gives you an opportunity to spruce up the new home and have some of the minor outstanding work completed before you actually move in. If you are moving from an owner-occupied home, bridge financing is necessary (see Chapter 16). For apartment dwellers, the extra cost of having two residences for a very short period of time is not that high. With a monthly rental of $540, each day of the overlap cost Jim and Tammy only $18. They'll save more than that expense in moving costs alone.

A scheduled closing date is little more than an educated guess at the offer to purchase stage. Be sure, though, that the offer contains a realistic closing date. If the subdivision is not registered or the services have not been installed, it is impossible to guarantee a closing date just two or three months in the future. In recent years, serious problems have been created by delayed and even cancelled closings when builders refused to extend closing past the originally scheduled date. These problems are discussed in more detail in Chapter 25.

Warranty and Condition

Although they have totally different legal meanings, "warranty" and "condition" are often wrongly used interchangeably in offers. This use of the word "condition" is different than *a conditional offer,* discussed below. Although it may not be possible to change a warranty to a condition or vice-versa, you should at least know what the expressions mean and what recourse you have against the builder if warranties and conditions are violated.

A *warranty* is a minor promise that does not go to the heart of the basic contract. In other words, when a warranty is breached, the buyer cannot simply cancel the contract. The buyer *must* close the purchase and sue the builder after closing for damages. By contrast, a *condition* is a promise that is fundamental to the very existence of the offer. Breach of a condition allows the buyer to back out of the deal before closing and get back his full deposit.

Issues of great importance to the buyer should be worded as conditions and not warranties, especially if you want the right to cancel the deal if the statement is incorrect. *To cancel a deal, the issue in question must be worded as a condition and not as a warranty.*

Premium Lot

Many builders charge a higher price for a premium lot — those wider than normal, deeper than normal, or that back onto a park, ravine or open space. When you're considering a home on a premium lot, examine what is being offered for the price and whether that premium will be recoverable on a resale. Will someone pay you a similar or larger amount for the feature, compared to other homes? If not, then the premium lot is not a good investment.

Mark and Angela felt the $3,000 they paid for a lot two feet wider than average would be fully recoverable at resale. Many people thought Richard and Maggie spent too much for too little when they paid an extra $10,000 for a lot that backed onto a park. Like home improvements, premium lots are fine within reason, but there comes a point where you can pay more than the value it adds to your house.

Colors and Materials

Buyers are usually given a very short period of time after acceptance (often seven to ten days) to select colors and materials from the vendor's samples. Items previously ordered, installed or completed (which would be the case if the house had been previously sold to someone else but did not close) cannot be altered. In either case, once the colors and materials are selected, you are not allowed to make any changes.

If you do not submit your color and material choices within the specified time, the builder may have the right to make the decision for you! It may be hard to believe, but some offers even give the builder the right to cancel the contract and keep your deposit if you don't select your colors and materials on time! This second type of clause is very unfair, but also very difficult to amend. Be sure you understand your rights and obligations under the offer, and then make sure you comply in full.

Despite these clauses, sales agents often tell buyers of pre-sale homes not to worry about making their selections promptly. This is especially true with pre-registration pre-sales. But agents will not give you an extension of time in writing. To protect yourself, you should send a letter to the sales agent confirming what you were told. No response from the agent is a sign the builder agrees with the arrangement. How could the builder later allege that you never chose your colors and materials on time?

In most offers, purchasers must also acknowledge that the colors used in the house might not be the same as the color charts or samples they view, and must accept whatever colors are used. So despite your precautions, you may not end up with your choice of light blue walls after all. Unless the offer says that no substitutions are allowed, the builder can change the colors, but you can't.

Substitution of materials

Most offers allow builders to use different materials than those shown in the plans, provided the substituted materials are of equal or better quality. Purchasers need not be notified of the changes. Sometimes the offer says the builder's architect will make the decision about substituting materials. In this form, the clause should be fair. But beware of several variations that could hurt a purchaser. In one, the "equal or better" expression is omitted, giving the builder *carte blanche* to substitute lower-quality materials. In another variation, the builder's own construction foreman must approve the substituted materials, again making the builder the final judge, without any input from the buyer. Try as you will, this clause is an untouchable.

Extras

Many builders offer numerous extras and upgrades to buyers —

at a price. A higher grade of carpeting and underpad, parquet floors, ceramic tile, an insulation package — the list goes on and on, and varies considerably from builder to builder.

According to most offers, extras are paid in full and up front when the offer is signed, and not when the deal closes. Little can be done to change this. In many offers, payment for extras is nonrefundable if the deal does not close *for any reason whatsoever,* even when the builder terminates the deal. As harsh as this seems, builders do not allow this clause to be altered. They argue that extras one buyer orders (such as an upgraded color-keyed bathtub) may not be desired by another. The builder might argue that it will cost him more money to change the extras for another buyer, if the first deal doesn't close. Still, allowing the builder to keep the money paid for upgrades and extras is unfair, especially when the builder is responsible for cancelling the contract or if the house is never even built!

An extension of this clause says that builders are not liable to purchasers if any of the extras or upgrades are uncompleted or if the builder decides not to provide them. In that case, the buyer must agree to accept a refund of the money paid for those items, in full satisfaction of all claims against the builder. In plain English, this means the purchaser cannot sue the builder for damages if the extras or upgrades are not installed. It also allows builders to cover up for their mistakes or oversights simply by refunding the money paid. Jeremy and Francine soon learned how unfair this clause was. Although they ordered ceramic floors and paid $2,500 for this upgrade, carpeting was laid throughout the house. On closing, their builder returned the $2,500 (without interest) and apologized for the error. And that was it. Jeremy and Francine had no recourse whatsoever against the builder.

On the other hand, any allowance given by the builder for an item you don't want should be clearly spelled out, either in the offer or in an amendment. Make sure your lawyer has a copy of the credit note, so the proper adjustment can be made in your favor on closing.

New Home Warranty Program (NHWP)
As we described in detail in Chapter 14, the NHWP (where applicable) protects buyers against defects in materials and workmanship, but not uncompleted items, for a limited period of time. A lengthy commentary appears in most new home offers about the pre-delivery inspection (PDI) and what will be recorded at that

time. Outstanding work will be completed within a reasonable time after closing, subject to weather conditions and the availability of materials and trades. Keep in mind that if you fail to complete the PDI on time, most offers allow the builders to cancel the offer and keep the deposit.

It is most unfortunate that the same paragraph of the offer which deals with the protection offered by the NHWP also deals with uncompleted items, which are not covered by the program. Unfinished work is a contractual matter between buyer and builder. No wonder buyers find this part of the offer misleading, since it erroneously implies that the NHWP covers both defects and unfinished work. Despite its inaccuracies, this clause is unalterable. Therefore, at least discuss with your lawyer before you sign the offer the coverage provided by the NHWP, so you fully understand what protection it provides.

According to most offers, only those uncompleted items listed at the time of the PDI will be finished after closing. You get only one kick at the can, one chance to list what is unfinished. That's why more and more people are hiring private home inspectors to accompany them on their PDI's, so that nothing is overlooked.

Access to the House before Closing

Everyone likes to see how work is progressing on their new house. Standing in the shell of your future home as it approaches completion is something many people look forward to. But remember what the offer says: you must not enter, examine or inspect the house without the builder's representative present. Legally speaking, entering the house without authorization before you take possesion makes you a trespasser. Builders are very concerned about people traipsing through a partially built home, for both safety and insurance reasons. If the builder allows you access before closing to do any work on the home, you must accept full responsibility for any loss, injury or damage that may result.

Substantial Completion

Few homes are totally finished when title changes hands. If closing takes place in late fall, winter or early spring, the sod and driveway may not be laid, the air-conditioner may not be installed and the grading and drainage may not be complete.

According to most offers, the house is deemed to be complete and ready for occupancy when the interior work has been "substantially completed," a term that is open to different interpretations by builders and buyers. Then comes an apparent inconsistency that new home buyers can do little about. Most offers go on to say that the deal must close and the entire purchase price must be paid to the builder, *without any holdback of funds,* when the house is "substantially completed," and not when it is fully completed. While you have to turn over 100 percent of the purchase price on closing you don't get 100 percent of the house at that time!

Ron and Nancy's house plan calls for three toilets. Once one of them has been installed, they could be forced to close since the house is "substantially completed." The other two toilets will be installed in the future. In return, the couple receives the builder's written undertaking to finish all uncompleted items as soon as possible after closing, depending on the availability of trades, material suppliers and weather conditions. An "indemnity" is also delivered by the builder, so that Ron and Nancy are not liable for any construction liens that are the builder's responsibility.

While this may sound fine, it can leave the buyer very vulnerable if the builder goes bankrupt shortly after closing, where work is still unfinished or where construction liens are registered. Remember that the New Home Warranty Program offers no protection whatsoever against unfinished work. The undertaking and indemnity the builder signed may not be worth the paper it is printed on. Yet builders adamantly refuse to alter this clause or allow any holdback of funds on closing, since it would cut into the money they get at closing. Any new home purchase that's closed without a holdback is a calculated risk, as getting work finished after closing depends on the reputation and financial security of the builder. Crossing your fingers and hoping for the best is not exactly comforting for purchasers of newly-built homes.

Try to avoid having to close when the property is considered to be only "habitable" or "fit for occupancy." "Habitable" certainly does not mean finished. It doesn't even mean "substantially completed." "Habitable" is a subjective term, and a very weak standard. A home not yet substantially completed could be considered fit for occupancy. Then you must close and turn over the entire purchase price, relying on the builder's good faith to complete everything that remains unfinished.

Many municipalities issue occupancy permits, certifying that the house is ready to be occupied. Be aware that some builder's offers force buyers to close the purchase even though the occupancy certificate may not be available. This too is unfair, but generally unalterable.

If you want your home to be totally completed before closing, make sure the offer is changed to clearly say so. But expect the builder to resist this alteration.

Right of Re-entry

As noted in Chapter 8, the municipality does not assume full responsibility for the subdivision services for some time (often three to five years) after closing. Before the municipality takes over, the developer must correct any deficiencies in the services, grading or drainage to comply with municipal requirements. Since this may require access onto your property, subdividers and builders reserve a right in the deed to come onto your lot during the period the subdivision remains unassumed. This way they can complete any remedial work, without being considered trespassers. This clause is nonnegotiable because it is imposed by the local municipality as part of the development agreement.

Grading and Drainage

As strange as it may seem, the storm sewer capacity for many new subdivisions is far smaller than even a generation ago. To reduce capital costs, a master grading and drainage plan is designed to complement this reduced capacity. The overland flow of water into swales and retention ponds is very important, especially during severe storms. Any interference with the drainage and grading patterns could prove disastrous. To ensure the master plan will not be affected, new home purchasers must agree not to alter the grading of the property and its surface drainage pattern. Like the right of entry clause this item cannot be deleted or omitted.

Find out how long the grading and drainage restrictions remain in effect (sometimes up to seven years), since they could affect your plans for the property (where you want to locate an outdoor shed, swimming pool or patio).

Fences and Other External Features

According to some offers, no fences, hedges, gardens, sheds, patios, swimming pools, TV antenna towers or satellite dishes can be erected for a set period of time after closing (three to seven years), without the builder's written consent. This also ensures that the grading and drainage of other homes will not be affected. Some of these privately imposed restrictions are reasonable, while others are not. Try as you might, you won't be able to modify this clause. So find out more about these private restrictions early on.

Basements

Some new home buyers must agree not to finish the basement for 12 months after closing. This allows the basement to properly dry out, and makes it easier for a builder to fix any leaks. In a related clause, buyers agree that nothing will be planted within six feet of an external wall over that same period of time. If the buyer does not comply, the builder has no obligation to repair any basement water leakage or seepage.

Other offers go further, and state the builder is not responsible for damage (called "consequential damage") caused to improvements, fixtures, furnishings or personal property in the basement from leakage, seepage or water infiltration. Your own insurance should cover this type of loss. But should damage to the basement itself be excluded from protection too, as is the case in most offers? Since NHWP protection applies, despite any agreement to the contrary, why is this clause inserted in the first place?

In effect, builders provide very little assurance the basement will not leak. Carefully review this nonalterable clause with your lawyer. Few new home buyers even know it exists.

Soil Settlement

Purchasers of newly-built homes acknowledge in the offer that the house, walkways, patios, driveways and sodded areas will settle. In the case of damage from settling, it is the builder alone who decides what will be fixed, and he will fix it only once. Minor soil settlement will not be corrected. Once again, the builder is both prosecutor and judge.

Access to the Interior of the House after Closing

Most offers allow builders free access to the interior of your house at reasonable times after closing to complete or rectify any outstanding work. If you refuse to give the builder access after he gives you reasonable notice, the offer says he has no further obligation to complete or rectify work inside your house.

This clause could prove quite harsh for single purchasers or two-income families. If you are worried about a tradesman entering your house when you're not there, then someone will have to stay home each time corrective work is scheduled. The alternative is to leave a key with the builder so the trades can come in when they are available. Theft and damage then become legitimate concerns for the home owner. But remember that according to the offer, the remedial work may never get done if you don't co-operate with the builder.

Conditional Offers

Basic contract principles apply to the purchase of a newly-built house. For a "firm and binding" contract to exist a written offer is needed, followed by acceptance of the contract and notification of that acceptance. Usually this is done by a telephone call, followed by delivery of the accepted offer to purchase. Once the offer is accepted, the transaction is set: "There shall be a binding Agreement of Purchase and Sale between the parties."

Although a deal has been struck, several loose ends sometimes need to be tied up before the buyer is ready to proceed with the offer. If these points cannot be resolved, then the buyer wants to be able to get out of the deal without losing his deposit. Very often other people who are not parties to the contract are involved in seeing that these outstanding items are resolved.

Purchasers following their home-buying strategy will consider asking that a conditional offer be prepared. Conditional offers give purchasers time *after an offer is accepted* to resolve these loose ends. Until these conditions are satisfied and waived, the contract is suspended and the deal is not really a deal. Once the conditions are satisfied, the offer becomes a legally binding and enforceable contract. If the conditions can't be satisfied, the offer becomes null and void.

Although conditional offers provide purchasers with considerable flexibility, unconditional offers will receive a much better reception from builders. Plain and simple, once the unconditional offer is accepted, the deal is on. An unconditional offer can be used to your advantage in negotiating other concessions from the builder such as extras and upgrades or even price. When faced with a choice between two identical offers, one conditional and the other unconditional, builders inevitably accept the unconditional version.

Be absolutely certain you can satisfy the would-be condition. Never forget that an unconditional offer is legally binding and enforceable, even if you learn later on that the would-be condition can't be met. It's always better to lose a particular home than to have signed a contract that can't be completed.

Most lawyers acting for purchasers will not process the deal while any conditions remain outstanding, unless you give firm instructions to the contrary. This avoids having to pay a large legal bill if the conditions cannot be satisfied.

Whenever a conditional offer is drawn, whether for a newly-built or resale home, make sure you carefully review and fully understand what the condition says and how it works. Not all conditions are alike, and noncompliance with the exact terms of a condition could cost you the property. To protect yourself, take the unsigned offer with the conditional clauses to an experienced real estate lawyer for review and comment.

A properly-drafted condition should contain the following:

1. The condition to be satisfied;
2. The length of time the purchaser has to satisfy the condition. Whenever possible, fix a specific date by which the condition must be satisfied. The old-fashioned approach of stating 15 or 30 business, calendar or banking days after acceptance can lead to considerable confusion in calculating the term of the condition.
3. What happens if the condition is not satisfied, and what if anything, must be done to cancel the deal?

    Two types of conditions appear in offers, and they have totally different consequences. It is absolutely essential to be able to tell the difference between these two types:

a) **Self-destructing:** Assume the condition is to arrange outside financing. If the financing cannot be arranged within a specified time, with a self-destructing condition the offer becomes null and void. The purchaser can sit back, do nothing, and let the offer die a natural death, following which his deposit will be returned. Or, if he wishes to keep the contract alive, he must waive the condition. Most people assume conditions are of the self-destructing type, but that is not always the case.

b) **Self-fulfilling:** If the condition to arrange financing is worded as a self-fulfilling condition, the contract *automatically becomes firm and binding* unless positive action is taken to cancel the deal. If the financing cannot be arranged within the specified time, with a self-fulfilling condition the purchaser must notify the vendor of that fact to terminate the deal. If the purchaser justs sits back the contract becomes valid and enforceable. With a self-fulfilling condition, to do nothing makes the contract firm and binding, not null and void! Understandably, self-fulfilling conditions can be dangerous.

    Make sure you understand the difference between a self-destructing and a self-fulfilling condition.

4. What steps are needed to firm up the offer (for self-defeating conditions) or destroy it (for self-fulfilling conditions)? Is written notice or verbal notice required? Even if oral notice is allowed,

put it in writing anyway to avoid any future misunderstandings. To whom should the notice be given? — the builder, the sales agent or the builder's lawyer? When? During the period the condition is outstanding, or beyond that date?

5. Will your deposit be returned in full, without deduction, and without interest? Clarify this at the outset to avoid future misunderstandings.

6. For whose benefit has the condition been inserted? Who can waive it? If the condition is for the buyer's benefit, then only the buyer can waive it.

Typical "conditional" clauses in new home offers include:

a) **Proper registration and permits** — Getting the subdivision registered, the services installed and the building permit issued are conditions inserted to protect the builder; they allow him to cancel the deal if this preliminary work cannot be completed. Many people are unaware that new home offers are conditional in this fashion. For more information on these conditions, see chapter 8.

b) **Financing** — Where the purchaser is to assume the builder's mortgage or the builder is to hold a vendor-take-back mortgage, the printed form requires the buyer to produce all required financial information and to be approved to assume the mortgage. If the purchaser does not qualify, then the offer is null and void. (Purchasers who arrange outside financing do not face this, as the offer with the builder is "all-cash.") In effect, then, the offer is made conditional on the purchaser being approved to assume the mortgage.

On the surface this clause seems to make sense. Unlike resale offers, though, the financing clause in most new home offers rarely allows purchasers to waive the condition, and this is most unfortunate. If Lewis and Lili are not approved either for the builder's mortgage or the vendor-take-back mortgage, they cannot try to keep the deal alive by making alternative arrangements for outside financing. This is extemely unfair to buyers whose applications are arbitrarily rejected by mortgage lenders, as was the case in 1981 when interest rates skyrocketed. At that time, many purchasers were denied mortgages despite their sound financial qualifications because current interest rates exceeded the ceiling previously arranged for the mortgage.

If they are initially rejected for the builder's mortgage, buyers should have one last chance to arrange outside financing within a specified number of days before the offer becomes null and void. Whenever possible, try to amend the offer this way. An amendment like this is reasonable and should be acceptable to most builders.

Even if closing is months away, most offers give purchasers only a very short period of time (often 21 days) after acceptance to apply to assume the builder's mortgage. Otherwise the builder can cancel the deal! Honor this time limit to avoid future problems. Just like color selections, if the builder or sales agent will not accept your mortgage application right away or does not even have the forms available, confirm these facts in writing. This will establish that the builder, and not you, was responsible for the late delivery of the mortgage application.

Only occasionally do purchasers of newly-built homes have formal approval for outside financing at the time they submit an offer to a builder. Buying a house without a mortgage in place then becomes a real risk. A commonly found condition in resale transactions allows purchasers to arrange satisfactory financing within a specified time before the offer becomes firm and binding. Rarely do builders allow this type of condition in a new home offer, especially where a builder's mortgage or VTB mortgage is available. Purchasers like Steve and Anita who want to arrange their own financing therefore must "go in firm," submitting an unconditional offer an offer to the builder. By doing this, Steve and Anita are gambling they can arrange a mortgage for closing. All the more reason to informally pre-qualify yourself for a mortgage as part of your HOBS.

Besides the purchaser being approved to assume the mortgage, offers are often made conditional in two other ways: the builder arranging his construction financing, and the builder arranging the builder's mortgage. If these mortgages can't be booked, the deal is off. Ask the sales agent if the construction financing is in place. If it is, delete that condition. For more information on the builder's mortgage condition, see Chapter 15.

c) **Sale of purchaser's property** — While "conditional on sale" clauses are inserted to benefit buyers, they are not the cure-all they initially appear to be. As part of your home-buying strategy, carefully consider and understand exactly what this clause means, before you sign the offer. Not all "conditional on sale" clauses are alike.

Like many buyers of newly-built homes, Chuck and Jody are trading up, so they must sell their current house before closing the new home purchase from Daddy Homes. One way to resolve the sell-first/buy-first dilemma is to buy the new home conditional on selling the old home. But be sure the conditional clause clearly says that "selling" means just signing the offer on the old house and not actually closing that deal.

Chuck and Jody's purchase from Daddy Homes was made conditional on selling their old house by March 15. Otherwise, the Daddy Homes deal would be null and void.

Builders' attitudes towards conditional on sale offers are an excellent barometer of the state of the real estate market. When the market is booming, Daddy Homes would likely shun the offer Chuck and Jody made conditional on selling their existing home. But when the market is soft, conditional on sale offers are much more acceptable to Daddy Homes. Better to have a signed offer, even a conditional one, and give the buyer a reasonable amount of time to satisfy the condition than to have no offer at all. If Chuck and Jody's existing home can be sold, then everybody wins. If not, Daddy Homes is really no worse off than before.

Many conditional on sale clauses say that construction on the new house will not begin until the condition is satisfied. Chuck and Jody can benefit from the longer conditional period this allows, since they can have as long as two or three months to sell their existing home. Because no work will be done until the offer is firm and binding, the closing of Chuck and Jody's new home purchase could be delayed if they need a lot of time to sell the present home.

In addition, Chuck and Jody should ensure that the conditional on sale clause gives them the option to waive the condition at their option. This way, if their old house has not been sold by, say, March 15, but they are confident it will be sold, Chuck and Jody can waive the condition and "firm up" the purchase from Daddy Homes. This flexibility is extremely important if considerable time must pass between acceptance and closing, such as in a pre-registration pre-sale. Of course, by waiving the condition without selling their current house, Chuck and Jody run the risk of still having to close the purchase if the present house remains unsold. This explains why not all builders will allow purchasers to waive the clause before the old house is sold.

Daddy Homes was also concerned that the conditional offer with Chuck and Jody effectively would take the new home off the market until March 15. Until then the house was sold, but not really. Just like Chuck and Jody, Daddy Homes wanted to keep its options open, in case another promising buyer came along.

To protect its interests, Daddy Homes's conditional on sale clause included a commonly seen escape hatch favoring the builder. It allowed Daddy Homes to continue selling the same house Chuck and Jody "bought " during the conditional period. If someone else wanted to buy it, Daddy Homes had to notify Chuck and Jody who then had three days to decide whether or not to waive the conditional on sale clause. By waiving it they would agree to close the purchase from Daddy Homes without first selling their existing home. By not waiving the clause, Chuck and Jody would lose the house and Daddy Homes would be free to accept the other offer — a real dilemma for which there is no easy answer. A lot depends on the state of the real estate market at the time.

Conditional on sale clauses often contain a hidden wrinkle that purchasers should know about. Fred is Daddy Homes' sales agent. As is usually the case, Fred agrees to a reduced commission per house sold of only 2 percent of the purchase price. In return, whenever anyone like Chuck and Jody buy from Daddy Homes "conditional on sale," the buyers must list their current home for sale with Fred. Selling homes listed this way during the conditional period for a full commission is where Fred's real profits lie. It also keeps Daddy Homes much better informed as to what is happening on Chuck and Jody's sale, and ultimately on their new home purchase as well. No wonder new home sales agents love these back-to-back or double-ender deals.

Chuck and Jody should realize they might face additional pressure from Fred to accept an offer on their current house while the condition remains outstanding on their new home. If they don't sell, Chuck and Jody are left with their old house and Fred earns nothing. Selling the old house is the key to buying the new house. And then Fred stands to earn two commissions.

Having to retain Fred as listing broker for their old house could have its own pitfalls for Chuck and Jody. What if he isn't overly familar with the real estate market in the community and neighborhood where the current house is located? Fred might list and sell the house for less than it is worth. If Fred works for a large real estate firm, this problem can often be avoided by having the listing transferred to a local office in that area. Then an agent familiar with comparable market values for Chuck and Jody's house would service the listing. Think twice before you sign a "conditional on sale" offer. It could mean you have to list your existing home with an "out-of-area" agent.

Most new home offers contain a catalogue of strange and unusual clauses that most people find surprising, to say the least. These bizarre clauses are known as "Zingers." We'll look at them in the next chapter.

Tips and Pointers

- Take a fully completed copy of the draft offer to your lawyer for review, comment and possible amendment.
- Be sure you fully understand what the contract says before signing it.
- Do not accept anything you are told at face value. Independently verify any statements made by the builder's agent.

19

Zingers

Everyone knows and accepts that offers for newly-built homes favor builders. What few people know is just how one-sided those offers are. They contain strange obligations and severe restrictions, and impose repressive conditions on purchasers far beyond what they anticipate.

"Zinger" clauses are usually buried in the fine print of a builder's offer. Often they appear in the middle of an extremely long paragraph. Rarely are they presented in bold type or in capital letters, underlined or indented. The fine print suggests these veiled clauses were not meant to be disclosed.

Sometimes a zinger clause will state that the buyer acknowledges that an issue has been adequately disclosed, that he understands its impact, and that the buyer agrees to close the transaction despite those consequences. Therefore it is absolutely essential that every buyer of a newly-built home understand what they are agreeing to do (and not to do) in the future. Whether these offensive clauses can be amended or deleted, depends on many different factors. But if buyers don't at least understand what the offer says, they could be stuck with clauses they have "acknowledged" that could seriously affect both the closing of the transaction plus their use and enjoyment of the property. All the more reason to take the unsigned offer to an experienced real estate lawyer for his opinion, comment and review first.

Termination of the Contract

Builders' new home offers are full of loopholes and trapdoors (builders call them opportunities) allowing them to cancel the deal, virtually at will. It's impossible for buyers to protect themselves adequately from these clauses, as a major rewriting of the offer by their lawyer will probably be rejected by the builder. Before they sign any offer, purchasers must realize how fragile and precarious a new home purchase is. For a deal to close, buyers literally must pray that the builder doesn't invoke any of the contractual rights the offer gives them. Not the most reassuring way to buy a newly-built home.

i) Closing Date

If the house is not completed on the scheduled closing date, the builder may have the right to terminate the contract right then and there, without having to extend the deal by even one day. This problem is especially prominent when the house has yet to be built (a pre-sale) and when the subdivision has not yet been registered (a pre-registration pre-sale). In these situations, the offer is conditional on events over which the purchaser has little control. This topic is examined in greater detail in Chapter 25.

ii) Mortgage

Unknown to most purchasers, new home offers are conditional on a) builder arranging his construction financing; b) the builder arranging a mortgage as stated in the offer, and c) the purchaser being approved to assume the mortgage. Otherwise the builder has the right to declare the offer null and void. See Chapter 15.

iii) Minor Breaches

A typical clause in a new home offer says "Any breach by the purchaser of any of the provisions of this Agreement shall entitle the vendor to give notice to the purchaser declaring this offer to be null and void, following which all deposit monies paid for extras shall be forfeited to the vendor." That's right, it means exactly what it says. *Any* breach of the contract, even the slightest, minor, technical breach, and the builder can cancel the contract and keep the deposit!

The builder doesn't need to give prior notice of the breach to the purchaser, only notice cancelling the deal. And no opportunity to rectify the breach has to be given, either! Obviously, this clause is extremely harsh and certainly very unfair, since the builder ends up being both prosecutor and judge. Would the clause stand up in a court of law? It might, since the purchaser agreed to it by signing the offer.

When the drastic implications of this clause are pointed out to a sales agent, the standard response is: "It'll never be used, so take it or leave it." Attempts to change the clause usually prove unsuccessful. If you decide to accept the clause as is, make sure you do everything the builder wants, when he wants it done, and how he wants it done. Or else the deal could become null and void.

iv) Builder/developer problems
No one wants to be a pawn in a battle between two competing interests. Yet this can be the case when one company develops, subdivides and services lots, and then sells them to a builder. Title to a lot is not usually "picked up" by a builder until the house is sold and ready for occupancy. Then two deeds are registered one right after the other: developer to builder, and builder to purchaser. Since the developer (and not the builder) is the registered owner of the property when the house is being built, the developer has a very powerful weapon if the builder fails to comply with the terms of the development agreement — he can withhold the deed.

Many offers say that if the contract between the developer/subdivider and the builder cannot be completed for any reason whatsoever, then the contract between the builder and the purchaser is terminated as well. If an offer is terminated this way, the builder is free of any liability to the buyer, once the buyer's deposit is returned. Once again, the new home purchase is made conditional on events taking place that have nothing to do with the buyer, without the offer expressly saying so. Almost every purchaser of a newly-built home is shocked to learn that his fortunes and future are controlled by a contract over which he has no control, and to which he is not even a party. And it's maddening to think the new home purchase could be terminated in ways that do not allow the buyer any recourse. Don't even try to change this clause. It's an untouchable.

v) "Keep your mouth shut and be a good boy or girl"
Builders must have very thin skins and be very uneasy about what buyers say about them. Why else would some builders reserve the right to cancel a signed contract if a purchaser (or anyone acting on the buyer's behalf) makes any "adverse representation" to the municipality or the lender about the construction of the house? Are builders worried that purchasers are going to criticize how the house is being built, or how long it is taking to finish the job? Is this clause really necessary? Those builders who include it must

think so, because once this clause goes into an offer, it doesn't come out.

Noise Problems

Some properties are built in areas where noise levels could be a problem. Prime examples are homes located on or near major thoroughfares, highways (and proposed highways), railway lines and airports. As part of their subdivision agreement with developers, municipalities require builders to make certain disclosures about noise to purchasers right in the offer.

A typical noise clause first states the source of the problem. Then it indicates that noise or vibration levels may increase in the future, based on increased volume or expansion of the source of the noise. Similar clauses must appear in any offer when the property is resold. While noise or vibration control measures are included both within the design of the subdivision and within individual houses to achieve acceptable indoor noise levels (dealing with the symptom and not the source of the problem), these concerns may continue to occasionally interfere with some of a home owner's activities.

Noise-control measures installed in individual homes may include central air conditioning, double-glazed windows, vibration pads and permanently sealed windows. One of the trade-offs Wally and Mary Ellen received when they bought a house backing onto a major rail line was central air conditioning. In some subdivisions, noise-attenuation fences and berms (mounds of earth) will also be constructed to disperse but not eliminate the noise.

The need for noise-control features differs at various locations within a subdivision, depending on how close a lot is to the source of the problem. Whenever a "noise" clause appears in your offer, get more information from the builder and then independently verify the facts. This could involve checking with the municipality or the appropriate government agency (such as CNR or CPR for railways; Transport Canada for airports; or the provincial highways department). Without doing this checking, how else could you ever make a final decision whether to buy a particular home? Remember that the more noise-attenuation features included in the purchase price, the greater the potential noise problem.

Gas Control Features

Land considered to be "way out of town" years ago is often now in the heart of urban development. Some prior uses of land would be incompatible with their use as residential subdivisions today, unless adequate safeguards were taken to protect the public. A sanitary landfill site (a nice way of saying a garbage dump) is a classic example of an incompatible former use.

Shouldn't buyers know that the home they are purchasing is built on, or adjacent to, a former garbage dump? Won't that affect its future resale value? A more serious problem with former landfill sites is methane gas. Excessively high methane levels could affect the use and enjoyment of your home. To properly protect residents, gas monitoring and control features must often be installed.

Like the noise-control situation, if you spot a clause dealing with gas control features in your offer, get as much information as possible from the builder. Then verify the nature of the problem as well as the proposed solution with the local municipality or provincial environment ministry. No one, absolutely no one who has a home-buying strategy should ever have to say they signed an offer while not fully understanding what this type of clause meant.

Schools
New areas may lack adequate neighborhood schools for years to come. Some development agreements force builders to be candid with purchasers, and tell them that even though schools sites have been chosen, there is no guarantee when or if a school will be erected there. Only when enough children live in an area will a neighborhood school be built. Until then, students may be accommodated in temporary facilities such as portables, or bussed to existing schools outside the area. It is crucial that parents of school-age children be aware of the school situation before signing an offer, so their decision to proceed is an informed choice.

Consent to Rezoning
Communities and neighborhoods are developed in stages, Over time, some land may be rezoned. Many developers/subdividers want total control as to how their adjacent landholdings will be developed. They do not want residents who have just bought and moved into the area halting or restricting the future development of adjoining or nearby land.

Unknown to most buyers, at the request of developers many builders insert a clause into the offer in which the purchaser automatically consents to any rezoning application that might be brought! In effect, the buyer approves future rezoning without knowing any of the details! When this clause and its implications are raised by the buyer, builders go on the defensive. While they maintain it is an unimportant clause, rarely can you have it removed. That has to be a sure sign of its importance to the builder and developer.

To find out whether the rezoning clause could be invoked, do an end-run around the builder. Check things out at the local municipality. Mel and Alice went in person to the municipal offices to learn more about vacant land situated a kilometer away from the house they were thinking of buying. Rarely is this type of information disclosed over the phone. There they asked questions about the present zoning of the lands: whether any rezoning applications were pending; whether there were any indications that the land would be rezoned in the future; and what the official plan allowed on that land. Although the information they got was no guarantee of what might happen, Mel and Alice could make an educated decision about the likelihood of future rezoning. Forewarned is forearmed.

Restrictions on Sale
Builders dislike speculators, especially those speculators who aim to turn a quick profit before the deal closes by selling the offer and "flipping" the property. Although many clauses have been inserted into offers in an attempt to eliminate speculation, the versatility of speculators in overcoming these obstacles has kept them in business.

Clauses aimed directly at speculators say that a) the purchaser must occupy the premises within 15 days of closing if a builder's mortgage is being assumed; b)the buyer will not sell (i.e, list, advertise or enter into an offer for sale)the property until the builder's mortgage is fully advanced; and c) the buyer cannot assign or sell the offer (as distinct from the property) before closing. People who intend to occupy the house they buy have nothing to fear from these clauses.

But because speculators have been successful in side-stepping these obstructions, builders have gone even further. Now they are demanding that buyers agree not to sell or transfer the property until the builder has sold *all* of his lots in the development. This restriction could be for a fixed period of time, perhaps one year after closing, or it could be more indefinite. Other clauses give builders an option to repurchase the property *at the same price* as the buyer paid, for up to five years after closing, or until all properties in the subdivision have been sold, whichever comes first! Now the pendulum has swung too far the opposite way. Clauses like these totally restrict the legal right of a home owner to deal legitimately with his own property. Buyers made aware of these clauses are shocked at their severity, and the potential for abuse. It's like killing a fly with a cannonball. Besides dealing with speculators, they also give builders a veto over any genuine transactions during the restricted period.

Bona fide sales of homes necessitated by death, company transfer, marriage breakdown or material change in circumstances — none of these may be permitted until the entire subdivision is sold out. If Lance and Lorraine absolutely had to sell their home subject to one of these restrictive clauses, they would have to go cap-in-hand to the builder, asking for a waiver of the clause. Having to plead for the legal right to sell their own home is degrading and offensive to most people.

Depending on the exact wording of the clause, an unscrupulous builder could keep one house for himself and effectively prevent any purchasers from ever selling their homes. As a condition to granting his consent to the sale, the builder could insist that he be paid any profit from the sale of Lance and Lorraine's home. Or he might demand the first right to repurchase their home at the original sale price for five years after closing, no matter how much the property has increased in value.

Purchasers of newly-built homes should not have to consider whether these clauses would stand up in a court of law. To legitimate buyers who plan to use their home as a principal residence, clauses like these are unorthodox, unfair and unjustified. Never rely on a statement by the sales agent that they will not be used, or only on the rarest of occasions. If they exist, they can be used. *Strike them out!* Surprisingly, many builders will delete them on request, to the relief of many purchasers.

Sufficient Sales
If Richard and Karen buy a house from a builder, shouldn't the builder be obligated to build it? Don't say yes too soon. The latest move up builders' sleeves, once again concealed in the midst of the offer, makes their offers conditional on a certain number of homes being sold by a certain date before they will proceed with the entire subdivision. Variations of this clause allow builders to cancel the contract if they are not satisfied with the "economic viability and feasibility" of the project by a specified date. These types of clauses originated with condominium projects, but are now being applied to residential subdivisions as well.

Once again the intent of the clause is clear. Building new homes is expensive and to bring in a full crew to construct just a few homes may not make economic sense. So this clause allows builders to put out feelers for their planned project. By allowing this clause to remain in their offer, Richard and Karen cast their fate to the discretion of the builder. Until the cancellation date passes, they really haven't bought a house; they just have a conditional offer. How can Richard and Karen plan a move if they don't know whether the house will ever be built? This is another unconventional and unjust clause that must and often can be struck out of the builder's offer. If it cannot be deleted, make sure you understand what it says and what it allows the builder to do. And be sure the "sufficient sales" clause is not open ended, but contains a target date fixed for the near future.

By now, purchasers with a home-buying strategy will have heard it many, many times — submitting the offer on a newly-built home should be one of the last steps you take and never the first. It should be the culmination of your HOBS. When you sign an offer, you must fully understand what it says, what rights the builder has and what your responsibilities are. Whenever possible, you should request appropriate changes to the offer to make it more acceptable, before submitting it to the builder. If changes are not allowed, at least you should know the downside risks of the clauses in question, especially those that allow the builder to cancel the contract prematurely. All hidden costs must be revealed and considered to ensure you can afford to buy the house and carry it in the future.

In short, newly-built home-buyers need full disclosure of all aspects of the transaction before they sign the offer, so they can make an educated decision to proceed. To assist you, have the unsigned offer reviewed by an experienced real estate lawyer. Instead of groping in the dark, you can then confidently proceed with the transaction.

Tips and Pointers
A checklist of clauses to look for:

- Agents are not responsible for statements they make unless the statements appear in the offer.
- Price escalation clauses.
- Conditional clauses such as:
  - registration of the subdivision

- servicing of the land
- issuance of a building permit
- builder arranging construction financing and builder's mortgage
- approval to assume the builder's mortgage
- sale of your existing house.
- "economic viability and feasibility" of the project
- The builder's discretion to build a different house from the one bought.
- Money paid for extras and upgrades will not be refunded if the work is not done.
- Clauses giving builders the right to cancel the deal, such as:
  - house not ready on time
  - purchaser not approved to assume mortgage
  - mortgage not arranged by builder
  - failure to apply for mortgage within a specified time
  - minor breaches by purchaser
  - failure to select colors on time
  - builder/subdivider problems
  - making statements that may harm the builder's reputation.
- Closing at substantial completion stage with no holdbacks.
- Noise problems
- Gas control features.
- Schools.
- Consent to rezoning.
- Restrictions on sales.

20

Buying a Newly-built Condominium Unit

What a transformation condominiums have undergone in recent years! First introduced to Canada in the late 1960s, condominiums (called Strata Titles in British Columbia and Co-ownership of Immoveables in Quebec) were at first criticized and rejected by most people. Developers had serious problems selling and maintaining units during those early years and buyers concerns were often neglected. Those were the days when condominiums were promoted as an alternative form of "affordable " housing for Canadians, a far cry from the elegant image that made them popular in Europe and the United States. Only in the mid 1970s, when condominiums were designed and built for the middle- and upper-income person, did the public begin warming up to the concept.

Condominiums are creatures of provincial statutes. While minor variations exist from province to province, the commentary in this chapter applies to most condominiums across Canada.

What is a condominium?

The word "condominium," often used to describe a certain type or style of building, really describes a system of land ownership. A buyer of a condominium unit, whether townhouse or apartment, acquires:

a) Title to a specific residential dwelling unit which is registered in the buyer's name. The legal description consists of a unit and level number, plus the condominium corporation number. Many high-rise buildings do not number suites on the thirteenth floor, but the thirteenth floor is included in the legal description. Also, the unit number need not correspond with the suite number. For example, apartment 1406 could be unit 8, level 13. Many of the expenses associated with home ownership (realty taxes, mortgage payments plus maintenance and repairs to the unit) are the unit owner's responsibility. Like single-family homes, the condominium unit is bought, sold and mortgaged as a separate entity. This means Jeremy's ownership of his unit will not be jeopardized if his neighbor, Bernie, fails to pay his taxes or mortgage.

b) A proportionate interest, together with all other unit owners, in the remainder of the condominium property and common areas known as the "common elements" or "common property." These shared title areas include the hallways, stairwells, elevators, lobby, driveway, walkways, parking garage, recreational facilities, grounds and playground, together with the land on which the building and these features are situated.

c) A right to use specific parts of the common elements called "exclusive use common elements." While they are legally owned and maintained by the condominium, their use is restricted to one owner. Typical examples of exclusive use common elements are exterior balconies, parking spaces and storage lockers in condominium apartments, and lawns in townhouse developments.

Since all unit owners own the common elements, they must share the cost of maintaining them. A monthly "maintenance" or common expense fee is levied against all owners for the expenses incurred in operating the condominium and maintaining the common areas. The more space you own in the complex, the higher the maintenance you pay. Eddie and Ellen, who own a three-bedroom unit, would own a larger percentage of the common elements and pay a higher maintenance fee than Carey and Sharon, who own a two-bedroom unit. All unit owners also become members of the condominium corporation, which is established to operate the business affairs of the condominium.

Types of Condominiums

Important differences exist between the two most common types of condominium developments: high-rise apartments and townhouses. Apartment condominiums have higher monthly maintenance fees because of the greater upkeep for apartment buildings. The cost of maintaining and repairing elevators, repairing and cleaning internal common elements, and maintaining, repairing and cleaning an underground garage are items owners of townhouse units rarely face. Also, in townhouse condominiums, utility charges such as electricity, water, gas, and cable television are usually billed separately to individual units. These items are usually bulk-metered to the whole complex in condominium apartments, to be passed on to the unit owners as part of the monthly maintenance charge. In this way, a townhouse owner doesn't end up subsidizing his more extravagant neighbor who always forgets to turn off the lights or turn down the heat.

Advantages of Condominium Ownership
Condominiums today are both an accepted and an acceptable form of home ownership. Probably the biggest advantage of owning a condominium is the "lifestyle" it offers. Condominiums give their owners the best of both worlds—home ownership and the opportunity for capital appreciation, while freeing its owners from the mundane responsibilities usually associated with home ownership. They are ideal for those who lack the time or inclination to maintain a conventional property. Simply put, condominiums offer convenience—for a price. Instead of tackling many of the chores most home owners face such as cutting the grass, shovelling the snow, landscaping the grounds and maintaining the exterior of the building, condominium owners pay a monthly fee to have this work done for them.

Many buildings today are designed as "luxury" condominiums. They cater to a certain type of buyer who appreciates elaborate recreational facilities like swimming pools, squash and racquetball courts. No wonder condominium marketing campaigns are aimed today at older people, especially "empty-nesters" whose grown-up children have moved out, and whose needs in a home are vastly different than 20 years ago. They want the benefits of home ownership without the headaches of maintenance, repairs and upkeep.

Condominiums are also attractive to many younger people, especially childless couples and career-conscious individuals for whom convenience is already an important part of their lifestyle. For those who find the allure of city living irresistible but want to own instead of rent, a condominium would appear to be the ideal choice.

Disadvantages of Condominium Ownership

By their very nature, condominiums limit many of the freedoms home owners have enjoyed in the past. After all, a condominium is a cross between owning a home and being a tenant. To ensure peace and harmony among condominium unit owners, restrictions are imposed on some personal freedoms so that the greatest protection is offered to the greatest number of people. All unit owners are subject to the "laws" of another level of government, the condominium corporation. In this private local government, the residents of the condominium enact laws to control and regulate activities within its boundaries.

Factors to Consider when Buying a Condominium Unit

First and foremost, it is important that you develop and apply your own home-buying strategy, the practical approach to buying any newly-built home or condominium today. Since most new condominiums are sold from plans before construction is completed, (often before construction even commences) take the time to reread Chapter 9, which deals with that issue. Then prepare your questions, and expect the sales agent to provide adequate answers about the specific project that interests you. As with any new home purchase, you may have to independently verify certain points. Don't forget to take the offer to your lawyer for review and comment *before* you sign it. This will ensure that you fully grasp the important legal issues involved with condominium ownership, especially if your unit is unbuilt and unregistered when the offer is signed.

Because condominium ownership is so different from conventional home ownership, additional topics must be addressed as part of your HOBS:

- adequacy and location of parking spaces for owners and visitors;
- adequacy, location and accessibility of locker and storage space;
- proximity to elevator and garbage chute. If noise bothers you, choose a unit away from garage doors, saunas, laundry rooms, elevators, garbage chutes, heating and electrical plants;
- floor level in an apartment condominium. Buyers often pay a premium for a unit on an upper floor, or with a certain view or "exposure";
- will the sound insulation be adequate to ensure proper soundproofing? If this concerns you, ask to see the acoustical plans and have an expert examine them;

- the availability of 24-hour security for the residents;
- availability of recreational and other facilities like a swimming pool (indoor or outdoor), sauna, tennis/squash/racquetball courts, health club, meeting/multi-purpose room;
- type of condominium such as adult only, or if a family complex are there adequate facililties for children?
- Rules and Regulations that govern what you can and cannot do, both within your unit and within the complex;
- costs and services included in the maintenance fee.

Many of these issues and others are addressed in the disclosure statement that the developer must provide to purchasers of an unregistered unit in provinces like Ontario (called a prospectus in British Columbia). Disclosure statements are so helpful that even some resale condominium buyers ask vendors for them. Written in everyday English, the disclosure statement is designed to help purchasers understand exactly what they are buying, what rights and privileges accompany the unit, and what duties and obligations they will face as a unit owner. It sounds tailor-made for the purchaser with a HOBS—and it is!

Besides describing the condominium complex in general terms, including the recreational and other amenities, the disclosure statement highlights the key points of the Declaration, By-Laws, and Rules and Regulations (all of which are examined in more detail below). A detailed budget statement for the first year following registration of the condominium, and the completion schedule for unfinished work are included as well.

In Ontario the *Condominium Act* gives buyers of new condominiums 10 days from the date they receive the disclosure statement to decide whether to proceed with the deal or back out. A similar 10-day rule applies in Alberta. Purchasers can do this without any penalty, and have their deposit returned in full! In other words, a signed offer to buy a new condominium is not binding on a purchaser in those provinces for at least 10 days after it is signed and accepted.

The details in the disclosure statement and the 10 day "cooling-off" period offer important protections for purchasers of unbuilt or unregistered units. Having 10 days to turn thumbs-up or down on a deal gives buyers a valuable opportunity to independently verify any verbal representations made by the sales agent. Any buyer who signed the offer before seeing a lawyer still has 10 days after acceptance to do so and still back out of the deal without penalty.

The cooling-off period gives buyers of new condominiums some breathing room and time to calmly reconsider the purchase after the fact, something newly-built home buyers never have the chance to do.

What do I own and what can I use?

The documents that establish the condominium are variously called the "Declaration and Description," the "Condominium Plan" or the "Strata Plan." They state precisely what is acquired when a condominium unit is bought, including the boundaries of each unit, areas designated as common elements and the unit owner's interest in each. In Ontario, draft copies of these documents must accompany the disclosure statement for unbuilt and unregistered units. Check later to be sure that the final version is substantially the same as the drafts. Major changes mean builders must give a further cooling-off period to purchasers.

While the boundaries of condominium units are almost always the same, some minor differences do exist from project to project. In layman's terms, a condominum dwelling unit consists of "a box in the sky," the area from wall to wall, and from ceiling to floor. Legally speaking, the unit boundaries generally are defined as the upper surface of the concrete floor slab, the lower surface of the concrete ceiling and the interior or backside surface of the unfinished walls. Everything else, including the space between the floors and units, is part of the common elements.

Knowing the precise boundaries of a dwelling unit is very important, as it determines who is responsible to repair damage. Unit owners like Greg and Marguerite must repair and maintain their unit, as well as the improvements and betterments within it. These include the customizing and upgrading made to a condominium unit like carpeting, wallpaper, window coverings, electric light fixtures, and upgraded kitchen cabinets and bathroom fixtures.

Maintaining and repairing the common elements is the condominum's responsibility. Recently, a leaky pipe damaged the walls in Greg and Marguerite's fifth-floor unit, plus the hallway outside their suite. The condominium corporation had to repair the wall itself and repaint its surface in the hallway, a common element. Since Greg and Marguerite own the surface of the wall inside their unit, repainting or wallpapering it is their responsibility.

Parking Spaces

Condominium unit owners can acquire a parking (and often a

locker) space in one of four different ways, depending on the project: a) freehold; b) leasehold; c) exclusive use; and d) allocated. While all of these entitle the unit owner to use a specific parking space, the legal interest acquired differs greatly.

From the disclosure statement, Ron learned that he will have a freehold parking unit, the best type for a condominium owner. Just like his dwelling unit, Ron will own the parking unit outright and receive a deed in his name for it. The second parking unit he is buying can be used by Ron and leased or sold to anyone else in the condominium complex. When available, some developers sell extra freehold parking units to unit owners.

Leasehold parking units are the next best choice. Owned by the condominium corporation as part of the common elements, they are leased to unit owners like Mark on a long-term basis, perhaps as long as 99 years. In that way, the dwelling unit and the leased parking unit go hand in hand as a package for the term of the lease. When Mark sells his unit, the lease is automatically transferred to the new owner of the dwelling unit.

Exclusive use is the most common way parking spaces are distributed among unit owners. Like leasing, the condominium corporation owns the parking spaces as part of the common elements. But instead of leasing them to unit owners like Karen, the condominium Declaration states that the owner of a particular residential unit has the exclusive right to use a specific parking space forever. As owner of dwelling unit 1, level 6, Karen has the exclusive use to parking space 53. When she sells the residential unit to Ken, he automatically has the exclusive right to use parking space 53, even though the deed does not specifically mention a parking space. This exclusive right of use is non-transferable, unless the dwelling unit is being conveyed.

The least advantageous way to acquire a parking unit is by allocation or designation. Although a unit owner like Earl is entitled to a parking space, the directors of the condominium determine its precise location, which can change over time. As properties are sold, the "prime" parking spaces indoors or near the elevator are re-allocated to long-term residents and those on the board of directors. New owners like Phil, who bought Earl's unit, end up with parking spaces in a less advantageous location. To get a better spot Earl must put his name on a waiting list, and sometimes pay an additional fee for a choice once it is available.

Balconies, Front Yards and Rear Yards

Most condominium owners are shocked to learn they do not own the backyard patio or front and rear yards of townhouses, or the balconies of apartment condominiums adjacent to their dwelling units. In fact, the condominium corporation owns all of them, as part of the common elements. According to the condominium Declaration, owners are given the exclusive right to use those areas to the exclusion of all other people. Most often, the condominium corporation will repair and maintain those areas, although occasionally these are the unit owner's responsibility.

Before signing any offer for a newly-built condominium, purchasers applying their HOBS should learn exactly what the unit includes, the location and type of parking space, and what exclusive use common areas accompany the unit. To do this, carefully review the disclosure statement, if available.

Rules and Regulations

Just like a mini-community, every condominium corporation imposes certain restrictions on the activities of its residents. Even townhouse condominium projects are subject to Rules and Regulations. Builders of new homes often impose restrictions to control the use of the land. Typical clauses prohibit outside clotheslines, TV antennaes and the permanent parking of campers and trucks on driveways. Similar rules and regulations are imposed on townhouses complexes to maintain the esthetic beauty of the development.

Only in the rarest of cases can a home owner be forced to spend money when he does not want to. That's not the case in a condominium. For example, Doug's condominium recently approved a major expenditure to upgrade the recreational facilities. All unit owners, even those like Doug who are opposed to the project, must pay their proportionate share of this additional expense. Remember that the condominium is just like another level of government, whose laws and rules must be obeyed.

Just as in landlord/tenant situations, representatives of the condominium corporation can enter a unit at any time without notice in an emergency, to repair the unit or protect the overall interests of all unit owners. To ensure that access is possible, a key to all locks for each unit must be left with the condominium's managers. Former tenants may be familiar with this arrangement, but it certainly differs from the privacy and security to which long-time owners of single-family homes are accustomed. Most of these restrictions appear in a document called, naturally enough, the Rules and Regulations, which are passed by the board of directors of the condominium corporation. Similar to the house rules in apartment buildings, such as those that prohibit barbeques on outdoor balconies, these practical regulations promote the safety, security and welfare of the unit owners.

Most house rules do not place restrictions only on the use of the common elements. *They also regulate and restrict how individual units can be used,* a point that bothers Norm, who owned his own single-family home for years. Typical house rules restrict pets, or require that specific areas of an apartment unit be carpeted to reduce noise levels to the floor below.

Rules and Regulations may affect an owner's unrestricted use and enjoyment of his unit, but that's the very nature of condominium ownership. Striking a balance among unit owners is important to prevent one person from unreasonably interfering with another's use and enjoyment of his unit.

As part of your home-buying strategy, learn all you can about the Rules and Regulations set by the condominium corporation before signing any offer to purchase. To wait could be too late. Are any of them unacceptable or incompatible with your intended use of the unit? Are you sure you have reviewed *all* the restrictions? Keep in mind that *all* the house rules and regulations may not appear in the Rules and Regulations!

For example, no rule is of greater concern to condominium unit owners than the one about pets. Some condominiums prohibit them altogether, while others restrict the type of pet allowed and where they are permitted. But in some condominiums, the restrictions dealing with pets do not appear in the Rules and Regulations, where they should be. Instead, they are buried in the condominium constitution, the Declaration. This makes the rule virually unalterable, since it requires the unanimous consent of unit owners and lenders before it can be changed. Rules and Regulations, on the other hand, can be easily changed by the directors of the condominium.

Just because the Rules and Regulations don't mention pets, never assume this means pets are permitted. If keeping a pet is important to you, carefully review *all* the condominium documents, especially the Declaration, before you sign any contract, to see if there are any prohibitions against pets. Don't rely on a verbal assurance from the builder's sales agent. If in doubt, take the draft condominium documents to your lawyer, and have him or her independently verify the point.

Remember that condominium rules can be enforced just like any other rules. If need be, the directors can take a unit owner to court for violating any of the condominium's rules and regulations.

Points to Know about Owning a Condominium Unit

1. *Condominium Corporation*

Once the Declaration and Description or Condominium Plans are registered, the condominium comes into being, together with a non-share company known as the condominium corporation to manage its affairs. All unit owners are members of the corporation. In some provinces each unit has one vote, while in others the size of the unit's percentage interest in the common elements ("the unit factor") determines the size of the vote.

Like any business corporation, the condominium corporation has officers and a board of directors elected by the unit owners. Since running the business on a day-to-day basis can be very time-consuming, most condominium corporations retain the services of a management company, whose fees are included in the common expenses.

The management company attends to the upkeep, maintenance and repair of the common elements and other assets of the condominium; updates the books and records; collects and disburses the common expense funds; enters into contracts and other agreements on behalf of the corporation; and prepares the annual budget that forms the basis for the following year's monthly maintenance charge. Policy decisions rest with the board of directors.

Many unit owners complain that decisions are made without their input or knowledge. Who makes these decisions? The directors. And who are the directors? Residents in the complex who have taken the time to get involved in the management and operation of the condominium corporation. Instead of complaining, participate in the decision-making process. Seek election to the board of directors. Don't leave it to someone else. As a member of the board of directors, you'll always know what is happening. Your voice will be heard and your ideas will be considered. It's an excellent way to meet your neighbors, make new friends and gain valuable experience — all at the same time.

2. Common Expenses ("Maintenance")

This is the monthly fee paid by all unit owners for the upkeep, maintenance and repair of the common elements as well as the operation of the condominium corporation. Typical items included in the monthly maintenance are utilities (if not separately metered); operating costs such as snow removal and grounds maintenance; the cost of repairs and maintenance of common elements; service contracts; personnel; supplies; insurance on the common elements; fees paid to the management company; administrative charges; plus contributions to the reserve fund. Many condominium owners are justifiably upset when garbage disposal fees are included in the common expenses. In a sense they pay twice for garbage pickup—once to the condominium corporation and once to the municipality as part of the property taxes.

If one unit owner does not pay his share of common expenses promptly, all unit owners end up bearing the burden. To deal with delinquents, the condominium corporation can place a lien against a unit when common expenses are unpaid. The condominium corporation even has the power to sell a defaulting owner's unit, if necessary, to recoup outstanding charges.

Before a condominium purchase closes, the buyer's lawyer orders what is called an "Estoppel Certificate," a status update report from the condominium corporation. Besides providing up-to-date information about any arrears in maintenance payments for the unit, this certificate also gives details about the condominium corporation itself, such as the size of the reserve fund. It also includes notice of any pending lawsuits or special assessments, and alterations and improvements planned to the common elements. Of course, with a newly-built unit, the report should come back clean as a whistle. Still, it is an important certificate to have on file.

3. Reserve Fund

In the early days of condominium development, a shortage of money for major repairs and emergencies often posed a problem. To generate sales, developers gave "low-ball" estimates for the monthly maintenance charge. In addition, they failed to set aside money for a "rainy day." When costly repairs were needed or major assets had to be replaced, condominium corporations often lacked the necessary funds to do the work.

Assume Condo Builders quoted a monthly common expense fee of $50 a month for the first year of operation, when it really needed to collect $150 a month. In the second year of operation, unit owners faced an enormous leap in the maintenance fee (at least $100 per month). More importantly, each owner had to make up his $1,200 deficiency arising from the unrealistically low maintenance fees in that first year. Unit owners faced special assessments to generate the needed cash, and liens against their titles if they were unable or unwilling to make up the shortfall. Some units ended up being sold by the condominium corporation, which pitted neighbors against one another. This very serious mess, of course, was created by the condominium developer.

Today, the problem of low-ball estimates for maintenance has been resolved by legislation. Developers now must state in the disclosure statement what the monthly maintenance fee will be for the first year. Any deficiency between those figures and the actual expenses incurred by the corporation during its first year in operation must be repaid by the developer to the condominium corporation. In effect, the developer guarantees the amount of the first year's maintenance payments.

In addition, reserve funds — money set aside "for a rainy day" — must now be maintained by each condominium corporation. The reserve fund can only be used to cover the cost of major repairs and the replacement of major assets such as roofs, sidewalks, heating, plumbing and electrical systems, carpeting, laundry machines, elevators, plus recreational and parking facilities. Each month, part of the maintenance fee must be paid to the reserve fund. The amount that must be contributed to the reserve fund depends on the state of repair, expected replacement cost and anticipated life expectancy of the common elements and condominium assets. In Ontario, at least 10 percent of the monthly common expenses must go to the reserve fund. Obviously, older condominiums need larger reserve funds because of the greater likelihood that major assets and equipment will have to be repaired or replaced.

To establish this "kitty" in new condominiums, purchasers must contribute one and sometimes even two months' common expenses to the condominium corporation, as an adjustment on closing. Buried in the body of the contract, this is another hidden cost which you and your lawyer should discuss before you sign the offer.

Rarely is the money in the reserve fund credited back to the seller on a future sale of the unit. A subsequent purchaser acquires the vendor's interest in the reserve fund *without adjustment* as an asset of the corporation, just like the bricks and mortar of the building.

To calculate a unit's proportionate interest in the reserve fund, multiply the total amount in the reserve fund (as stated in the Estoppel Cerificate) by that unit's share of the common elements. The amount involved could easily be hundreds of dollars per unit.

4. *Insurance*

The distinction between an individual's unit and the condominium's common elements is most apparent when you consider insurance. The condominium corporation arranges insurance coverage on the common elements *only*, for protection against loss by fire, water, smoke and other major perils on a replacement cost basis. The corporation must also arrange liability coverage for the common elements. The insurance premiums for this common element coverage is passed onto the unit owners in the monthly maintenance fee.

But the condominium corporation's coverage offers no protection whatsoever to the unit owner, the unit, improvements and betterments made to the unit, or the contents of a unit. If there was major damage to a unit, the corporation's insurance would restore the unit to its orginal, unfinished condition — drywall and concrete. Repairing the interior of the unit would fall under the owner's insurance coverage. Public liability coverage for a unit is also the responsibility of the unit owner.

The insurance industry has developed "Condominium Unit Owner's Package Insurance," which recognizes that a condominium itself is a cross between conventional home ownership and a tenancy. In some respects this coverage resembles a home owner's package as the unit itself is owned. It also parallels a tenant's package in some ways, because the unit being insured is only one part of a much larger complex.

As with any insurance coverage, several options are available including "all-risks" coverage, which provides much broader protection than the standard named-perils basis, as well as replacement cost coverage. Personal liability coverage, which protects the unit owner if he is sued by someone who suffers personal injury in the owner's unit, should also be included. As with any other type of insurance, you should find out what losses and perils your policy does and does not cover.

Some insurance companies also provide low-cost coverage for any losses a unit owner may suffer if the condominium corporation has insufficient insurance coverage. How could this ever happen? Suppose the common elements in Bruce's building were severely damaged by a fire. When the repair bill was to be paid,

Bruce learned the condominium corporation's insurance coverage was inadequate to repair the damage in full. But somebody had to make up the difference, and that "somebody" is the unit owners. Over the next few years, Bruce and the others face a sizeable special assessment to cover the cost of the repairs. With this additional insurance coverage, called Loss Assessment Coverage, Bruce was reimbursed by his own insurance company for the amount of the special assessment. By paying a nominal premium, Bruce was able to avoid the expensive special assessment.

Two incidents at a party held in Ed and Trixie's condominium apartment illustrate the two different types of insurance needed for complete coverage. Their guest, Alice, broke her ankle when she tripped on a rug in the foyer of the building. Since the injury occurred on the common elements, Alice must make a claim against the personal liability coverage provided by the condominium corporation. Her husband, Ralph, tripped on a rug in Ed and Trixie's suite, and also broke his ankle. Since the injury occurred within Ed and Trixie's apartment, Ralph will have to claim against the couple's personal liability coverage. The same holds true for a fire. Whether the property damaged was common elements or within a unit would determine which insurance policy would have to bear the cost of repairing the damage.

To get the right type of insurance coverage, advise your insurance agent that you have bought a condominium unit. But to ensure that there are no gaps in coverage, deliver the certificate of insurance provided by the condominium's insurer to your own insurance broker. Let the broker review what coverage it provides and where it is lacking. Your personal coverage should make up any shortfalls in the condominium's policy.

5.   *Selling/Leasing Unit*

According to the provincial condominium acts, dwelling units can be freely sold, subject to any restrictions in the Declaration. This begs the obvious question: Are there any such restrictions in the Declaration of your condominium? It may not be an important question to ask when you're buying now, but it could ultimately have a serious impact on the resale of your unit in the future.

In the United States, the board of directors of condominiums often must approve any subsequent purchaser of a dwelling unit. In effect, the board has a veto on who can own a unit in the complex, and to whom you can sell your unit. Though this practice is permitted by condominium legislation in some provinces, these restrictions on sales are not nearly as prevalent here. Still, the time to find out about this kind of restriction is before you even submit an offer.

Renting out a unit is a different situation altogether. A unit owner has the right to rent out his property, provided the criteria set out in the Declaration are met. Once again, the condominium corporation has the power to place restrictions on the leasing of units, but this is rarely done. Like any other type of rental arrangement however, the tenant still must provide certain information to the condominium corporation, so that it can update its occupancy records. The tenant must also agree in writing to comply with the Rules and Regulations, the Declaration and the By-Laws of the condominium corporation.

Where the condominium is not yet registered and an occupancy agreement is in effect, developers have the power to withhold their consent to a transfer of the unit. Designed to curtail the power of speculators to "flip" units before the deal closes, this shouldn't affect the purchaser who intends to live in the unit he buys.

6. *Mortgage Clauses*

Mortgages registered against condominium units include a number of special clauses that recognize the uniqueness of condominium ownership. Here are some typical clauses:

- to protect its investment, lenders have the right to exercise the borrower's vote at a meeting of the condominium corporation, although this right is rarely exercised.
- copies of all relevant notices and documents must be given to the lender, to keep it abreast of developments.
- if the borrower does not punctually pay all common expenses, the lender can pay the arrears and add it to the mortgage debt. Many lenders do this, since in most provinces unpaid maintenance fees rank higher than that first mortgage!
- borrowers must observe and perform *all* duties and obligations imposed by the provincial condominium act, the Declaration, By-Laws, Rules and Regulations of the condominium corporation. Noncompliance gives the lender the right, *at its option*, to demand that the mortgage be repaid in full, and the borrower has no opportunity to rectify the situation! Taken to its extreme, keeping a pet in the unit contrary to the Rules and Regulations could be grounds for the lender to terminate the mortgage.

Some lenders are still concerned that a condominium borrower only owns the unit plus a percentage interest in the land. Reflecting this concern, some lenders grant mortgages for only 70 percent of a condominium unit's value, somewhat lower than the 75 percent financing granted on conventional housing.

The Unbuilt/Unregistered Condominium

An increasing number of new condominium units are pre-sold before construction commences on the project. This parallels the pre-registration pre-selling of other newly-built homes. Offers on condominiums sold this way are usually made conditional on a number of events taking place, including:

a) the builder arranging financing for the construction of the complex;

b) rezoning the land, if necessary, to permit the condominium building to be constructed;

c) having the Declaration and Description registered to formally establish the condominium corporation.

As with any purchase of a newly-built home, you should get more information about these conditions. If either of the first two have already been satisfied, then have them deleted from the offer. If not, find out when the developer expects the conditions to be met. Is there any time limitation on complying with the conditions, failing which the builder could arbitrarily cancel the deal? If so, the deal really is not a deal yet. Registering the necessary documents, of course, must be done before individual units can be transferred to purchasers. This is one condition that builders will never remove.

Registering a condominium is a costly and time-consuming procedure. Approvals are needed from numerous government departments. More often than not, new condominiums are built in less time it takes to than complete the paperwork and formally register the condominium!

Yet developers cannot afford to leave that building empty once it is ready for occupancy. Many purchasers like Darryl and Robin are anxious to take possession as well, especially if the unit is in "move in" condition. There's only one problem. While Darryl and Robin can move into their unit, how can the builder, Adar Construction, give them a deed if the condominium is not yet registered? Without a deed to prove their ownership of the unit, Darryl and Robin would be understandably reluctant to turn over any money to Adar Construction.

To resolve the dilemma a two-step procedure has been developed that allows purchasers to move into a unregistered condominium, followed by a transfer of ownership at a later date. To protect buyers like Darryl and Robin (and their money) when they take possession of a condominium unit before it is registered, (a period of legal limbo), an elaborate series of statutory safeguards has been enacted. In fact, the provisions found in some provincial condominium acts are so forward-thinking and consumer-oriented, they are the envy of purchasers of other newly-built homes.

Darryl and Robin's unit was substantially completed even though the condominium complex was not yet registered, and some work remained to be done on the common elements. Their offer, like most, required that they take possession of their unit immediately. This stage in the transaction is variously called "interim closing," "occupancy closing," "escrow closing" and "possession closing." The period of time between that date and "final closing," the actual closing date when the deed is registered, (the condominium itself now being registered) is dubbed "interim occupancy." During this time, the builder must provide all the services that the registered condominium will provide later, including the maintenance and repair of the future common elements. With an interim closing, Darryl and Robin's occupancy date (the day they take possession of their unit) is *not* the same as their closing date (the day title changes hands). With newly-built condominiums, possession and ownership are separated in time.

On the occupancy date of June 5, Darryl and Robin obtained possession of their unit from Adar Construction, but no deed was delivered. Before they picked up the keys, they delivered to the builder the entire unadjusted balance due on closing ($100,000 less the $10,000 deposit previously paid) together with six post-dated cheques for the monthly interim occupancy charge.

Understandably, Darryl and Robin were very reluctant to part with their money without getting a deed in return. No need to worry, their lawyer assured them. Just as they did not get a deed in the usual fashion, Adar Construction would not get the money paid in the usual fashion. It would either have to hold the funds in a trust account until final closing or else give Darryl and Robin prescribed security (at its own expense) in the form of excess condominium insurance coverage from the Mortgage Insurance Company of Canada. With Darryl and Robin's money now fully protected, Adar Construction could use the closing proceeds as it sees fit.

Starting June 5, Darryl and Robin began to pay Adar Construction an occupancy charge, similar to the rent a tenant would pay. In all other respects, however, the parties dealt with the property as if the transaction had formally closed that day. This meant, for instance, that Darryl and Robin were now responsible for repairing and maintaining their unit. Following registration of the condominium, the transaction was formally closed on December 2, at which time the deed to Darryl and Robin was registered. Only then could Adar Construction use the closing proceeds without having to insure them. Only then did Darryl and Robin really own their unit.

When you're reviewing the offer, be on the lookout for a clause that gives the builder the right to cancel the transaction even after a buyer moves in. Typical clauses allow builders to fully refund all money paid (except the monthly occupancy charge) on written notice to the buyer if the condominium is not registered by a specific date, perhaps 18 months after interim closing. Builders claim this clause is necessary so they can obtain vacant possession of the building if they encounter serious problems registering the condominium. But what about the purchasers who may have to look for alternative accommodation on very short notice, after perhaps a year of occupying the building they thought was going to be their home!

Sales agents constantly reassure anxious purchasers that this clause would only be used if absolutely necessary. Not good enough. Anything can happen between now and then. Therefore, try to strike this clause out of the offer. If you can't, then seriously think twice about dealing with that builder. Who knows what else the builder might have up his sleeve if circumstances of the real estate market change substantially? If you still decide to buy from that builder, at least you now know the possibility exists that you could be evicted from the premises in the future.

Remember, too, that a builder could not afford to throw several hundred families out on the street at one time. What about his reputation? How will he pay the ongoing costs of operating the building if there is no money coming in? What about our politicians? Will they stand idly by and let this happen? Will the public not heap its contempt and scorn on any builder trying to pull such a stunt? While these are strong arguments, the best way to eliminate the problem is to eliminate the clause.

Usually, details of the interim occupancy arrangement appear right in the offer to purchase. Sometimes a lengthy contract that sets out the rights of both the buyer and the seller must be signed before the buyer takes occupancy. If a "lease" of this type is required, ask to see a draft of it before you sign the offer to purchase. This way you will know in advance the terms governing your future occupancy of the unit.

Most interim occupancy agreements try to label the arrangement between the builder and the buyer as a "licence" rather than a "tenancy." This explains why the money Darryl and Robin pay to Adar Construction each month is called an "occupancy charge" and not "rent." Despite a bold statement in most builders' offers that no landlord and tenant relationship is created during this time, most interim occupancy arrangements are in fact governed by the applicable provincial laws dealing with residential tenancies. If the transaction does not close, the builder must rely on that legislation, rather than the builder's own remedies that appear in most offers, to obtain vacant possession.

Some provincial condominium acts spell out the maximum interim occupancy charge a builder can levy. If Darryl and Robin were the registered owners of their unit, they would be responsible for payment of i) the realty taxes on their unit, ii) the monthly maintenance fee, and iii) possibly a mortgage payment, depending on how large a mortgage (if any) they had arranged. The occupancy fee paid to the builder between interim and final closing for their unregistered units should be no different.

The maximum interim occupancy charge purchasers/occupants like Darryl and Robin should pay is made up of three components, which cannot exceed the total of:

a) One-twelfth of the estimated realty taxes for the unit. This amount is often readjusted once the final tax assessment for the building is complete. All purchasers pay this item, whether or not they have a mortgage during interim closing;

b) the projected monthly common expense charge. Whether they pay all cash for their unit or have a mortgage, Darryl and Robin must pay this component; and

c) *interest only* monthly, on the unpaid balance of the purchase price. Of course, the unpaid balance of the purchase price is the amount that would have been secured by a mortgage, if a mortgage could have been registered at this stage. (Remember that it can't be done yet, since the condominium itself isn't registered.) Purchasers who pay the balance of the purchase price in cash on interim closing are not responsible for this component. Those who do not pay all cash at that time pay interest on the difference between the purchase price and the amount of money paid on interim closing. If Darryl and Robin had only paid $25,000 of the $100,000 purchase price on interim closing, they would have to pay monthly interest to the builder on the remaining $75,000.

It is unclear whether the interest rate on that $75,000 is fixed or subject to change, upwards or downwards. The condominium legislation is vague, simply stating that the interest component shall be the interest paid on any mortgage to be assumed or given on final closing. Very often the interest rate on this mortgage is set only shortly before final closing, although the interest component is collected starting with interim closing. What happens if interest rates fall 1 percent between interim and final closing? Will the 1 percent interest rate differential be refunded to purchasers as part of the final closing adjustments? What if interest rates increase 1 percent during interim occupancy? It's hard to say which is better–an interest rate fixed on *interim* closing, or one that is temporarily established on interim closing but that will be fixed on *final* closing.

Remember that this component applies only if the buyer does not pay the full amount of the purchase price on interim closing. It does not apply if the purchaser pays "all cash" on interim closing.

During interim occupancy, Darryl and Robin will pay these sums to Adar Construction, which turns over the money to the appropriate party. In effect, the buyer pays the builder *before* final closing the same amount of money he will pay *after* final closing to the municipal tax department, the condominium corporation and the mortgage lender (if he has a mortgage). The builder is little more than a middleman at this stage. (Although it is rarely done, see if these payments can be credited towards the purchase price.)

Besides learning the amount of the total occupancy charge, ask for a detailed breakdown of its components. Although it may be difficult to do, try also to independently verify these items, in case you're being overcharged. Ask other condominium owners in similar complexes how much they pay for realty taxes. The monthly maintenance component should appear in the disclosure statement. And what is the interest rate being charged on the unpaid purchase price? Since no condominium corporation exists at this stage, any excess sum paid is usually a windfall to the builder.

The "Phantom" Mortgage

What is a "phantom" mortgage? Either you owe money on a mortgage or you don't — right? How can there be such a thing?

In recent years, purchasers of yet-to-be registered condominium units have learned through painful experience that during the period of interim occupancy they must assume a phantom mortgage (also dubbed a "notional" mortgage, a "provisional" mortgage or the "peek-a-boo" mortgage). Bucky and Pat were shocked to learn that they couldn't pay the total purchase price for their unit when they moved in! Instead, they must assume this phantom mortgage on interim closing, a form of temporary occupancy financing. *Today, virtually all buyers of unregistered condominiums cannot pay all cash to the builder on interim closing, even if they want to!* That's right. The builder does not want all Bucky and Pat's money when they get the keys to their unit. It's amazing but true — builders would rather wait until final closing to receive the balance of the purchase price from Bucky and Pat! But why do builders refuse to accept money and insist on a mortgage instead? There's something strange going on here!

In fact, phantom mortgages reflect the statutory obligation of condominium builders to pay interest to purchasers on money paid prior to final closing. In Ontario, interest must be paid to purchasers on all funds paid to the builder on or before interim occupancy, excluding the monthly interim occupancy charge. This interest is paid on final closing, as part of the closing adjustments. Since the prescribed rate of interest varies over time, some builders pay interest at a fixed but higher interest rate for simplicity's sake. *The builder must pay this interest, despite any agreements that would deny it to purchasers.*

Neil and Jane are buying a newly-built condominium for $100,000. On October 1 they paid a $10,000 deposit. Interim occupancy took place nearly eight months later, on May 20. When an interim occupancy closing occurs, the right of purchasers to receive interest falls into two different categories:

i) Interest is payable on the deposit from the date of payment until interim occupancy begins *only if the offer provides for it.* There is no legal obligation on the builder to pay interest on the deposit during this period. Whether Neil and Jane receive any interest on this $10,000 deposit before interim occupancy begins (the period from October 1 to May 20) is strictly a contractual matter between them and their builder.

ii) Interest is payable on all money paid before or on interim closing *by law*, whether or not it is stipulated in the offer and despite any agreements to the contrary, from interim closing to final closing. Therefore, the $90,000 Neil and Jane paid on interim occupancy plus the $10,000 deposit they paid earlier would begin bearing interest on the interim occupancy date of May 20. Interest would be payable up to the final closing of November 20.

Paying more cash on interim closing benefits buyers in two ways. Obviously, the more cash paid by purchasers on interim closing the more interest they receive. In addition, the monthly interim occupancy charge will also be smaller. Remember that interest on the mortgage assumed (the unpaid purchase price) is one of the three components of the monthly occupancy fee. With a smaller or nonexistent mortgage from interim to final closing, the obligation to pay this part of the monthly occupancy fee can be reduced or even eliminated.

Suppose Neil and Jane had paid the full $100,000 in cash to the builder on interim closing. This means the builder would receive no money for the third of the three components — the mortgage — as no mortgage exists at this time. Each month their occupancy charge would consist only of taxes (say $120) plus maintenance (say $250), for a grand total of $370. Remember too that the builder must pay Neil and Jane interest on that $100,000 until final closing. Assuming the rate of interest paid was 7.5% for an interim occupancy period of six months (May 20 to November 20), the builder would have to pay $625 per month in interest to Neil and Jane. Total monthly net gain to Neil and Jane: $625 — $370 or $255; over 6 months: $1,530. Instead of interim occupancy costing Neil and Jane money, they earned money each month! Of course, provided the appropriate security arrangements were in place, the builder could use this $100,000 to offset the interest payable to the purchasers or to pay off other expenses. If the builder received a 7.5% return on the $100,000, his net cost would be nil.

By contrast, consider the situation of Jason and Kylie, who also have $100,000 in cash to pay for a comparable unit. Instead of paying the full $100,000 on interim closing, they decided to pay only $25,000 cash at that time, keeping $75,000 in the bank. With an unpaid balance of $75,000, Jason and Kylie would have to pay interest to the builder on a $75,000 mortgage during the period of interim occupancy.

Assuming the interest rate charged on this $75,000 mortgage was 10%, Jason and Kylie would have to pay $625 monthly to the builder. Remember that the smaller the amount of cash paid by the purchaser on interim closing, the larger the amount of interest *paid to the builder*. Interest would also be payable by the builder to Jason and Kylie, but only on the $25,000 actually paid on interim closing. In other words, the smaller the amount of cash paid by the purchaser on interim closing, the smaller the amount of interest *received from the builder*. Having a "mortgage" on interim closing costs purchasers money.

Interest paid at 7.5% would total $156.25 monthly. Assuming the tax and maintenance components were exactly the same as in Neil and Jane's situation, Jason and Kylie would pay $995 monthly ($250 maintenance, $120 taxes and $625 mortgage), and receive $156.25 interest monthly from the builder. Total monthly net cost to Jason and Kylie: $995 − $156.25 or $838.75; over six months: $5,032.50. Of course Jason and Kylie still have $75,000 in the bank which is earning interest until the condominium is registered. At 7.5%, this would generate $2,812.50 interest, reducing Jason and Kylie's overall cost to $2,220. Investing the money at a higher interest rate would help reduce this cost even further. Still, Jason and Kylie's occupancy expense is much higher than the $1,530 Neil and Jane *earned* by paying all cash on interim closing!

Looking at the other side of the coin, builders stand to gain handsomely from having a mortgage outstanding on interim closing. Interest at 7.5% on the $25,000 paid by Jason and Kylie on interim closing will cost their builder $156.25 monthly. More importantly, the $75,000 unpaid purchase price will generate $625 interest monthly at 10%. The net gain to the builder: $625 − $156.25 or $468.25 monthly; over 6 months: $2,812.50.

When builders began to realize how much all-cash or large cash payments on interim closing hurt them financially, they devised ingenious schemes to avoid paying interest to buyers on the funds received at interim closing. In different formats, buyers were asked to waive their rights to the interest; to transfer it back to the builder immediately after getting it on final closing; and to pay the interest back to the builder immediately after final closing as an increase in the purchase price. All these schemes were struck down by the courts, which confirmed that only purchasers are entitled to the interest on the money paid on or before interim closing, notwithstanding any arrangement to the contrary.

To counter this, the builder's latest strategy, and the one that seems to be working, forces *all* buyers into Jason and Kylie's situation. *In other words, all buyers are forced into assuming a mortgage on interim closing, whether they want to or not. Buyers are not permitted to pay "all cash" on interim closing, even if they want to. Payment of the entire purchase price in cash is delayed until final closing.*

To do this, the builder places a ceiling on the amount of money all buyers can pay on interim closing, usually 25 percent of the total purchase price. With 75 percent of the purchase price still unpaid, purchasers must pay interest to the builder. A short-term vendor-take-back "notional" mortgage secures the mandatory unpaid 75% of the purchase price. This "mortgage" takes effect on interim closing and is repaid in full on final closing. Although it exists in the Offer to Purchase, this "phantom" or "peek-a-boo" mortgage is not registered on title.

Phantom mortgages disregard the type and amount of any permanent financing purchasers arrange. Due on demand with interest payable monthly, phantom mortgages are designed to cover only the period of interim occupancy. People like Neil and Jane who want to pay all cash for the condominium unit, or Howard and Marsha who want to assume a builder's mortgage for less than 75 percent of the unit's value, or Fred who wants to arrange outside financing with a separate lender, cannot do so on interim closing. All of them must await final closing, when the deed is registered.

Phantom mortgages turn the payment of interest completely on its head. Instead of builders paying interest to buyers, the reverse occurs. With less money paid on interim closing (say $25,000 instead of $100,000), a builder's interest expense is reduced considerably. More importantly, it increases the revenue coming in from buyers between interim and final closing, because part of the purchase price (the $75,000 secured by the phantom mortgage) remains unpaid. This scheme allows builders to convert what would have been an interest expense into a substantial source of revenue. For this reason, few if any builders today will allow purchasers to pay all cash on interim closing.

On final closing or shortly afterwards, Neil and Jane can finally pay cash for their unit and the phantom mortgage is cancelled. The same is true for Howard and Marsha, who only want to assume $50,000 of the $60,000 phantom mortgage. By paying $10,000 to the builder and assuming the builder's mortgage on final closing, everything is settled. As for Fred, he learned that phantom mortgages on interim closing make it extremely difficult for purchasers to arrange outside financing for final closing. In his case, he'd paid $20,000 of the $80,000 purchase price on interim closing, with the remaining $60,000 to be paid on final closing from the new mortgage Fred was arranging with a bank.

Some builders ask purchasers to provide proof that the money to pay off the phantom mortgage will be available for final closing. Acceptable forms of security include the delivery of a certified cheque for the full amount of the phantom mortgage; an unconditional and irrevocable letter of credit from a chartered bank; or a mortgage commitment confirming that the lender will be advancing sufficient funds on final closing to retire the phantom mortgage. This presents no problem to Neil and Jane, since they planned on paying all cash anyway. The same is true for Howard and Marsha, since their $10,000 cash plus the $50,000 builder's mortgage takes care of the peek-a-boo loan. But for Fred, the $60,000 is money he doesn't have yet.

The crucial question Fred must ask is "*When* must this security be given to the developer?" Some builders ask for it on *final* closing, which makes sense. Yet as strange as it seems, some builders demand that a letter of credit or certified cheque be delivered on *interim* closing. But how can Fred get a letter of credit or a certified cheque for the unpaid balance of the purchase price at interim closing if he lacks the funds? Before either form of security can be issued to a builder, Fred must have sufficient funds on deposit with the bank to cover the security. Unfortunately for Fred, it's a requirement he could never fulfill.

Thankfully, Fred's builder was prepared to accept a mortgage commitment on interim closing as security. But this created another dilemma for Fred. Although his bank could deliver the commitment on interim closing, unfortunately for Fred it is little more than an assurance that the money will be advanced on final closing. The mortgage commitment will not be a guarantee as to its other terms and most importantly its rate, which cannot be pegged so far in advance.

Seeing a lawyer before an offer is signed always the most prudent course. As part of your home-buying strategy, be especially careful if you're planning to arrange your own financing when purchasing a unit in an unbuilt or unregistered condominium, which requires an interim closing with a phantom mortgage. Be absolutely certain you know before the offer is signed what type of security the builder wants to cover the phantom mortgage, and more importantly, when it must be delivered. If you must provide security at interim closing, see if the delivery of a mortgage commitment will suffice. The entire transaction could be jeopardized unless you can satisfy the builder's requirements. The time spent now reviewing this point with your lawyer could avoid considerable aggravation, anxiety and frustration at the time you would expect to be happiest — when you're ready to move into your new condominium unit.

Tony and Margaret faced a slightly different, but very common, situation in arranging outside financing. To their relief, their builder did not want any form of security delivered until final closing. Arranging a mortgage prior to interim closing would only assure them that the funds would be available for final closing. It would not guarantee Tony and Margaret good mortgage terms and the interest rate they would pay — these would only be set just prior to final closing! Practically speaking shopping for a mortgage at interim closing made little sense. Tony and Margaret could not really compare different lenders' mortgage packages until the condominium was registered.

David and Zena recently learned how expensive the phantom mortgage could be. They bought a unit for $120,000. To avoid a large prepayment penalty on the sale of their existing home, they arranged to transport the $70,000 mortgage with Huvey Trust to the new condominium unit. Since the condominium was unregistered when the unit was ready for occupancy, the builder insisted on an interim closing and a phantom mortgage. As David and Zena have no deed, the portable mortgage could not be registered against their new unit. Faced with a long and uncertain interim occupancy period, Huvey Trust decided it could not wait for the portability of the mortgage to be completed. Instead it insisted that David and Zena pay the prepayment penalty. The interim closing with a phantom mortgage effectively destroyed the benefit of the portability feature.

As Fred, Tony and Margaret, and David and Zena all learned, a builder's insistence on an interim closing with a phantom mortgage scuttles buyers plans to have their financing firmly in place when they move into their new units. The phantom mortgage limits the choices available and, more importantly, postpones setting the final interest rate and terms until final closing at an uncertain future date.

What options are open to purchasers of a new condominium unit like Aron and Frieda who will need a mortgage on final closing? The need for a phantom mortgage steers them away from arranging outside financing, and towards assuming the builder's mortgage. Yet any builder's mortgage they assume will not reflect current interest rates, but only the rates in effect at final closing. Even if the mortgage rate is "capped"(as discussed in Chapter 15) so many variables in the cap could make the quoted rate meaningless. For Aron and Frieda, agreeing to assume the builder's mortgage will assure them of a mortgage, but little else.

Remember, too, that not all condominium builders offer builders' mortgages. With no builder's mortgage to assume, Aron and Frieda have no alternative but to arrange their own financing and pay all cash to the builder on final closing. Just like Tony and Margaret, Aron and Frieda will be subjected to the vagaries and uncertainties of the interest rate market when the deed is registered, months or even years down the road.

When will the condominium be registered?

One of the most common complaints involving newly-built condominiums is the considerable delay in getting the project registered, especially when purchasers have been occupying their units for a considerable period of time. This is the condominium quandary — owners paying a large monthly occupancy fee, with no deed to show for their money.

Under provincial condominium legislation, builders must register the condominium as soon as possible, following which deeds must be registered without delay. What "reasonable" period of time it takes to complete the registration process will vary from project to project. Yet one thing is virtually certain — the paperwork to establish the condominium will take longer than the actual construction of the building.

Some people feel builders deliberately go slow in registering a condominium, to make additional money during the interim occupancy period. Rarely is this the case. Until the condominium is built and registered, and the individual deeds registered, the builder must hold the money paid by buyers on interim closing in trust, or pay an insurance premium in order to use it. Either way, it costs the builder money. Considerable time must be spent answering purchasers' inquiries about when the registration process will be completed, time that could be spent more valuably elsewhere. Time also is spent as a middleman, collecting the monthly occupancy fee and paying the ongoing obligations for the building, costs payable by the purchaser and the condominium corporation after closing. Remember, too, that the builder must guarantee a complex's first year's common expenses. The one-year clock only starts to run with registration. Too long a delay in registration could make those projections obsolete.

During interim occupancy, builders must also take reasonable steps to sell the other units in the complex. This prevents a shift in emphasis from selling to renting unsold units, until the builder takes certain steps. In addition, to prevent developers from taking (but not delivering) funds earmarked for the condominium corporation, once it is registered the builder must not collect money from purchasers on behalf of the condominium.

What happens after the condominium is registered?

The original directors and officers of the newly-created condominium corporation are nominated by the developer. Once more than half the units are sold and those transactions closed, a "turnover" meeting is held within a very short period of time. At the turnover meeting, the new owners elect new directors and take control of their own destiny. All corporate and financial records, together with plans, guarantees and warranties, are delivered to the new directors at that time.

Developers often try to continue their relationship with the new condominium corporation by contracting to provide management services. Property management has become a very lucrative industry in recent years. Builders can earn future profits from a project they have just constructed and sold by being its manager. From the new condominium's point of view, having an experienced property manager is extremely important to efficiently run the business on a day-to-day basis.

These management agreements were open to serious abuse with early condominiums. Some builders/developers made long-term deals with the condominium corporation when they still controlled it; that is, before the turnover meeting. When the new directors were elected, they inherited these "sweetheart" deals builders had made for themselves.

These days, to ensure the management is competitive and in the best interests of the condominium, in some provinces the directors can terminate the agreement signed by the developer on 60 days' written notice. Other service agreements signed by the developer that run for more than 12 months are automatically terminated after one year, unless ratified by the new directors.

Included here are leases of common elements for business purposes, such as the right to place coin washers and dryers in a laundry room. Current rules make it very difficult for a builder to perpetuate a relationship with the new condominium corporation, unless the new directors decide to continue it. Current legislation gives the new board of directors a broom to sweep away any commitments made by the builder for that very short period of time when he controlled the condominium corporation.

Tips and Pointers
All purchasers must thoroughly understand the substantial differences between condominium and conventional home ownership before making any type of commitment. Make sure the comdominium lifestyle is compatible with your personal lifestyle. Talk to other owners of condominium units to see how they enjoy the conveniences and restrictions associated with condominium living. Was the adjustment for them really all that difficult? Were the minor sacrifices worth it in the long run?

This need for a good grasp of both the lifestyle and legal concept called "condominium" is heightened when you buy an unbuilt, unregistered unit. Make certain you fully understand the unique issues associated with interim closing and what interim occupancy and phantom mortgages are all about, before you make any purchase commitment. Check out the clauses in the offer that deal with interim closing and final closing, and spend some time with your lawyer reviewing your rights and obligations during this most bewildering of times. One of the key elements of HOBS, your unique home-buying strategy, is to avoid future surprises by learning all the facts *now*. Designing and applying a HOBS takes on added importance when buying a new condominium from a developer. Only then can you make the best possible educated decision on *your* purchase of a newly-built condominium.

Questions to Ask
Before you sign any offer to purchase an unbuilt or unregistered condominium, be sure to get thorough and complete answers to the following important questions:

- Have you received the disclosure statement, if available, and reviewed it carefully? Are there any parts of it that require further clarification?

- When is registration expected? Does the developer have the right to evict occupants if registration is delayed?
- Is the parking space (and locker space) freehold, leasehold, exclusive use or allocated? Is there any additional fee for parking?
- What are the boundaries of the unit? Does the unit owner have an exclusive right to use the patio/balcony or the front and rear yards?
- How much will the monthly maintenance be for the first year? Does it include electricity, water, heating, and cable TV? Will any "up-front" contribution to the reserve fund be necessary?
- Are the Rules and Regulations acceptable? Have you reviewed them *all*, including those that appear elsewhere in the con-dominium documents?
- Are there any restrictions in the draft declaration or by-laws on the sale of the unit that could affect its future sale?
- What will be the condominium corporation's insurance coverage? What areas must be covered by a condominium unit owner's package?
- What will be the occupancy fee? Are any of the items subject to readjustment?
- What rate of interest will the money paid on interim closing earn? Will it also cover the deposits from the date they were delivered?
- Will there be a phantom mortgage on interim closing? Must the purchaser post security for the phantom mortgage? When must this be done: on interim or final closing?

21

All Systems Go

Chapter 2, "HOBS for the Newly-built Home," stated the purpose and goal of your home-buying strategy: "In its simplest form, HOBS emphasizes the need to carefully plan and arrange every stage of a purchase transaction, *before signing any offer to purchase*. Without HOBS, buyers could find themselves signing an offer before all the important details are in place. With HOBS, the heady enthusiasm and excitement most people experience at house-hunting time can be maintained and even enhanced until well after they take possession of the house."

Followers of the HOBS approach are now prepared to buy that newly-built house. Look at what you have accomplished so far. After creating the all-important needs and wants lists, you began putting your home-buying strategy to work. Locations where you might want to buy have been carefully considered — communities and neighborhoods — as have factors affecting specific sites. As the house probably hasn't been built yet, you learned how to buy from plans, translating impressions and words into reality. You reviewed financial concerns from several different points of view — what you can afford, and how much money you will need to carry the house each month. The more you learned, the more your HOBS was constantly being modified and redefined.

What to look for in a lawyer and especially a builder have been thoroughly examined, important concerns that too many new home buyers tend to overlook. But still, at that point you were not quite ready to make a serious commitment to buy. First you wanted to learn more about new home warranties, hidden closing costs and builders' offers. Only then could you make an informed choice, knowing what you were committing to before making that commitment.

Now that you're ready, you're probably very excited and enthusiastic. On weekends you've toured new home sites, picking up brochures and asking pointed questions of sales agents. The information you have received has been carefully reviewed and compared against your home-buying strategy. Your goal has been to see which builder is offering "the right house" — one that satisfies your needs and as many wants as possible, and one that you can afford to buy and maintain.

But before dashing headlong to sign an offer to purchase, keep several important points in mind. First, don't rush into things. Be patient and don't get discouraged. Finding the right house rarely happens overnight. Usually it takes time, and many visits to different sales trailers to see which builder best fills the bill. Each house you see represents another opportunity to gain precious experience and confidence, to continue learning more about the market as well as your own unique needs and wants.

An important part of your home-buying strategy has been to look at matters as objectively as possible. So keep it up when you are out looking at homes. Be as business-like as possible. Keep your composure, and make decisions with your head, not your heart.

Don't be upset if you have to lower your expectations and standards somewhat. Everyone gets caught up in the emotion of shopping for a newly-built home. But being too emotional could lead to an impulsive decision. Being realistic is so very, very important. Before you buy, be absolutely sure you can live up to your obligations. Imagine what would happen if you bought a house beyond your means, and later faced a continuous struggle just to keep it. Or even worse, if you lost the struggle and the house.

Occasionally a quick decision must be made or else a prime opportunity will be lost. This is not a problem for purchasers who have a HOBS, where all the preliminary decisions have been made well ahead of time. Imagine the extra pressure and anxiety of having to make a snap decision without a HOBS!

Signing an offer is serious business. With no "cooling-off" period (except for newly-built condominiums), once a commitment is made the deal's a deal. You can't change your mind and walk away. Once the die is cast, there's no turning back.

Buy a house for the right reasons. Don't be swayed to sign an offer just because of a pending price increase or because another party's interested in the same home. Stand back and think things through one last time. Be certain the house satisfies the criteria in your home-buying strategy. Make sure that everything is in place, and that all systems are go, before saying yes.

And then comes the final status check — take the offer to a lawyer with extensive real estate experience for his review and comments *before you sign it.* Take the time to understand what it says, and to discuss possible pitfalls, before the document becomes a contract. Too often, though, agents will pressure buyers to sign, sign, sign, and buyers don't really think about what they're committing to.

Fewer than one in ten offers for newly-built homes are reviewed by a lawyer before buyers sign them and this is most unfortunate. Lawyers do not want to review unsigned offers simply to pump up their fees. By taking the draft offer to Ray, their lawyer, Mitch and Lucy have a golden opportunity to review and possibly revise the contract before its terms are fixed. Before he processes the transaction Ray has to read the offer to purchase anyway. So why not let him review the offer at a time when he can do something with it? Once the offer is signed and the ink is dry, the contract is etched in stone and unalterable.

Whether Ray receives a signed or unsigned offer he will need the same amount of time to review it. The only extra charge involved is his time spent meeting with Mitch and Lucy to discuss the contents of the offer, before they sign it. Mitch and Lucy, not Ray, decide how long that meeting must be, and it depends on how long it takes them to understand what the offer says. When compared to the amount of money at stake, the cost of consultation could be the best investment Mitch and Lucy make in the whole transaction.

Preparing to sign an offer to purchase a newly-built home is a very emotional time for most people. Even the coolest and calmest of people become nervous and jittery. With nothing directly at stake in the transaction, Ray can provide Mitch and Lucy with the unbiased advice they probably need.

Some new home sales agents mistakenly fear that taking an unsigned offer to a lawyer first will "blow the deal." But few lawyers are hired to talk buyers out of deals. As Mitch and Lucy's lawyer, Ray's role is to ensure they understand their legal rights and obligations; to discuss what it will cost to buy and carry that house; and to make sure that they appreciate the commitment they are about to undertake. He can also help to independently verify the facts given to them by the sales agent. Experienced real estate lawyers know what can and cannot be amended in an offer. They also know that too many proposed changes could cost Mitch and Lucy the house, so only clauses that might prejudice their best interests should be amended. Sincere new home agents will not discourage, but will rather encourage, purchasers like Mitch and Lucy to have the unsigned offer reviewed by their lawyer first.

If Mitch and Lucy decide not to proceed with the deal, Ray will probably be looked upon by the agent as the culprit. More likely, Mitch and Lucy have realized that they would have problems in closing the deal or in maintaining the home afterwards. Isn't it better for potential buyers to learn this sooner instead of later, before instead of after a contract is signed?

Two areas where Ray will not offer comment are the purchase price, and whether Mitch and Lucy should buy the house. With a home-buying strategy, Mitch and Lucy will have a much better understanding about purchase prices and market values in a particular community and neighborhood than Ray. Similarly, the ultimate decision whether to sign the offer must rest with Mitch and Lucy alone.

Time is crucial in real estate transactions, and not every lawyer will always be available when you need him or her to review an offer. Despite your home-buying strategy, it is *occasionally* necessary to sign the offer before your lawyer can review it. In that case, you should include the following condition in the offer, to give your lawyer ample time to protect your interests:

"This offer is conditional on the purchaser's lawyer, _____ having an opportunity to review this offer to determine that it is satisfactory to the purchaser, and to approve it in full without requiring any changes whatsoever. To satisfy this condition, a letter from the purchaser's lawyer to this effect shall be delivered to the seller's agent on or before 11:59 p.m. on _____ Otherwise this offer shall become null and void, with the purchaser's deposit being returned to the purchaser without interest or deduction. This clause has been inserted for the sole benefit of the purchaser, who reserves the right to waive it at his option."

The period of time you request should be reasonable — no more than 48 hours.

This clause does two things. First, it gives your lawyer time to review and comment on the offer. More importantly, it gives you a very short "cooling-off" period you wouldn't otherwise have, to reconsider and even cancel the contract after it is signed. If you decide the next day not to buy the house, backing out of the deal is very easy. If you find even one clause to be unsatisfactory, the self-defeating condition will automatically kill the contract.

"Never on Sunday?"

Without a doubt, Sunday is the most popular day for people to visit new home sales trailers. Hoping to strike when the iron is hot, real estate agents would naturally like to get purchasers to sign offers on Sunday. Until April of 1985, what stopped them was the federal *Lord's Day Act* which invalidated any contract made on a Sunday.

That month, however, the Supreme Court of Canada unanimously struck down the *Lord's Day Act,* because it infringed on the freedoms guaranteed in the *Canadian Charter of Rights and Freedoms.* Now it is generally accepted that a real estate offer submitted or accepted on Sunday is valid.

With this obstacle out of the way, some new home agents now encourage purchasers to submit an offer the same Sunday that they see a house they like. Purchasers with a home-buying strategy, of course, won't be *that* anxious to sign an offer. Instead they will take the unsigned offer to their lawyer before they put pen to paper.

Acceptance Procedure

Once you sign the offer and give it to the sales agent, it is up to the builder to decide whether to accept your offer. While resale offers go back and forth quickly between the purchaser and the seller, as they are rarely accepted the first time out, new home contracts are treated somewhat differently. Often it's a "take-it-or-leave-it" fixed-price proposition; purchasers have little room to negotiate terms, conditions and prices. Unlike the resale market, long bouts of negotiating, sign backs and counteroffers are rare with new homes, especially when the demand for new homes is strong. This is why the part of your home-buying strategy that compares what different builders offer is absolutely crucial.

After the signed offer is submitted, purchasers face an extremely nerve-wracking period of uncertainty, until they receive word that the offer has been accepted. Very often builders are slow to accept offers, which adds to the pressure and anxiety. Of course, the fewer changes proposed, the greater likelihood the offer will be accepted, and accepted quickly. Any substantial changes a buyer makes to the offer will be reviewed with the builder's lawyer, accounting for additional delay. This phase of buying a newly-built house is not for the faint of heart.

While "waiting for word," the best thing you can do is to forget about the deal and keep busy with other activities. It's out of your hands, and worrying won't speed up the process. Keep cool, calm and collected. Any changes the builder might make in his counter-offer must be initialled by the purchaser for a binding contract to result. Once the offer is accepted, even if conditions remain outstanding, get a copy of the signed offer to your lawyer as soon as possible. This enables him or her to begin processing the deal. Any amendments or waivers of conditions should also be delivered as soon as they are available.

All systems are now "go." But before pressing that final button, remember: *Never sign any offer to purchase until it has been thoroughly reviewed by your lawyer.*

Once the offer to purchase that newly-built home has been signed, the emphasis of your home-buying strategy shifts from finding the home to making the final preparations for closing. Here too, a well-thought-out game plan is essential to help avoid many of the problems other people have faced up to closing.

Tips and Pointers
- Be patient and don't get discouraged. Finding the right house takes time.
- Be sure your lawyer reviews the offer before it is signed.
- While waiting for word, put the deal out of your mind; worrying about the purchase won't speed things up.

Part Four

CONTRACT TO CLOSING

22

Your Lawyer's Role from Now To Closing

Congratulations! The offer has been accepted. You'll now be most concerned with the final details — when will the house be ready; when do we sign the closing papers; exactly how much money is needed to close; when will the deed be registered, the keys be available, and when will the house be ours? It's important that you understand what your lawyer is doing on your behalf between acceptance of the contract and closing to help keep your peace of mind.

Lawyers rarely have clients sign a formal engagement contract in any real estate transaction. These professionals understand what the buyer wants — a formal legal opinion that the purchaser becomes the registered owner of the property on closing with a "good and marketable title in fee simple." "Good" means appropriate for the purchaser's purposes, and "marketable" means adequate to transfer to someone else. "Fee simple" means the buyer has acquired the most extensive, unrestricted and unconditional interest possible in the property. In short, "perfect" title.

The first step in any purchase transaction is to search title to the property. Title searches are historical investigations of previous ownership and prior dealings with the property. Depending on the province and the land registration system involved, all registered documents affecting the title for 40 years or more may have to be examined. Your lawyer's opinion on title is based on the information that appears in the title search.

Usually the buyer has a very short period of time (30 days from acceptance) to examine title and raise title defects. Even if closing is months in the future, title should be searched immediately if the subdivision has been registered. Since your lawyer reviewed the draft offer, all you need to get the wheels in motion is a phone call to your lawyer that the offer was accepted. The actual offer can be delivered later.

If the final plan of subdivision has not been registered at the time the offer is signed, work on the search will be delayed. Keep in touch with the sales office to find out the date of registration and the subdivision's registration number. Give this information to your lawyer as soon as it's available, so title can be searched quickly afterwards.

Serious title defects are uncommon in newly-built home purchases. Most problems are corrected before the subdivision is registered. Occasionally, unexpected matters such as an utility easment or a right-of-way are revealed, which detract from the "perfect" title buyers expect to receive. Unfortunately, little can be done about these qualifications on title, since the builder's offer obligated you to take title subject to them. If a serious problem is uncovered in the title search, your lawyer should contact you immediately to discuss the problem and to seek your written instructions about whether to proceed with the deal.

Following a careful review of the title search, your lawyer will forward a "requisition letter" to the seller's lawyer, setting out all matters affecting title that must be dealt with before closing. The most common requisition is the need to discharge any existing mortgages. Other requisitions may include the need for proof that development agreements and building schemes on title have been complied with; the need to register the builder's mortgage being assumed on closing; plus outstanding monetary obligations such as taxes, utility charges and condominium expenses. Before closing, some lawyers obtain a written acknowledgement from their home-buying clients that lists all items to which title will be subject. This way, everything qualifying "fee simple" title is noted, discussed and approved before any money changes hands.

While your house is being constructed, your lawyer won't be too busy with your file, but he or she should always be available to talk and meet with you if the situation warrants it. Problems may arise between contract and closing with the construction of the house; with a sales agent or builder who will not give you straightforward answers if a problem arises; or with a delayed closing or an attempt by the builder to cancel the contract. In any case, don't be afraid to pick up the phone and call your lawyer, who should be able to get the information you need from the builder's lawyer or from an independent source. With an experienced real estate lawyer on your side, you're never alone.

About a month or so before closing, the lawyer's work on your behalf should begin again in earnest. Part of a lawyer's job is to ensure everything is up-to-date and has been complied with on closing, so the purchaser can turn over his or her money without inheriting any problems from the builder. The lawyer orders numerous clearances, reports and certificates to ensure that no liens or other deficiencies are outstanding. The cost for these documents is included in the out-of-pocket disbursements lawyers incur on behalf of their clients.

For example, the lawyer obtains a realty tax certificate to ensure that all property taxes have been paid. The local municipality provides a number of reports showing that the home complies with all zoning by-laws; detailing any outstanding work orders or deficiency notices affecting the property; making sure all the terms and conditions of development agreements on title have been complied with in full; stating if an occupancy permit for the home has been issued and, if not, when it will be available; and assuring that the municipality has sufficient security to guarantee completion of the subdivision services if the developer does not complete its work.

A lawyer checks with the local utilities — electricity, water and gas — to see if any charges are outstanding. At the same time, the utilities are notified that the property has been sold, and who the new owner will be. The buyer's lawyer requests a final meter reading on the date of closing, with the final bill to be sent to the builder or his lawyer. A search is conducted for outstanding judgments and liens against the builder and possibly even previous owners of the land. And personal property security records may be reviewed for liens or chattel mortgages affecting personal property being purchased from the builder as part of the deal.

In condominium transactions, the lawyer orders an Estoppel Certificate from the condominium corporation, which states whether common expenses for the unit are in arrears, and whether any actions are pending by or against the corporation. In a new condominium project, this certificate should show nothing of the kind.

As noted in Chapter 8, there is usually no problem obtaining a survey for a newly-built home. The survey should be carefully reviewed to ensure that the dimensions of the lot correspond with the offer. Any encroachments onto this property by adjoining buildings, or by this building onto adjoining lots, should be noted.

Then the survey is sent to the local municipality, along with a request for a by-law and work order report. Remember that the survey you have obtained will be technically out-of-date by the time the deal closes. To avoid any misunderstandings some lawyers get written acknowledgements from clients to confirm this fact. This qualification is then repeated in the lawyer's title opinion.

Shortly before closing, the draft deed, Statement of Adjustments and other closing papers are reviewed by the purchaser's lawyer. To ensure its accuracy, the figures in the Statement of Adjustments should be independently verified, and any discrepencies should be quickly resolved.

Your lawyer's role in the mortgage arrangements depends on how the purchase is being financed. If a vendor-take-back mortgage is being given to the builder, his lawyer will probably prepare it. If you are assuming a builder's mortgage on closing, documents will be forwarded to your lawyer for your signature by which you agree to make the mortgage payments to the lender after closing. Your lawyer will ensure the terms of the mortgage being assumed correspond with those in the offer.

If you are arranging a new mortgage, the lender's instructions will list the documents to be prepared before any funds are released. Usually your lawyer can save you money by also acting on behalf of an institutional lender. Draft documents are sent to the lender for approval, and the buyer's lawyer makes arrangements to receive the net mortgage advance on closing. Private lenders ofter prefer to have their own lawyer act for them in the mortgage transaction.

Too many purchasers, especially first-time buyers, are afraid to ask their lawyers simple, straightforward questions. Why? That's what your lawyer is there for. If you had all the answers, you wouldn't be asking the questions. To help their clients, some lawyers provide them with information sheets that answer the most commonly asked questions, and give an overview of events between acceptance and closing. In any case, never let your questions pile up until the final meeting before closing; ask them as they arise. Routine questions can be handled by the secretary or law clerk; discuss your most serious questions directly with your lawyer. Unasked questions could become unresolvable problems if they're not answered early on in the transaction.

Followers of the HOBS approach, of course, should not be surprised when their lawyer tells them the exact amount of money needed to close, usually the week before closing. Long ago they received from their lawyer a reasonable estimate of what the hidden and other closing costs will be. Now it will be interesting to see just how accurate their lawyer's estimate was.

When it comes to closing a real estate purchase, it's true that the early bird definitely catches the worm. Most builders are ready to finalize the deal early on the day of closing, as all the closing papers have already been signed days previously. To expedite closing, buyers must do two things *no later than 3:00 p.m. the day before closing:* see your lawyer to review and sign the closing papers, and deliver the closing funds. *Both* of these tasks must be done on the day before if you want the deal to be completed as early as possible on the day of closing.

Whenever possible, try to meet with your lawyer one or two days before closing: Avoid scheduling this pre-closing meeting on the actual closing day because who knows what could happen that day? The car could get a flat tire, the kids could be sick, bad weather could make travel impossible or traffic could be jammed. Besides, your lawyer's office is probably the last place you want to be on closing day. You're much better off to check on the final progress of your new home and start moving! Most papers can be signed several days ahead of time, so why leave it for the last minute?

But you won't get any keys at this meeting. They won't be available until the transaction is closed and the deed is registered. In any case, if you don't meet with your lawyer until the morning of closing, how can you expect to receive your keys early? This is especially true for buyers selling an existing house without bridge financing. Before the purchase can close, the sale must be completed. If you wait until closing day to meet with your lawyer, that means a late-in-the-day closing with the builder's lawyer, and an even later delivery of the keys.

Remember that much more paper work must be signed on a new home purchase than for a resale transaction. Few documents, though, will be given to you by your lawyer following the pre-closing meeting. Too often, papers delivered at this time get misplaced. Instead, your lawyer will send all relevant documents to you with the reporting letter.

Arranging a pre-closing meeting with your lawyer ahead of time is only half the battle, because hitches in getting the closing proceeds to your lawyer can also delay finalizing the transaction. Meeting to sign papers several days before closing only to deliver the funds the day of closing defeats the purpose of an early meeting. How can you expect to get the keys early on the day of closing if you don't get the money to your lawyer until noon that day? The money still has to be deposited into your lawyer's trust account, and withdrawn as a certified cheque. Only then can the transaction be closed and the keys released to you. Therefore, make sure your lawyer is "in funds" (in receipt of the closing proceeds) no later than 3:00 p.m. the day before closing. Unless you're told otherwise, deliver a certified cheque, money order or bank draft to your lawyer, payable in trust to the law firm.

Some smart buyers meet with their lawyers several days before closing to sign the closing documents, and then deliver the funds by noon on the day before closing. It's an excellent way to give themselves a fighting chance of completing the deal early on the day of closing.

Closing proceeds come from different sources such as your savings account, the mortgage lender, and the bank that provides bridge financing. These funds are assembled in your lawyer's trust account for use on the purchase. To expedite closing, make sure each source forwards his share of the closing proceeds to your lawyer no later than the afternoon before closing.

Some purchasers like Paul and Louise wondered about losing a day's worth of interest by "putting their lawyer in funds" a day early. Yet when they realized that the cost is really quite nominal, they had no further reservations. On a $125,000 purchase, for example, the cost of having both the balance due on closing *and* the proceeds of an 11% mortgage delivered a day early was only $37.67. That's a small price to pay to be able to finalize the purchase and get those all-important keys as early as possible on the day of closing. In fact, Paul and Louise actually saved money, compared to the delay and extra moving costs Herb faced because he didn't put his lawyer in funds the day before closing.

Your lawyer's role does not end with the registration of the deed and the mortgage. Immediately after closing the tax department and the condominium corporation (if applicable) must be given the names of the new owners. An amortization schedule should be ordered for any mortgages you arranged or assumed on closing.

Proper preparation of the reporting letter by your lawyer takes time, so don't expect it for at least a month after closing. But you'll need certain information immediately such as mortgage particulars (date of first payment and amount, address for payment and mortgage number), taxes and condominium maintenance fees. With so many things to remember around closing, purchasers tend to forget a lot of the details. To help their clients, some lawyers mail an interim report immediately after closing to highlight the important information. For many home buyers, this is the first letter they receive at their new home address.

The reporting letter that summarizes what your lawyer did on your behalf also contains that all-important title opinion. A proper reporting letter is not just a form letter with the blanks filled in. It should be drafted to reflect this particular transaction. Since most people want to know "where the money went," the reporting letter should highlight every item in the Statement of Adjustments and how each credit was calculated. The same is true for deductions made by the mortgage lender at source. Copies of all relevant documents should accompany the reporting letter, such as the deed, mortgages, amortization schedules, the Statement of Adjustments, survey and copies of the documents that verify the credits and deductions. A separate report is sent to any mortgage lender your lawyer may also have represented in the transaction.

The lawyer's bill to the buyer will indicate the fee charged plus disbursements incurred on your behalf. There may be a separate account for other services connected with the transaction. A Statement of Receipts and Disbursements will provide a complete account of the funds passing through your lawyer's trust account.

A properly prepared reporting letter and enclosures should answer all outstanding questions you might have about the transaction. It should also form the basis for any future mortgage or resale transaction with the property.

Tips and Pointers

- Never be afraid to contact your lawyer's office to ask any questions you have about the purchase.
- *Always* meet with your lawyer and "put him in funds" *at least one day before closing.*
- Before closing or *immediately* afterwards, get full particulars of the payments due after closing.

23

A Buyer's Work Is Never Done

While your lawyer has a lot of work to do between acceptance and closing, you also have much more to do than just pack. Here are some of the tasks facing purchasers of newly-built homes:

1. Arrange for your lawyer to get a copy of the accepted offer as soon as possible. If you have only one signed original, a photocopy will do. If your lawyer is seeing the offer for the first time (if he or she did not review it in draft form), arrange a meeting instead of just sending the offer. Go through the offer thoroughly, but remember that no changes can be made to the now firm and binding contract.

   Tell your lawyer who is to be the registered owner of the property, including full names, birthdates and spousal status of all parties, depending on the particular province. Further details on "taking title" appear in Chapter 31. If you're in doubt, check with your lawyer.

2. Attend to any outstanding conditions *immediately,* in the manner and within the time set out in the offer. Usually conditions must be satisfied in a very short period of time. Be absolutely certain you understand whether the condition is self-defeating or self-fulfilling, so that you'll know what needs to be done, either to keep the deal alive or to kill it. Strict compliance with terms and conditions is essential. If in doubt, consult your lawyer.

   Once they are satisfied, individual conditions can be removed from the transaction either by amending the offer or by waiving the condition. Once *all* conditions have been satisfied (assuming they are self-defeating conditions), a waiver of conditions should be prepared by the builder's sales agent, signed by you and returned to the agent. Be sure this is done on time. If the condition is worded properly, the builder does not have to sign the waiver. Once all the conditions have been waived, the unconditional offer becomes a "firm and binding" contract.

Like most buyers, Fred and Wilma think they have "bought" a house once the offer is firm and binding. But, legally speaking that isn't quite true. All Fred and Wilma have at this stage is a legal interest in the property. They don't formally own the house until the deal closes.

3. Current tenants must either cancel their lease, transfer their tenancy or sublet their apartment, if permitted. Be sure to give the appropriate amount of notice to the landlord in the prescribed manner as set out in your province's residential tenancy legislation. If in doubt, contact your lawyer. Where possible, arrange an overlap period so the lease terminates after the closing date of your purchase.

4. Your lawyer will contact the local gas, electricity and water utilities to request final meter readings on the day of closing, and for accounts to be set up in your name. To ensure that these services are maintained after closing, call the utilities yourself several days before closing. It's better to double-check than to find yourself without these vital services when you need them.

   Remember that it's up to you and not your lawyer to contact the telephone and cable TV companies. Telephone companies will not guarantee a phone number until it's actually installed. Arranging for a date when phone service can be hooked up is very difficult if closing is delayed for any reason.

5. Arrange home owner's insurance coverage as soon as possible, to take effect on the day of closing. Make sure a binder letter is forwarded to your lawyer well before closing. Insure the building only and not the land, for its full insurable value. See Chapter 24.

6. Make the necessary arrangements for your move as early as possible. Remember too that packing takes much more time than people think. Get quotes from movers or for a rental truck, and start collecting boxes from stores now. Demand for movers and vans peaks in the middle and at the end of the month, on Fridays (especially the last Friday in the month) and the week before summer holidays begin and end.

7. Keep in touch with the sales office and even the construction office to see how work is progressing on your house. Make one person *your* contact person to check with periodically. This will give you a better indication whether closing will be delayed.
8. Arrange with your builder for the pre-delivery inspection of your house several days before closing. See Chapter 26.
9. Make arrangements with the home inspector who will accompany you on the pre-delivery inspection. Retain him much earlier if you plan to hire him to make periodic inspections of the house while it is being constructed. More information on this topic appears in Chapter 27.
10. Visit the site regularly and check on the progress of the house. (Most purchasers of newly-built homes would do this anyway!) Get to know the different foremen on site — the construction foreman in charge of the basic work on the house and the finishing foreman, who is responsible for getting the house ready for occupancy. Often there is a third foreman, in charge of after-sales service. Many new home purchasers will tell you that they spent considerable time at their house talking to the foremen, and especially the trades. They'll also tell you how important it is to establish a good relationship with the trades and the foremen on the site.

Keep a log of major problems encountered during construction. Instead of leaving them all until the job is done, discuss them with the construction foreman as the house is being built. Problems left too late might not be correctable! New home buyers who visit the site must walk a fine line between checking out their future investment and becoming a pest. Remember to exercise common sense if you feel like screaming at a tradesman working on your house who is not doing something right.

Occasionally something is overlooked or improperly constructed. While it is most unfortunate that purchasers sometimes must police the construction of their home, it seems to be a fact of life. Otherwise, what you bought may not be what is built. Andy and Joan ordered a sliding glass walkout at the side of their house as an extra. But when the house was being framed, they noticed that the walkout was being built at the rear. Only by raising the point with the foreman during construction were Andy and Joan able to have the walkout relocated. And it's a good thing they spotted the problem in time. If the brickwork had been in place, the builder said he would have refused to correct the error, and would have offered a refund according to the refund clause in the offer.

Many people would like access to the property before closing for many different reasons. It may be to add extra insulation to the walls and ceiling; to wire it for an intercom or security system; to store or install some items such as appliances several days before closing; or simply to periodically "see how it's coming along."

Understandably, builders are very reluctant to let purchasers or their property into an unfinished home before closing. A home under construction can be a very dangerous place, with nails, projections, loose boards and holes everywhere just waiting for an accident to happen. Any items stored in the house or garage before closing are not covered by the builder's insurance in the event of fire, theft or damage. Legally speaking, entering the home or even the lot without the builder's consent is trespassing, and entitles some builders to cancel the contract.

Travelling on the roads in the new subdivision is a different matter. While the roads may not be assumed yet by the municipality, they are considered public thoroughfares once the subdivision is registered. So although the construction superintendent can keep you out of the house, he can't keep you away from the site.

In many cases, *some work* may have to be done by the buyers or their representatives before closing. Steven and Elyse took a credit for the carpeting supplied by the builder, so that they could lay hardwood floors throughout. Their offer allowed this work to be done before closing, provided the builder approved in writing. Before giving his consent, the builder insisted on receiving a detailed description of the work to be done, and a timetable of when it would be finished. Steven and Elyse also had to accept responsibility for any delays that arose if their work interfered with the builder's own timetable for completion.

11. Meet with your lawyer at least one or two days before closing to sign the closing papers and put him or her in funds.

Checklist of purchaser's work between acceptance and closing

1. Review transaction with lawyer.
2. Satisfy outstanding conditions quickly.
3. If you're a tenant, give proper notice to landlord.
4. Double-check with utilities to ensure continuation of service.
5. Arrange home owner's insurance.
6. Make arrangements for the move.
7. Check with sales office on construction progress.
8. Conduct pre-delivery inspection.
9. Retain home inspector for PDI.
10. Visit site to check on house.
11. Book pre-closing meeting with lawyer.

24

What About Insurance?

Insurance is bound to cross your mind sometime before closing. How much coverage for the house do you need? Does the mortgage need to be insured? What does the expression "mortgage insurance" mean?

Four totally different types of coverage come under the umbrella "mortgage insurance": one insures the property, one insures your life, one ensures that payments will be made to the lender on the mortgage, and one ensures the mortgage interest rate on renewal. Despite what you might be told, not all of these types are necessary, and some are more important than others.

Home Owner's Insurance

This is one type of insurance everybody needs. Commonly dubbed "fire insurance," the coverage should protect your home and its contents against destruction by fire, provide public liability protection, and coverage against theft. All of these features are available in the "Home Owner's Package" many insurance companies offer today.

The most basic type of coverage in a package is on a "named perils" basis. It protects against loss by fire and certain other specified losses, including explosions, lightning, windstorm, smoke damage, falling objects, vehicular impact, riots and vandalism. For a higher premium, more comprehensive coverage is available against additional possible sources of loss, on an "all-risks" basis. Even here, though, coverage is subject to certain exclusions and deductibles.

Mortgage lenders are very concerned about how much home

owner's insurance coverage is in effect. Suppose Lenders Trust is financing Matt and Ruth's purchase of a newly-built home. Lenders Trust is considered to have an insurable interest in the property, since the insurance proceeds would replace the building as security for the loan if it was destroyed. To get first claim to the insurance funds, Lenders Trust must be shown as first mortgagee in the loss payable clause of the insurance policy. Once the mortgage is paid off, the insurance policy will be amended to delete Lenders Trust's interest.

Since the actual insurance policy is rarely delivered on closing although coverage commences that day, insurance agents issue "binder letters." These contain full particulars of the insurance including the name of insurer, the amount of coverage, the policy number, the expiry date, and the name of the lender or lenders in the loss payable clause. Be sure the coverage takes effect at 12:01 *a.m.* the day of closing. If you are arranging your own insurance for closing rather than assuming the builder's coverage, make sure your lawyer gets the binder letter at least several days before closing, because it might have to be forwarded to the lender for approval. Once the lender is assured by the binder letter that adequate insurance coverage is in place, the mortgage can be advanced as scheduled.

Purchasers of newly-built condominium units do not have to arrange for a binder letter this way, since condominium insurance is handled differently. In this case, both the condominium corporation and the individual unit owners must arrange separate insurance coverage to protect their respective interests. For further information, see Chapter 20 on condominiums.

How much insurance coverage will you need? Don't fall into the trap of considering only the size of your mortgage financing, because this could result in overinsuring or even underinsuring the home. Consider the only meaningful figure — the "full insurable value" of the building (the premises). By insuring the premises to that figure, you guarantee that the maximum insurance coverage is in effect.

Ask your insurance agent what the full insurable value should be, based on data available to him for houses in your area. If the mortgage lender had the property appraised, ask for the breakdown between the value of the land and the building. This should confirm how much insurance coverage is needed for the building only.

Consider arranging this coverage for the building on a "replacement cost" basis. For a slightly higher premium, this guarantees that the cost of rebuilding the premises *at current prices* will be paid, with no reduction for depreciation. Without a replacement cost policy, the insurance company will not pay the full cost of replacing the home with one of similar type and quality in the event of an insurable loss.

Ignore the value of the land when you're arranging insurance coverage. Land does not have to be insured because it can't be destroyed. Even if your home was totally destroyed in a fire, the land would still exist.

While full insurable value may be the proper amount of coverage to arrange, some lenders confuse the issue by requiring that the full amount of the mortgage be insured, even if the size of the mortgage exceeds the full insurable value of the property. The additional insurance coverage is useless. It's an unnecessary expense buyers must bear.

For example, Archie and Edith's new house cost $120,000. Vaughan Trust's appraiser valued the lot at $45,000 and the full insurable value of the house at $75,000. Since the couple needed only a $70,000 mortgage to close the purchase, Vaughan Trust insisted on only $70,000 insurance coverage. To give themselves the maximum coverage they need, however, Archie and Edith should still arrange $75,000 worth of insurance, based on the full insurable value of the building.

Mike and Gloria are buying an identical house for $120,000, but need an $85,000 mortgage to close. Since the full insurable value of the building is only $75,000, any higher coverage is unnecessary. Still, Vaughan Trust insisted that the full amount of the $85,000 mortgage be insured. This meant that Mike and Gloria had to arrange an extra $10,000 worth of needless insurance coverage in order to get the mortgage. Although the additional insurance premium for this $10,000 coverage may be small, by insisting that the full amount of the mortgage be insured, Vaughan Trust acted somewhat unreasonably.

The home buyer normally arranges and pays for his own insurance coverage. So if a loss is incurred, how could the insurer pay the insurance proceeds to the lender when there is no direct contractual link between them? To protect themselves, mortgage lenders insist that the Standard Mortgage Clause approved by the Insurance Bureau of Canada be attached to the policy. This allows a direct payment to the lender in the event of a loss, and assures lenders that coverage will not be cancelled without written notice from the insurer.

Some builders transfer insurance policies to purchasers on closing. If you decide to arrange your own coverage and cancel the builder's coverage, often the full premium you paid as a closing adjustment will not be refunded because of an administrative charge. Sometimes the builder's insurance cannot be cancelled until after the builder's mortgage is fully advanced, which could be months away. Review your offer and Chapter 17 for more information about insurance policies that are transferred by builders on closing.

Prudent purchasers will shop for insurance well in advance of closing, obtain quotations and compare coverage to get the best possible terms. This will also help them decide whether or not to keep the builder's insurance coverage, if it is available. Consider dealing with an insurance broker who deals with many insurance companies instead of an agent who markets just one company's product. Brokers should be able to get you a better overall package at a lower cost.

Using a chart similar to the one below, record the insurance quotations you receive from various companies.

Agency/Broker
Name
Address
Phone Number
Contact person
Amount of coverage
Insurer
Cost
Replacement cost coverage

Remember that in the event of fire or theft, more precise information about your possessions will result in a more complete claim. Compile a complete inventory of personal possessions, prepared on a room-by-room basis. Describe each item in detail, including serial numbers. Keep one copy of the list in a secure location *outside* the house, such as your safety deposit box. Many police departments will also loan home owners engraving guns at little or no cost. You can mark a unique identification code such as your Social Insurance Number on items such as TV sets, stereos, VCR's, appliances, cameras, china and tools. If your marked property is ever stolen and later recovered, there is a greater chance it will be returned to you.

Term Life Insurance

Many institutional lenders offer term life insurance to borrowers at a nominal cost. If the mortgage is outstanding when you die, the insurance proceeds are used to retire the loan. Hence the name "mortgage insurance," although it's really nothing more than declining balance term insurance. You can get it from any life insurance agent.

Before you buy this type of coverage, consider the following question: Do you already have sufficient life insurance to pay off your obligations if you die, and still leave adequate funds from which your family can live comfortably?

Mortgage Payment Insurance

High-ratio mortgages for more than 75 percent of a property's appraised value are considered high-risk investments. This means institutional lenders need some assurance the mortgage will be repaid if the borrower defaults. To protect the lender, on high-ratio loans borrowers must arrange and pay for mortgage payment insurance on the full amount of the mortgage. This insurance is available from two sources: a private insurer, the Mortgage Insurance Company of Canada (MICC); and a federal government agency, Canada Mortgage and Housing Corporation (CMHC).

In addition to their regular mortgage payment, Ward and June pay a monthly charge to the lender for payment insurance. Although Ward and June pay the payment insurance premium, the benefits go to the lender. Despite what some borrowers believe, if Ward and June default on the mortgage, the payment insurance *will* not make the mortgage payments on their behalf. Payment insurance simply guarantees the lender that all payments will be made, either by Ward and June or by the insurer.

Because of its high cost, you should never arrange mortgage payment insurance unless it is absolutely necessary. Depending on the size of the mortgage in relation to the value of the property, the insurance fee could be 1.25 percent to 2.5 percent of the total amount of the mortgage. It is usually added to the outstanding principal and paid off monthly so that its true cost is concealed. Few people realize, for example, that a $1,000 insurance premium on an 11 percent mortgage amortized over 25 years will cost an extra $9.63 each month, and $1,887.59 in additional interest over the amortized life of the loan.

There are other ways to restructure your mortgage financing and eliminate the mortgage payment insurance premium. For further details, see the Canadian bestseller *Hidden Profits in Your Mortgage*.

Mortgage Rate Insurance

With great ballyhoo, the federal government introduced the Mortgage Rate Protection Plan in 1984. Its aim was to protect home owners againt sharp rises in interest rates. But despite its noble intentions, the plan has been largely ignored by the public for a number of reasons.

Under the terms of the plan, the interest rate on the renewal term (which matches the initial term) is protected once the initial mortgage term expires. But the plan does not completely guarantee the interest rate to borrowers, because no protection is available if rates on the renewal term increase by 2 percentage points or less. Above 2 percent, the plan protects only 75 percent of the increase. The rest is the borrower's responsibility. If rates increased from 10 percent to 16 percent, the borrower would still pay 13 percent for the renewal term (10% plus 2% plus one-quarter of 4%).

Even with this plan, mortgage rate insurance is still very expensive. A one-time premium paid to CMHC of 1.5 percent of the outstanding principal is added to the amount borrowed and repaid monthly, just like mortgage payment insurance. However, the premiums are not pro-rated for the number of years in the initial term. Borrowers who have a one-year mortgage pay the same premium for one year's worth of protection as borrower with a five-year mortgage, who gets five years' coverage. No wonder the scheme has been such a flop.

Vendor-take-back and second mortgages are excluded from the plan.

Tips and Pointers

- Arrange home owner's insurance coverage for the full insurable value of the building. Disregard how much money you owe on your mortgage.
- Arrange to have term life insurance only if you don't have sufficient coverage already.
- Avoid payment and rate insurance if at all possible.

25

Problems with Home Delivery

Probably the most common complaint about buying a newly-built home involves late or delayed closings. Builders are notorious for not closing new home transactions on time. Because they have more than 25 different trades to deal with, delays are inevitable. Sometimes legitimate reasons exist for extending the closing date — strikes, shortages of materials and supplies, the lack of skilled labor and unfavorable weather conditions. In addition, as the construction industry is one of boom and bust, in good times some builders "oversell" — that is, they sell more homes in a year than they know can be built. Better to sell houses now, they feel, and work out problems with closing dates later.

Although purchasers awaiting delivery of a newly-built house must be patient, they still rely very heavily on the closing date, and plan many of their activities around it. Existing homes may have been sold with the two closing dates tied together. Tenants may have given notice to their landlords based on when the new house should be completed. Children may have already been transferred to a school in the neighborhood where the new house is located.

A missed closing date is bound to cause great inconvenience — even hardship — depending on individual circumstances. Too often a delayed closing means purchasers must scurry about, rearranging plans on very short notice, all at their own expense. Because they have no place to live, they must find alternative accommodations with friends or family or in a motel or apartment. Arrangements must be made for two moves instead of just one, plus storage of non-essential furniture and personal items. Although they are not responsible for the delay, the buyers are paying the price in terms of grief and anxiety, not to mention the additional costs. Most offers say that if closing is delayed, the builder and the agent are not liable to pay any costs, compensation or damages to the purchaser.

The problem of delayed closing has become so serious in some areas of Canada that a delayed closing syndrome has developed in which people *expect* their new home to be delivered late. Buyers treat the closing date in their offer as a meaningless number. What's more, they rarely ask for their deposit back when closing is delayed. Instead, they make the necessary adjustments to their lives and then wait for closing to take place at some indefinite time in the future.

As part of your home-buying strategy, you should have a contingency plan ready that affords you an alternative place to live for a short period of time if your house isn't ready as scheduled. Whether "Plan B" will be needed depends on many factors, all of which are totally beyond your control. That's why it's important to have this back-up system ready, just in case.

Some offers stipulate a maximum number of times the deal can be extended, and others impose a maximum extension period (often six months) that closing can be delayed. All this assumes, of course, that the deal will still close, but somewhat later than expected. This is a dangerous assumption to make.

When the original closing date cannot be met, practically all new home offers give builders the option to extend closing and the buyer must grant the extension. Yet the builder also has the option *not* to extend closing. If that happens, the deal is terminated, and the new home buyer loses the house! In other words, only the builder — not the buyer — can decide whether or not the deal is to be extended. Builders insist on these powers, in case delays beyond their control prevent the house from being finished on time.

Here is a typical clause about closing dates that appeared in Alan and Hannah's new home offer:

"If for any reason whatsoever except the vendor's wilful neglect the dwelling is not completed on or before the closing date, the vendor shall, in its sole discretion, be permitted such reasonable extension or extensions of time for completion of the work as may be required by the vendor and the date of closing shall be extended accordingly. If the vendor should be unable to substantially complete the dwelling by the closing date, or if extended, within such extended time, the deposit shall be returned to the purchaser without interest and this Agreement shall be at an end and the vendor shall not be liable to the purchaser in any way for damages or otherwise."

Alan and Hannah's purchase was scheduled to close June 5. Throughout the winter and early spring, they were constantly assured and reassured by both the construction office and the sales agent that the house would be ready on time. By early May, Alan and Hannah could see that this was impossible. The frame of the house hadn't even been erected.

Plain and simple, the builder's problem was that the demand for his homes was so brisk, he couldn't keep up. He couldn't hire enough tradesmen to finish the house on time. Since Alan and Hannah had already sold their old home, they had to arrange for an alternative place to live. But finding an apartment on such short notice and for such a brief, indefinite period of time was no easy task. Alan and Hannah also had to bear the extra expense of a second move and put some of their furniture and belongings into storage. Their lives were thrown into absolute turmoil.

What Alan and Hannah didn't yet understand was the potential problems they could still face, based on the wording of their offer. To appreciate this, let's translate the delay cause into straightforward English.

First, it assumes no "wilful neglect" on the part of the builder, whatever that means. Probably only a judge in a court of law would be able to decide that question. Thankfully, Alan and Hannah did not have to face this.

If the original closing date of June 5 arrives and the house is not substantially completed, *the builder* has two choices "in his sole discretion," without any input from the purchasers. One is to "reasonably" extend the time to substantially complete the work on the house. This means that no limit exists on either the number of extensions Alan and Hannah must endure, or on the total length of time for such extensions. The builder can take as many extensions as he wants. This type of extension, which automatically reschedules the closing date, is the route Alan and Hannah assumed the builder would follow.

But Alan and Hannah did not realize that there was another option open to the builder. *He could cancel the contact and return the deposit if the original scheduled closing date of June 5 could not be met because the house would not be substantially completed that day. There was no obligation on the part of the builder to extend closing even one day.* That's correct; the builder was under no legal obligation to extend closing at all!

Unknown to Alan and Hannah, this clause also allowed the builder to back out of the deal if closing was extended, say for a month, and the house was not substantially completed on the extended closing date. In other words, just because closing has been extended once does not mean it has to be extended a second time. Imagine how bothersome this would be to purchasers who already have experienced one delayed closing!

With these typical clauses in most offers for newly-built homes, the issue of whether the deal will close and the actual date of closing is completely at the builder's discretion. Unsuspecting buyers are genuinely shocked to learn how much depends on the good faith of the builder, who literally controls the purchaser's fortunes. He *alone* has the power to decide which deals close, and when. Purchasers must hope and pray the builder won't invoke his full legal rights before the deal closes. Not very reassuring for purchasers of newly-built homes. The only certainty is uncertainty!

Looking at another example, assume house prices have increased dramatically since an offer was accepted. An unscrupulous builder like Shyster Homes could use this clause to its advantage by constantly delaying closing. This will cause some purchasers to throw up their hands in frustration and despair. Because they need a place to live and can't wait any longer, they will have to look elsewhere for a home, and back out of the contract. Shyster Homes can anticipate losing some buyers, and need only deal with buyers who dig in their heels and refuse to go away.

But Shyster Homes holds all the cards with them, too. After months of anxiety and frustration, Len and Gail still have no right to demand an extension of the contract. Yet nothing stops Shyster Homes from aborting the deal at this stage and reselling their partially built home to someone else at substantially higher price. Although it is unethical, what the builder is doing is legally permissible by the rights Len and Gail gave him in the contract. No wonder it has been said these clauses give builders an incentive for delay.

Although this didn't actually happen, what could Alan and Hannah have done if the builder had cancelled the contract on the original or an extended closing date? Not much, because according to the clause:

a) the agreement is terminated, meaning it's null and void;
b) the purchaser's deposit will be returned without any interest;
c) the builder is not liable to the purchaser in any way for any damages.

In other words, if the builder had decided to pull the plug on Alan and Hannah's deal, they would have gotten their initial deposit back, but no interest. And the builder would not be liable — even in a court of law — for any damages or expenses Alan and Hannah incurred!

As unfair as the clause seems on the surface, it also has several hidden meanings. When Alan and Hannah's lawyer told them of the delayed closing, he suggested that they not rock the boat too hard. If they were too vocal or critical of the delay, the builder could refuse an extension and abort the deal, meaning Alan and Hannah would lose the house. So they would have to keep their opinions to themselves.

It is fairly common today that house values are increasing between the time the offer is accepted, and closing. If the offer lacks a price escalation clause, the builder cannot demand more money for the house. A contract is a contract. Purchasers would be happy, since the house they bought months ago is now worth more money. Builders would be upset because other people are profiting from their as-yet unconstructed product.

But don't forget that builders do not have to extend closing, if closing is delayed. The deal could be terminated. Some builders might revive the contract with the same purchasers and extend the closing date, if and only if the purchasers agree to renegotiate the price for the house (i.e. pay more)! Again, the builder calls all the shots. Used this way, the delayed closing clause becomes an "indirect" price escalation clause, a back-door method for builders to demand more money for their homes. This is precisely what happened during the unprecedented building boom in Ontario in 1986, when more than one builder cancelled what purchasers thought were valid and binding unconditional offers.

Talk about double jeopardy! If house prices had risen substantially in the interim, Alan and Hannah would have lost the home and its increase in value. To buy another equivalent home they would have to pay a substantially higher current price. Losing the house undoubtedly would be a severe enough setback. But through no fault of their own, Alan and Hannah might also find themselves priced right out of the market, and unable to afford any other home.

Some offers do impose a cap on "reasonable" extensions, so that the closing shall be extended a set amount of time, perhaps 60 days, from the original scheduled closing date. After that, any further extensions require the mutual consent of builder and buyer, or else the contract is cancelled. All this does for purchasers is deny builders the automatic right to terminate the transaction if the closing is delayed on the initial closing date — nothing more. Once the 60 days are up, the builder does not have to extend closing. And if the builder agrees to an extension, once again it's on his terms — including a possible price increase. Purchasers often have no practical choice but to agree to any further extension that builders are prepared to give, on the builder's terms.

Be on the lookout for other clauses dealing with closing dates in new home offers. Some allow builders to close the deal *earlier* than expected, provided they give you at least 60 days' prior written notice. Builders could use this clause if the closing date set was an extremely long time in the future (say 18 months), and the house is constructed faster than the builder anticipated. If this clause is in your offer, and work proceeds ahead of schedule, you could be forced to close sooner than you'd planned.

Another clause can force purchasers to take possession of their home on an interim occupancy basis (just like a newly-built condominium), if the house is ready for occupancy but a deed can't be registered yet. The balance due on closing is paid to the builder's lawyer and held in trust until a registrable deed can be delivered. After this "escrow closing," you are responsible for all expenses, including payments on the mortgage as if the deed was registered.

An interim occupancy closing may be necessary if the builder encounters delays in getting the deeds registered, or if minor zoning infractions exist. Review interim occupancy in chapter 20 on Condominiums.

In recent years there has been a lot of talk about the need for builders to set realistic closing dates. A complaint often made against builders is their failure to tell new home buyers when they buy a house of delays they may encounter. Buyers themselves should determine how realistic the suggested closing date is, remembering the various stages in building a house. If you are unsure about what you are told (or not being told) by the builder, check out these points with the local municipality:

1. Learn whether the subdivision is registered and, if so, its registration number. Just because an offer is signed does not mean that construction of the house can immediately begin. While yet-to-be-built homes are pre-sold, in some provinces homes can also be sold as "pre-registration pre-sales" from draft (not registered) plans of subdivision. Only when the subdivision is registered, the services are in place and a building permit is issued can work actually start on the house. Until then the offer is a conditional offer.

   Trying to give a meaningful closing date so many months in the future is difficult enough when the subdivision is unregistered. When you are buying a pre-registration pre-sale home, the sheer number of variables make it impossible for any builder to guarantee the deal will close on time. He can't even guarantee when and if the subdivision will be registered! Closing dates are little more than guesses.

2. If the subdivision is registered, find out if it has been serviced. If it hasn't, additional time will go by before construction will begin on your home. Remember that the builder of your home is not necessarily the same company that developed the subdivision. If you are clamoring for more details on the status of your land, your builder can adequately answer your question only if he has received the information from the developer. That's all the more reason to check things out with the municipality.

3. If the subdivision is registered and the lot serviced, see if the necessary building permit has been issued. To properly construct a new home on a serviced lot under ideal conditions, a builder generally needs between 14 and 16 weeks *after* the permit is issued. Getting that permit could take several weeks once the other preliminary work is out of the way.

4. Only when work begins can a builder give you a realistic target closing date, no matter what the offer says. Even then, closing on time depends on the assumption that construction will proceed smoothly. Simply by listening to the news you'll find out all about shortages of material and labor, strikes and poor weather conditions. Once the frame is erected, the builder will need at least two months to ready the house for occupancy, assuming everything goes according to schedule. Delivery of the house is still another three to four weeks away after the drywall has been put up.

Beware of builders who sell new homes based on attractive "lowball" closing dates that they could never meet. All these builders are doing is baiting the hook for unsuspecting buyers. In late March, Fuddle Homes told Sy and Marcie that a pre-sale home would be ready for occupancy that September. Another builder down the street, Duddle Construction, assured them of delivery in late July. The subdivision was registered in both cases, but servicing had not yet begun. Sy and Marcie dealt with Duddle Construction, solely on the appeal of the anticipated July closing date. But the deal didn't close until September. On further investigation, Sy and Marcie learned that Duddle Construction's July closing date was just a gimmick to get the sale. The builder knew full well the closing date was unrealistic. Fuddle Homes, which had been honest and candid, lost the deal.

Carefully consider the various trade-offs when you're buying a newly-built home. Remember that the earlier the house is sold in the development process, the more uncertain the closing date. Yet the earlier the house is sold, especially with a pre-registration presale, the more purchasers may see their house values rise between acceptance and closing. Yet the earlier the house is sold, especially with a pre-registration pre-sale, the more opportunity the builder has to cancel the contract. Most buyers presented with these trade-offs choose the house and the benefits of a fixed sale price, and reluctantly accept the consequences of a delayed or possibly cancelled closing.

Many of the problems that cause delayed and cancelled closings arise in the pre-construction stage. Once work begins, deliberate delays are not in the builder's best interests. "Carrying" that unfinished home, including mortgage interest, is expensive. The easiest way for a builder to gain relief is to complete the home and transfer title as soon as possible. Unfortunately, this is something that many new home buyers overlook.

No buyer should ever be in the dark about anything as important as the closing date of his new home. Builders must be more forthright with new home purchasers than they have been in the past. Before signing an offer, purchasers must be informed at what point the land is in the development process, and how the closing date might be affected. Realistic closing dates must be given, not just dates buyers want to hear to placate them.

Better communications and more thorough, timely disclosure about delayed closings is needed as well. Too often, purchasers' biggest complaint is not the impact of the delayed closing but the fact they were not told what was going on. Work came to a grinding halt on Glen and Joy's house when all other homes were being built, and their closing was postponed. No reasonable explanation was given them despite their many requests. All they were told by the builder was that there were "unavoidable construction delays." Through their own sources Glen and Joy found out why — a minor violation of the zoning requirements had been committed. Now they were starting to wonder what else the builder wasn't telling them — and whether construction problems and defects were being concealed, too.

How much better it would be if builders at the earliest possible opportunity volunteered information to purchasers on any delays that could affect the closing date. This would considerably reduce the inconvenience, grief and hardship caused by the delay in closing. With sufficient advance notice that closing must be extended, purchasers living in apartments can delay giving notice for terminating their leases. Those who have sold existing homes can either try to extend the closing of their sale, or arrange short-term alternative accommodations. It would also do much for the image of builders in the public eye. Waiting until the last possible moment does not help the situation or the tie between builder and buyer.

To their credit, some builders regularly contact their purchasers and bring them up-to-date on the progress of their homes. This approach is bound to improve these builders' reputations.

Builders know that everyone who faces a delayed closing wants to get into their new house as quickly as possible. But yelling and screaming at the builder won't get you into the house any faster, while good human relations sometimes will.

Like everyone else in their subdivision, Wayne and Karen's closing was delayed by a construction strike. Once it was settled, everyone wanted to be the first to move in. Wayne and Karen's situation was somewhat different, since they were living in a basement apartment with a newborn baby. Instead of making demands of the builder, they calmly asked if completion of their house could be put near the top of the list because of their circumstances. The builder was amenable. Here was a rare purchaser who wasn't kicking up a fuss. For that reason alone, the builder arranged for them to be among the first to get possession of their new home.

What changes are needed to best protect purchasers of newly-built homes? People expect work to begin on their house once they have "bought" it. This means sales of a new home should not be allowed until a building permit has been issued, or until a builder can guarantee that one can be issued for the model and type of house being sold on a lot. Only this way can reality correspond to the public's impression of reality. Only then can a closing date be meaningful at all.

But such a dramatic change could lead to hardship in the new home industry. Instead, a possible compromise might be to prohibit the sale of any new home before the subdivision plan is registered. By removing many of the conditions that presently must be satisfied before the first shovel can be put into the ground, much-needed certainty would be added to the process. However, the offer would still be conditional on a building permit being issued.

If closing is delayed, *purchasers and not builders* should have the right to decide if the transaction will be extended or cancelled. The way most clauses are worded today, the builder arbitrarily and unilaterally decides the point. Even a mutual consent clause would work against a purchaser's best interests, since builders could refuse to extend closing if they saw fit. If the decision rested with purchasers, delivery of the house would be guaranteed, as long as the buyer still wanted it.

The right to extend closing should apply if closing was missed *for any reason whatsoever*. As we have seen, an extension of the closing date may be necessary for a whole host of reasons. A delay in the actual construction of the home is just one of the possibilities.

Any extension should be made *on the same terms and conditions* as stated in the offer. This would guarantee purchasers that whatever they bargained for — most importantly price and mortgage terms — would be retained if closing is delayed. Delayed closings are rarely the buyer's fault. Why should they be forced to pay more or assume a different mortgage if the deal can't close on time?

Besides this, purchasers should be paid a reasonable rate of interest on their deposits during the delay period, from the original scheduled closing date to the actual closing date. Builders often say this is a matter of contract and negotiation between the parties. Rarely, though, are the parties negotiating from equal positions of strength. As with holding back money on closing when work on the house is not completed, the builder has all the clout. If you want the builder's house, you accept the builder's terms, plain and simple.

The standard builder's argument is that the purchase price reflects the builder keeping the interest on the deposit paid from acceptance to the originally scheduled closing date. Otherwise, the sale price would be higher. However, the builder's argument loses its validity if the original closing date is missed. If interest on the deposit is taken into account in setting the sale price, any interest earned after closing is delayed must represent an unfair windfall to the builder. In effect the deposit becomes an interest-free loan to the builder. Most purchasers faced with a delayed closing must bear some additional costs. Why shouldn't buyers earn this interest to help defray those extra expenses? It will make an extension somewhat more palatable to a buyer.

To properly protect newly-built home buyers, a pre-determined penalty should be spelled out right in the offer, stating what will happen if the closing is delayed. This way, nothing is left to chance or to the builder's discretion. New home purchasers would not have to negotiate from a position of weakness at the worst possible time, when closing is delayed, to get compensation.

Compensation would be payable from the original scheduled closing date to the date the deal actually closes. The inconvenience and extra expenses purchasers incur — additional moving and storage charges, living expenses and the cost of temporary accommodations plus, of course, interest on the deposit would be covered. Most commercial construction contracts are secured by a performance guarantee or bond and impose a penalty if the job is not performed on time. Why should new home contracts be any different?

Whenever possible, try to delete from your offer the clause that allows the builder to terminate the transaction if closing is extended, and the house is not ready on the extended closing date. Or as an absolute minimum, insert a penalty clause *if closing is extended and then cancelled.* Otherwise, you could face the same dilemma as Randy. When his house was not ready on July 15, closing was extended to August 26. When the house was not completed on August 26, the builder said he wanted no more extensions, and he cancelled the contract. Although Randy relied on the revised closing date, he is not entitled to any compensation from the builder whatsoever.

The way things stand now, all buyers can do is sue for these costs if closing is delayed. To most buyers, even this is not a practical solution, since suing for small amounts is expensive and time consuming. Because builders know this, they take a very tough stand on paying compensation for late closings. (This assumes purchasers have not signed away their rights in the offer to sue the builder for damages.) Therefore, it is unlikely builders would ever voluntarily consent to compensation clauses appearing in their offers.

This is especially true in a seller's market, when a heavy-handed "take-it-or-leave-it" attitude prevails.

The only effective way to bring about these much-needed reforms and protections for the home-buying public is through legislative change at the provincial level. A voluntary, self-policing approach may be commendable and a step in the right direction, but rarely is it totally effective. The potential for abuse and the consequences of it are just too severe to be left to self-regulation. Besides, most of the necessary changes are so sweeping that it is unlikely the residential construction industry would ever agree to them. The only way the home-buying public can be adequately protected against unscrupulous builders (and occasionally themselves) is by government intervention.

Legislative action in the new home field is not new.* Purchasers of the new condominiums have been protected for years by significant legislative safeguards, guidelines and disclosure requirements. New trails do not have to be blazed, as the precedent is in place. Existing trails need only be extended further.

Buyers should never assume that the escape clause won't be used, regardless of the builder's size and reputation. Practically speaking, it is not used too often, especially by the larger builders. But it's always sitting in the offer, waiting. Whether the clause can be amended or eliminated from your offer depends on many different factors, although during a seller's market attempts to alter this clause generally prove fruitless. If the builder assures you that the clause won't be invoked, but won't amend the offer to say so, you have to wonder why.

At first glance, buying a newly-built home may seem like sitting on a powder keg. Clauses dealing with closing delays are slanted toward the builders, with little apparent room for maneuvering. But most new home purchases do close, although not necessarily on time. For the most part there appears to be a major inconsistency between what builders say in their contracts and what they actually do.

All the more reason as part of your home-buying strategy that you review the contents of the offer with your lawyer before it is signed. At least you will know that trap-door clauses like these exist, and understand the potential consequences in the worst case scenario. Until legislative change is introduced to protect purchasers from these unfair clauses, this is the best, and the least, you can do.

Tips and Pointers

- Remember that in most new home offers, the builder is under no obligation to extend closing if it is delayed.
- If closing is extended, the builder can literally rewrite the terms of the contract, including the purchase price.
- Make sure you fully understand what rights you are giving the builder in the offer if closing is delayed, before you sign the offer.

---

*As part of its new home reform package, the Ontario government endorsed an "Addendum" to new home offers prepared by the building industry, which was scheduled to take effect March 1, 1987. This document certainly did not offer the protection new home buyers needed from one-sided contracts. For example, the Addendum pointed out five types of clauses in new home offers that purchasers should be wary of: the right of a builder to cancel the transaction; that purchasers must be approved to assume the builder's mortgage; that the interest rate in the builder's mortgage may be higher than the rate quoted; the right of a builder to alter plans and substitute materials; plus the fact new home offers contain many hidden costs. What the Addendum did not do was give details of these clauses! No information was given how the offer could be cancelled prematurely; how the quoted interest rate could be increased; and what closing costs new home purchasers might face. Effectively, the Addendum only disclosed that pitfalls exist in new home offers; the home-buying public still must figure out itself what those pitfalls are, and maneuver around them!

In addition, an elaborate scheme was established dealing with delayed closings. Initially, closing must be extended up to 120 days if it cannot be completed on time. After that, closing would be extended for a further 120 days at the purchaser's request only. If closing was delayed for more than 240 days, the transaction would be cancelled. Interest on the deposit would be paid during this second 120 day extension if the agreement is terminated after 240 days.

Several problems exist here as well. The addendum dealt only with closings that must be postponed due to delays in the actual construction of the house. Of course, closing could be delayed for many other reasons — such as the subdivision not being registered on time; services not being installed or building permit not being issued prior to originally scheduled closing date; problems arranging construction financing or builder's mortgages; and the builder not being satisfied with the "economic feasibility and viability" of the project—none of which would be covered by the Addendum. Purchasers do not receive interest on the deposit or compensation if closing is delayed but still takes place. Interest is payable only for a limited period of time if the deal never closes. Finally, nothing in the Addendum specifically guarantees that the offer will be extended on the same terms and conditions. Therefore, there is no assurance that the original purchase price and mortgage arrangements will be maintained on the extension.

Overall, a very small step in the right direction.

26

The Pre-Delivery Inspection

Before they took delivery of their new car, Joe and Tillie spent considerable time with the dealer's service rep examining the vehicle inside and out. During the test drive Joe and Tillie checked out the handling and braking, making sure the car operated smoothly. Only after this pre-delivery inspection (PDI) was complete, and minor deficiencies noted, did Joe and Tillie drive their new car home.

The PDI of a newly-built home is a lot like the PDI for a new car, in that buyers should examine the house inside and out with the builder's service representative. The equipment and features in the house should be put through a "test drive" to make sure they operate smoothly. Only after the PDI is completed and minor deficiencies noted should you close the deal and take possession of the house.

The PDI of a newly-built house should take place several days *before* closing. At this stage, the house should be substantially complete and ready for occupancy. Although the builder should contact you to schedule the PDI, don't wait for his phone call if closing is less than a week away. Do the PDI during the daytime, so the exterior of the house can be examined fully. All systems in the house should be totally functional — electrical, plumbing and heating.

During the PDI, record *all* outstanding and unfinished work, even the most obvious items, since most new home offers say that the builder will complete only whatever is shown as outstanding at the PDI. In addition, all visible and known defects in materials and workmanship should be listed. Be as thorough and complete as possible. Your goal is to establish that any damage arose before closing, *which makes it the builder's responsibility to repair.* Otherwise, it will become increasingly difficult after closing to establish that the problem existed before closing. In Ontario, where all houses must be enrolled in the New Home Warranty Program, all defects and uncompleted work are listed on the plan's Certificate of Completion and Possession form.

After closing, Ken and Barbie noticed that they had failed to list a cracked window on their PDI. At this stage it was impossible to prove that it had been damaged before closing. The builder claimed the window must have been broken by Ken and Barbie or their movers. And even if the defect had existed before closing, the builder said Ken and Barbie had accepted the imperfection anyway, by not mentioning it before closing. The question became one of evidence, Ken and Barbie's word against the builder's. In fact, once they took possession, Ken and Barbie were stuck. They had no choice but to repair the window at their own expense. Therefore, *never* conduct the PDI after closing.

No PDI will reveal all flaws in a newly-built home. Some defects will arise after you take possession. Others could not be uncovered on the PDI no matter how thorough you are. Usually these problems become evident quite soon after you close. Where the New Home Warranty Program applies, all defects in materials and workmanship discovered during your first year of occupancy are protected. This is true whether or not these defects are listed on the PDI, even though you signed the Certificate of Completion and Possession. But the more you record on the PDI, the fewer items that could come back to haunt you later.

While the PDI may be your first chance to see the house in its completed state, don't let your excitement overcome you. The PDI is serious business. Before long the present situation will be reversed — you will have the builder's house while the builder will have your money. Therefore, now is the time to thoroughly inspect and inquire, not to admire. This means a complete examination of the house, finding out where items are located and how they work, and scrutinizing the materials and workmanship. The PDI also provides an excellent opportunity to familiarize yourself with key elements of the house, such as the main water shut-off and the main electrical panel. Leave no stone unturned. Look for the obvious but more importantly the not-so-obvious problems.

Inspect the house from bottom to top. Start in the basement and work your way upstairs, room by room. Note surface defects that would be easy for the builder to blame on you after closing. Test features which can easily be tested, to ensure everything works. Record everything that concerns you, both defects and unfinished items, despite whatever comments the builder's rep might make. And don't be rushed. An incomplete list or one prepared in haste is not in your best interests.

Basement
Are any cracks visible in the walls? Check the walls and floors for water stains and evidence of present or previous water infiltration. Do the laundry taps (hot and cold) work properly? Make sure the furnace, air conditioner and humidifier all work. Is the hot water tank hooked up? Locate the main water shut-off and fuse box/circuit breaker. Are the stairs securely fastened? Do all windows open and close properly? Is the insulation properly covered with plastic vapor barrier?

Plumbing
Do all sink faucets (hot and cold) work properly? Test the showers and tub taps to make sure the hot and cold water is working properly. Is the flow of water adequate? Flush every toilet. Are they adequately secured? Check under all sinks and around the toilets for leaks.

Electrical
Test all light switches and electrical outlets. (A small plug-in radio or night-light is ideal for this). Do all light fixtures work? Has the heavy-duty plug for the stove and dryer been installed? Locate all telephone and cable television outlets. Turn on the range hood light and fan.

Ceiling, Walls and Floor
Check the ceiling, walls, floors and floor coverings for defects, scratches, dents, gouges, marks and chips. Carefully examine the paint job on walls, baseboards and doors. Are the colors correct? Are any drywall seams showing? What about nail pops? Have the correct floor coverings been laid? Are the baseboards, quarter-round and heat vents installed? Do the floors and stairs squeak? Do the floors "buckle" when you walk on them?

Windows and Doors
Open and close all windows to make sure they don't stick. Are any

window panes cracked? Are all screens installed? Make sure all doors hang straight and open properly, without rubbing on the carpet. Does the hardware on the doors operate properly? Have door stops been installed? Does the sliding door operate and lock properly? Test all other locks. Do the exterior doors open and close properly? Does the garage door open properly?

Built-in Items
Examine all bathtubs, mirrors, counters and toilets for scratches, chips and dents. Are all cupboards and countertops properly installed? Ensure all cabinet doors open properly.

Miscellaneous
Test the smoke detector and the door chime. In the attic, check the roof, insulation and ventilation.

Exterior Items
Does the brickwork and masonry appear sound? Are the "weep holes" at the base of the brickwork open? Check the exterior lighting and electrical outlets. Test the exterior hose bibs. Are all the concrete walkway and patio slabs in place? Does the driveway need more stones? Check the condition of the soffits, fascia, eavestroughs and downspouts. From your vantage point on the ground, are there any shingles missing? Is there adequate caulking around the doors and windows? Do you feel any drafts coming into the house? Has the house been properly graded, with the grade sloping away from the side of the house? If you have an attached garage, make sure it has been adequately "gas proofed" so carbon monoxide can't enter the house.

The exterior of the house may not be totally complete when you do the PDI. If any exterior work remains outstanding, even as obvious as the laying of sod or the paving of the driveway, mark it down. Ignore protests by the builder's rep that he knows these items are outstanding. Remember that according to the contract, it won't be completed unless it's listed.

Remember to take along a copy of the offer on the PDI. Make sure all the "standard" items listed in Schedule "A" of the offer have been installed or supplied, as well as *all* extras and upgrades that were paid for. If you're unsure where various features are, ask the builder's rep to point them out.

A proper PDI takes at least an hour. Never be rushed into a 20-minute cursory examination of the house. Don't feel intimidated if the builder's service rep says this is the longest PDI he has ever conducted, and that you are being overly picky. Obviously the more critical he is, the better a job you must be doing. Treat his complaints as a disguised compliment.

Many buyers are pleasantly surprised on a PDI. Reputable builders will have gone through the house before you, so that only a handful of items remain outstanding. And they may point out defects and deficiencies you didn't even notice. While this is the way a PDI should be handled, consider yourself lucky if you find yourself in this situation.

Once the PDI is complete, carefully read over the list of defects and uncompleted work before you sign it. Be sure nothing was missed. Avoid the word "touch-up" if something major must be done. And make sure you get a copy of it for your records.

Next, try to get firm written commitment from the builder's rep as to when the outstanding items will be corrected. Of course, you want these items completed as soon as possible after closing, but don't be surprised if he avoids any firm promises. Constructing a house involves hiring numerous subtrades, and it's often cheaper to lump together all "call-backs" (corrective work) with one subtrade. This way a number of problems in different homes can be cleaned up at one time.

Some items, though, will have to be completed and fixed before you close and move in, such as the installation of kitchen cupboards, laying the balance of the carpeting, and repairing a missing window. Sometimes a quick follow-up inspection may be necessary the day before or even the morning of closing, just to be sure these bare essentials have been taken care of.

Contact your lawyer and let him or her know how the PDI went. This is especially important in the event that so much work is outstanding that closing must be delayed. In that case, arrangements will have to be made with the builder's lawyer to postpone closing for several days.

Besides being the first formal introduction to your new house, the PDI is your first real introduction to the builder, and vice versa. You have probably visited the home site during construction and talked with the tradesmen, possibly even the construction foreman. But conducting a proper PDI is vital, not only for what it shows you about the house, but more importantly what it tells the builder about you. A thorough, no-nonsense PDI will help set the ground rules early on for your dealings with the builder after closing. It won't take long for the builder and his staff to realize that you are an educated consumer who is not easily fooled. If problems arise, you expect them to be corrected properly and promptly. The way you handle yourself on the PDI will be the first real indication of how you expect to be treated by the builder after closing.

To add credibility to this approach, more and more purchasers of newly-built homes are taking professional private home inspectors with them on their PDI's. This makes very good sense. Home inspections are gaining increased acceptance in the resale field. Why should newly-built homes be any different? The next chapter focuses on home inspectors.

Tips and Pointers
- Make sure your PDI is conducted *before* you close, to eliminate any misunderstandings about who is responsible for what damage.
- Test and record all outstanding, incomplete and defective items, even the most obvious.
- Be thorough on your PDI: how you handle yourself on your PDI will set the tone for your dealings with the builder after closing.

27

Home Inspectors for Newly-built Homes

Building a newly-built home is a complex process with many intricate details that could go wrong. Hundreds of man-hours and thousands of dollars of construction materials are needed to convert the artist's rendering you first see in the builder's construction trailer into a dwelling that is ready for occupancy. Although new homes today are expensive, running into the hundreds of thousands of dollars, they are still mass-produced, meaning mistakes are bound to be made. But as a purchaser you can't afford to accept any mistakes. To protect yourself and your investment, it's necessary to try and discover as many of these defects in materials and workmanship as early as possible, preferably before money and title are exchanged.

To that end, pre-delivery inspections (PDI) give you an opportunity to record flaws in the house. But how many people, even those who have a friend or relative who "knows what he's doing," really know what to look for? How many new home purchasers can tell whether the construction specifications listed in Schedule A of the offer, plus the extras and upgrades, have been fully and properly completed? How many people are familiar with the technical and ever-changing standards of the local or provincial building codes?

More often than not the PDI, no matter how carefully you carry it out, is still a superficial inspection of the house and its key operating features. It is a cursory examination of visible imperfections, conspicuous defects and cosmetic blemishes. What will probably go unnoticed are the potentially serious problems — structural defects; faults in the plumbing, electrical and heating systems;

sloppy roofing; poor insulation; flaws in the brickwork and cracks in the foundation walls. These are the major defects and deficiencies that will cause grief for purchasers in the weeks and months after closing. Yet most purchasers are still more concerned with the cosmetic problems like a broken window or a non-functional electrical outlet. Despite the PDI, most purchasers of newly-built homes still rely on blind faith, because they are unable to verify for themselves that everything has been properly completed.

In recent years, more and more purchasers of resale homes have been hiring private home inspectors to thoroughly examine a "used" home before buying it. Following this diagnostic evaluation of the house, both inside and out, the inspector reports in detail on its condition, listing flaws and defects. Isn't this exactly what the purchaser of a newly-built home needs to take the guesswork out of buying? Granted the house is brand new, but does that mean everything has been done properly? Ask any new car buyer if newness means perfection!

Whether or not the house is protected by any type of new home warranty, an expert inspection should be an essential component of your home-buying strategy. Where the NHWP applies, any defects must be spotted early to ensure they are protected by the warranty coverage. Purchasers who buy a newly-built home without any warranty have all the more reason to hire a professional inspector before closing. Because it's caveat emptor, what protection do you have if a serious flaw is discovered after your money is in the builder's hands? In both situations the time to identify these hidden defects, which might not otherwise become apparent for years to come, is before closing.

A home inspection is not the same as an appraisal of the property conducted for a lender if you are arranging outside financing. That is nothing more than a estimation of its fair market value for lending purposes. Sometimes the lender will send out its own inspector to ensure the work is substantially completed before advancing the mortgage funds. Quality of construction is not considered nearly as thoroughly as your private home inspector will examine it. Purchasers who are arranging a new mortgage will have to pay for both the home inspection report and the appraisal report of the property the lender needs.

Purchasers of newly-built homes will find home inspectors useful in three different ways:

1. To accompany you on the PDI and examine the property with

the builder's rep before you close and take possession of the house. Together you objectively prepare the detailed itemized list of defects, deficiencies and uncompleted work *you* give to the builder. If applicable, it can be filed with the New Home Warranty Program as part of your Certificate of Completion and Possession.

Builders are not too keen to have a home inspector tag along with you during the PDI, fearing what may be uncovered. Unless the offer specifically excludes them (and few do), the builder has no legal grounds to prevent you from bringing a home inspector on the PDI. If worst comes to worst, you can always say he's your brother who has just come along to help out!

2. While the PDI examination is the most obvious role home inspectors have to play in the new home field, it is far from the only one. A home inspector should examine the property with you immediately before the basic warranty period (usually one year) expires. Some structural and cosmetic problems due to substandard building materials or workmanship take time to show. Any outstanding deficiencies and defects noted and reported to the builder before the warranty period lapses will continue to come under the warranty program, even after the basic coverage ends.

3. *While the house is being built,* the home inspector can monitor its construction. The inspector can prepare interim lists of oversights, defects and deficiencies to be forwarded to the construction foreman. Too often, and especially when builders are under pressure to complete homes quickly following a delayed closing, problems will be covered up rather than corrected. Unless you are constantly on site viewing the house *and know what to look for,* you may never get a chance to note the problems. Construction monitoring eliminates this.

In effect your private building inspector becomes your trained eyes and ears on the job, as he looks for construction imperfections and flaws (not just cosmetic ones) that you might overlook or know nothing about. How better to ensure what you are supposed to get is actually built? New home purchasers who use independent home inspectors in this capacity now have the necessary resource person to talk the same language as the builder, without feeling intimidated. No longer do they have to fear that the builder will be playing on their ignorance.

Home inspectors have to be very careful with construction monitoring. As the builder, and not you, own the house, technically speaking the home inspector is a trespasser every time he enters the uncompleted home or even sets foot on the lot. (Purchasers are trespassers too, although no one ever thinks that way). Different builders take different approaches to purchasers and their representatives scrutinizing the quality of construction. So be understanding if your home inspector encounters difficulties in monitoring the progress of the house.

While the industry is new to Canada, the home inspection concept is not. For years home inspectors have operated in the United States and in the United Kingdom. Usually home inspectors hold engineering degrees or have construction backgrounds. But that is not always the case.

One of the most serious problems with the home inspection industry in Canada today is the fact it is ungoverned, unlicenced and unregulated. As self-proclaimed experts, anyone with no appropriate background can open up shop as a home inspector, just like that. No standards or criteria exist to protect the home-buying public, despite the increased reliance being placed on home inspectors and their reports. Also, many home inspectors do not carry liability insurance, which could jeopardize a new home buyer in case an error is made.

To avoid this problem, find out more about your home inspector before hiring him. What is his background and qualifications? How long has he been in the business? Who has he acted for in the past? What type of a report does he provide, and how extensive? Better reports include recommendations for preventive maintenance. Can you see a sample report first? Does he carry errors and omissions (liability) insurance? If you are unsure as to which inspector to use, check with your family, friends and lawyer. Like other service industries, home inspectors rely very heavily on referrals. To ensure objectivity, never choose a home renovator as your home inspector, either. His major aim may be drumming up future business.

From the resale side of the market, home inspectors have learned to operate with very short time limits. Often they have as little as two or three days to inspect the house and prepare their written report. Why not make life easier for the home inspector and yourself? Contact different inspectors early in the process, getting at least three price quotations. If the inspector will be monitoring construction of the house, retain him shortly after the offer is signed, even though work may not begin until months in the future. Based on his knowledge of developments in the area, the inspector might be able to tell you when work will begin. For pre-delivery inspections, ask him to be "on standby," ready to accompany you on the PDI once you get word the house is ready for occupancy.

Compared to the price of the house, the expense of having your newly-built home expertly inspected is minimal. PDI and 12 month inspections run in the $200 to $300 range, while the fees for construction monitoring vary, depending on how often and how extensively the house will be viewed. Rarely do they exceed $1,000. To buy a newly-built house and not have it expertly examined at some stage is being penny wise and pound foolish. If you consider hiring a home inspector to be another form of insurance, just like seeing a lawyer before the offer is signed, it's a small price to pay for the peace of mind it brings.

Tips and Pointers

- As an absolute minimum, have a home inspector accompany you on your PDI.
- Consider having your home inspector do "construction monitoring" while the house is being built.
- Before hiring any home inspector, look into his qualifications and speak to his previous clients.

28

It's Closing Time

It's finally here. Closing day. By the end of the day, that "artist's rendering" which you nurtured along from a simple hole in the ground will be yours. While your major concern is getting the keys, what happens in between?

Closing is a simple procedure of exchanging documents and funds in the local registry office, so the purchaser winds up with what the builder had, and vice versa. Most closings are handled by trained, para-legal conveyancers. Meanwhile, your lawyer remains in his or her office, available to discuss matters with you and other people whose deals are closing. Last-minute instructions can easily be relayed this way from client to conveyancer through the lawyer's office, while information about keys is reported in reverse fashion.

With your home-buying strategy, all preliminary work — meeting with your lawyer to sign the closing papers and delivering the closing funds to him or her — should have been attended to well in advance. How else can you hope to get the keys as soon as possible on closing day? Ideally, closing day itself will be quick and smooth. At the pre-set time, your lawyer's conveyancer hands over the purchase funds, any vendor-take-back mortgage and all other required documents. In return, the builder's rep delivers the deed and all other documents from the builder, and authorizes the release of the keys, as discussed below. Once everything is carefully checked against the lawyer's closing memo, the conveyancers wait in line to register the deed, mortgage and other items. Only then can each side formally release to his or her client the items received at closing.

While the actual exchange of documents on closing can be completed in a few minutes' time, considerable delays may be faced in registering them. On busy days — the middle and the end of each month, Fridays, and the days before summer holidays begin and end — registration clerks simply can't handle the sheer volume of business. Hours on end can be spent waiting in line to register documents. Even on quiet days, afternoons tend to be busier than mornings. All the more reason to see your lawyer and put him or her in funds no later than the day before closing. Give yourself a fighting chance to close first thing the following morning.

Undoubtedly, the most often-asked question on closing is: "When and where will my keys be available?" Everyone knows how anxious buyers are to get their keys early, so the moving van can be unloaded. Unlike resale transactions where the keys are delivered to the purchaser's lawyer in the registry office on closing, most builders keep the keys at the site, either in the sales office or the construction trailer. Once the deal has closed, the keys are released with a phone call from the builder's lawyer. Keeping the keys in the vicinity of the new house is much more convenient. It also will save you considerable time and money. There is no need for the keys to be forwarded first from the registry office to your lawyer's office, while a moving van is waiting.

Unlike purchasers of resale homes, new home buyers do not need to worry about what time on closing day the current owner will be out of the house. Too often purchasers of resale homes complain that while they are ready to move in, the seller hasn't yet moved out. With a newly-built home, immediate access is possible once title and funds change hands.

On closing day, there is usually some last-minute work being completed at the new house. Most buyers will be at the house on that day to make sure that the final items are finished properly. While you may be on site, unless you have access to a telephone it is very hard to know what is happening. Many purchasers will drop over periodically to the sales office or construction trailer on closing day, just to see if the keys have been released yet. They also take a pocketful of quarters, to check every so often with their lawyer from a pay phone. Once the deal has closed, it's just a short drive to the sales office or construction office to pick up the keys.

Still, it's impossible to guarantee a precise hour when the keys will be released. So much must happen before the house is yours. Even the slightest hitch may be compounded into a long delay. Realistically, purchasers of new homes should not expect keys to be available at the site office until mid-afternoon the day of closing, at the earliest.

One of the unknown problems purchasers of newly-built homes face is learning that the home has been approved for occupancy by the municipal building inspector. Usually the final inspection is made at the builder's request, either the day before closing or more likely the day of closing. The builder may claim that according to the contract, the deal must close when the house has been substantially completed on the interior. What lawyer though, will deliver your money to the builder without first getting confirmation from the municipal inspector that the house has been approved? What assurance would you then have as a purchaser?

Procedurally, the problem is one of timing. Most inspectors begin their rounds early in the morning, and are unavailable until they report back until late in the afternoon. Unless the house was approved the day before closing, it is impossible to know until late on closing day whether your house was approved for occupancy. This virtually guarantees a late-in-the-afternoon closing, despite all your efforts to close early that morning.

If you know the house has not yet been finally inspected, there's no need to load up the moving van too early on the morning of closing. Delay is inevitable. (Don't worry that the people buying your old home will be getting late possession, either. Legally speaking, unless the contract specifies to the contrary, you don't have to be out of your old house until 11:59 *p.m.* that night.)

Premature occupancy of newly-built homes is a great concern to buyers and municipalities alike. No one can afford to move into a house that is incomplete, possibly hazardous, and that does not meet minimum standards. To ensure compliance, many development agreements do not permit a newly-built home to be occupied until the municipality has issued an occupancy permit following this final inspection. Where external work needs to be done such as laying the grass, lot grading and drainage, laying sidewalks, paving driveways and applying the final layer of asphalt to the road, a provisional occupancy certificate is issued.

Some purchasers are desperate to move in, and often do so without an occupancy certificate. This is a very dangerous practice. If need be, municipalities can cut off all municipal services to the property. Some municipalities go even further to prevent premature possession of unapproved homes. Title restrictions are imposed, prohibiting title from changing hands until the municipality grants its written consent and signs the deed. Of course consent is only granted if a occupancy permit has been issued. Purchasers are greatly protected this way, because it ensures that the municipality has approved occupancy of the newly-built home before the deed is registered.

Unavoidable delays also occur if back-to-back deals are closing the same day, as the sale of your old house must be completed before the purchase of your new home is finalized. Even longer delays are possible if your sale hinges on another transaction closing first. Consider the following scenario where you are Stan, who is buying a house from Terrific Homes.

Quincy ————→ Roy ————→ Stan ————→ Terrific Homes.

As Stan's sale to Roy had to close first, Stan expected some delay in completing the purchase from Terrific Homes. What slowed up the works even more was the fact that Roy was selling his house to Quincy. Stan had no control over this situation and never even knew about it until the day of closing.

Like dominos, the Quincy/Roy deal had to be closed and registered first, before the Roy/Stan and then the Stan/Terrific Homes transactions could be completed in that order. Having to close both deals the same day, Stan faced a very lengthy delay completing his purchase from Terrific Homes. Of course, all this could have been avoided if Stan had arranged bridge financing for his new home purchase (discussed in Chapter 16).

Sometimes it's impossible to complete everything the day of closing. Documents and funds may change hands, but there may be a hitch preventing the transaction from being finalized. The registry office may be closing before Stan's deed from Terrific Homes can be registered. On a busy day your lender may have been late in forwarding the mortgage proceeds to your lawyer. The registration line-ups may be lengthy. Or as is often the case, Buddy and Sally's lawyer has not yet heard from the building inspector that the home has been approved for occupancy. However, Buddy and Sally are confident that everything is in order from what their own home inspector told them at the PDI. What do they do?

Buddy and Sally obviously need a place to live. To put their possessions into storage overnight will be expensive. The builder will not reimburse them for the additional cost of storage, moving and accomodation, even for one night. Their builder would like the money as soon as possible, too. While it is unfortunate the deed cannot be registered, everything is ready to go except the paperwork.

When registration is delayed like this, the usual arrangement is to close the deal "in escrow." Here, the deed and all other documents are delivered to Buddy and Sally's lawyer on Wednesday, the scheduled closing date. The keys are also released to them from the site office, so they can move into the house that same Wednesday. In return, the closing funds are delivered to the builder's *lawyer*, but not to the builder. Effectively the deal has closed on Wednesday, except for the actual registration of the documents and release of funds. But no one does anything with the items received from the other side until registration takes place the following morning. Most importantly, the builder's lawyer holds Buddy and Sally's money until the deed is registered Thursday.

As part of the terms of the escrow closing, Buddy and Sally's lawyer must agree to reattend at the registry office first thing Thursday morning. Once the documents are registered, he or she must notify the builder's laywer that the funds can be released. Then the deal has formally closed, back-dated to the previous day. Although it seldom happens, any problems encountered in registering the closing papers must be reported to the builder's lawyer immediately, so arrangements can be made to correct them as soon as possible. Unless notified of any such problems, the builder's lawyer can release the funds to the builder at a pre-set time, usually before noon that Thursday.

Closing in escrow gives Buddy and Sally's lawyer the necessary time to ensure the house has been approved for occupancy. Of course, if it turns out that occupancy is denied, then it becomes necessary to undo everything that has taken place, putting both sides into the same position they were in before the escrow closing took place. Rarely does this happen, though. Instead, the necessary completion work is immediately done to the house so the inspector can approve it for occupancy, followed by the formal registration and release of funds.

Escrow closings can be dangerous if you have no idea whether the house will be approved for occupancy. Buddy and Sally had a home inspector accompany them on the PDI. If they hadn't, they literally would be taking their chances, even closing in escrow, before the house was municipally inspected and approved. In those circumstances, there might be no choice but to make some last-minute alternative plans — postpone closing one day, keep the moving van loaded up and rent a motel room. The risk of being wrong is just too great.

Occasionally purchasers are given access to the property the day of closing, before the deal actually closes. Perhaps it's to have some appliances or furniture delivered. Sometimes when registration of the closing papers is delayed, the sales office may even open up the house for you, so the movers can begin unloading the truck. Be aware, though that moving into the house before the deal closes is risky and is never recommended.

What if the house is not approved for occupancy by the municipality? What if some last-minute title problems are encountered? Most importantly, what if a mover injures himself before the deed is registered? Will your liability insurance be in effect at that time, or does it only take effect once you are the owner? The potential downside risks purchasers face could be horrendous. As annoying as it may seem, never take possession of the house or even accept the keys until the deal has closed.

Remember, that communications are a two-way street. While you anxiously are waiting word from your lawyer, your lawyer will have information to relay, perhaps even questions to ask of you. If you stay at work, fine. Purchasers who move the same day as closing will be unavailable for extended periods of time. Checking on things at the house, the change-over in telephones, running errands and the move itself are just some of the reasons you may be out of earshot. Make sure your lawyer knows how to reach you *at all times* on the day of closing. Be it a friend, relative or neighbor at either house, make sure that contact person can reach you quickly, if necessary.

And every so often, check in with your lawyer's office to see what is happening, or has happened! Developments at the registry office and at the site occur independently of each other. However you do it, keep in touch. As harried, anxious, excited and nervous as you may be, don't lose your cool on the day of closing. Imagine if the deal had closed and the keys had been released, but no one knew how to tell you! Coordinating communications through your lawyer's office the day of closing is crucial.

Tips and Pointers
- Expect to pick up your keys on the site rather than from your lawyer.
- Stay in contact with your lawyer's office throughout the day, to learn when the keys have been released.
- "Early access" to your home could be dangerous; avoid moving anything in until the property is yours.

Part Five

AFTER YOU CLOSE

29

Getting Your Act Together

The period from contract to closing has been both long and difficult. But now the house is legally yours. You are the proud registered owners of that piece of the earth and the building located on it. Even though the "move" is over, you are still not on easy street. There's a lot more work still to be done, all as part of your home-buying strategy — much more than just unpacking those cardboard mountains of boxes.

Builders of newly-built homes have access to all homes in the subdivision with a master key. Immediately before closing, the tumblers are changed to give each home a unique locking system. Many purchasers are satisfied with this, and do not change the locks any further. Because the builder will need access to your home after closing to correct problems and complete outstanding items, it may be necessary to leave a key with the service department, either permanently or each time work is done. Who knows what is done with those keys when they are out of your control? Once all the required service work has been completed and the basic warranty period expires, get the key back and resecure the house by changing the locks or at least the tumblers.

As soon as possible after you move in, get the following emergency numbers and stick them right on your phone. The time to look them up is now, not when the first emergency arises.

Police   Fire
Ambulance   Poison information center

And know where the nearest hospital is located, too.

Right after closing, notify *everyone* of your change of address. Start with the post office, which charges a nominal sum to redirect mail for several months to your new address. Or perhaps do this in the days immediately before closing. If the redirect period isn't long enough, renew it. Pick up change of address cards at the post office as well, for friends, neighbors and relations.

Who do you contact with your change of address? For starters, list all mail you receive for at least a month before you move from: credit card companies; magazines and subscriptions, car, life and home insurance; your health insurance plan; the federal government for family allowance payments; your dentist and family doctor; clubs and associations you belong to; your accountant; financial institutions — bank, trust company or credit union. A quick flip through your wallet will add several more names to the list. Don't forget the newspaper carrier. *For both your car ownership and your driver's licence, inform the provincial department of transport of the change of address within the specified time. Otherwise, you might face a fine for not doing so.*

Using the form below as a guide, list the names and addresses of everyone who needs to be sent a change of address. Once it has been sent, tick off the completed column.

Reminder list for changes of address

Name	*Address*	*Completed*

Expect to receive your lawyer's formal reporting letter about a month to six weeks after closing. To provide key information to you as soon as possible, some lawyers mail interim reports right after closing, highlighting payments due in the near future. Using the form below as a guide, list the names, addresses, payment dates, amounts payable and account numbers for payments due shortly after closing. If your lawyer does not provide an interim report, call for the information as soon as possible after closing.

Payment Dates	Name Address	Amount Payable	Account Number
First mortgage Second mortgage Realty taxes Condo maintenance Other items			

For newly-built homes, the land has already been assessed for realty taxes. The house itself will be reassessed shortly after closing. Expect to receive a supplementary tax bill a month or so after closing. Added to the earlier bill, this will represent the amount payable for property taxes for the year of closing. A combined bill will be issued the first full year after closing.

When the purchase closes early in the year, before the final tax bill is issued, the adjustment for taxes on the Statement of Adjustment is probably based on last year's figures. If this is the case, contact your lawyer later in the year about the possible readjustment of realty taxes in your favor.

Set the wheels in motion now if you are cancelling the insurance coverage transferred to you by the builder on closing. The longer it takes to notify the builder's insurer about your own insurance coverage, the smaller the premium that will be returned to you. It's your money, so don't delay.

Many builders collect considerable sums of money on the closing adjustments for the readjustment of taxes, interest on the unadvanced portion of the mortgage, and damage to the grading and subdivision services. Remember to contact your lawyer both when the supplementary tax bill is issued, and when the external work has been completed permitting the final mortgage advance to be made. The builder may owe you money!

Some items in your house will be covered by separate guarantees and warranties. Included here are the furnace and air conditioner, air cleaner, humidifier plus any appliances bought with the house. Even if your house is covered by the New Home Warranty Program, it does not apply to these items. Ask your builder for these warranties and put them in a safe place.

Make a note for two months after closing to get the Warranty

Certificate from the NHWP, if applicable. If you haven't received it by then, contact your lawyer.

First-time home owners will have to buy many household items in the days and weeks after closing. While this list is far from exhaustive, it includes garbage cans; snow shovels; a lawn mower and other lawn accessories; lawn fertilizer and spreader; rake, hose, nozzle and sprinkler; shears; numbers to be affixed to the front of the house; mailbox (not for mail service, but for newspapers, flyers and items dropped off); extra keys; household tools and supplies such as a hammer, wrench, pliers, screwdrivers, nails and screws; and rock salt or sand to melt the ice.

Some purchasers of newly-built homes leave the front and rear yards untouched until the property is graded, followed by the laying of the sod. Besides being unsightly, the ground is covered with bricks, bits of concrete, aluminum siding, paint cans, metal brackets, wires, pipes, nails, styrofoam, drywall, insulation and wood. These are safety hazards, especially for young children.

Not only that, but once the garbage and debris is plowed underground it remains there forever. This causes lumpy lawns and spawns the occasional growth of mushrooms! So clean up the grounds. Make it a family project. Gather up all the unsafe and unsightly items on your yards. Both you and your lawn will appreciate it.

Speaking of lawns, make sure you water that newly-laid sod thoroughly. To root properly, freshly-laid grass must be watered for several hours each night. When in doubt, ask the builder or the landscapers how long you must water. Don't expect the builder to replace any dead or burnt sod. Most offers say the home owner is responsible for maintaining the sod once it is laid. If you want replacement sod, you pay for it.

Besides cleaning up the exterior of the house, consider cleaning the interior as well. Not the floors and walls, but the heating ductwork. Tradesmen treat heating outlets as garbage pails and basketball nets. It is amazing how much garbage accumulates in those ducts. Before closing, the builder will do a general clean-up of the house and will clean out the ducts. But it's never been done adequately.

Duct cleaning companies are a growing industry in Canada. Armed with a powerful vacuum cleaner, they literally suck out all the garbage and dust in your home's ductwork. Ask any purchaser of a newly-built home, and they will tell you about the lunch bags, styrofoam cups, concrete, nails, wires, pieces of wood, drywall and even bricks removed from their ducts. All this debris, of course, blocks the flow of warm air in the winter and cold air in the summer, making your furnace work overtime. For a charge of several hundred dollars, you will be helping your furnace and air conditioner properly climatize your house for years to come.

Tips and Pointers

- Make sure you request a refund of all money owing to you by the builder.
- Notify everyone about your change in address as soon as possible.
- Get a new list of emergency telephone numbers as soon as you've moved in.

30

After-Sales Service

Today's new homes are mass-produced, built on an assembly-line basis. The construction crews move from house to house, completing their task. Just like the automobile industry, no item is built perfectly. Problems do arise which must be corrected. Just like the automobile industry, customer service departments are maintained to repair the defects which arise and are noticed after closing.

Speak to purchasers of newly-built homes, and many will have critical impressions of their builder's after-sales service office. One of the two most common complaints is the extreme delay encountered in having outstanding items completed, and in getting defects and deficiencies corrected. The second is the negative attitude some builders exhibit towards their purchasers.

All that purchasers of newly-built homes want is what they bargained for, no more and no less. Whatever is defective should be repaired and whatever is outstanding should be completed as soon as possible. Builders never seem to complete the work as quickly as purchasers would like. Because the builder is the focal point for many different trades working on the house, some delays in after-sales service are inevitable. Compounding this are external factors over which the builder has no control, such as weather conditions and the availability of trades and materials. Purchasers who expect all defects and uncompleted work to be done immediately after closing are being unrealistic.

Unfortunately, too often the reverse holds true. Too often once the money and title have changed hands, purchasers feel abandoned by their builder. Having to live with the defect or uncompleted work is annoying enough. Delays in having the necessary work done doesn't help matters. Getting the trades to return for service work seems to take forever. Promises are broken and target dates are missed, and the work remains uncompleted.

Compounding the defects and delays is the disposition some builders have towards their buyers. Complaints fall on deaf ears. Phone calls are ignored, leading to letters from buyers. When builders pay no attention to these letters, they are followed by lawyer's letters and then threats of lawsuits. All the while the problems persist. Quite often a simple letter from the builder explaining the reason for the delay is all that is needed to reassure purchasers that the builder is aware of the problem, that the work will ultimately be done, and that the builder is not abandoning his purchasers. Builders too seldom prepare this type of letter.

Over time, purchasers are bound to get worn down and tired through constantly being ignored. Some frustrated buyers simply lose interest in fighting the builder any further, and throw up their hands in despair.

Other buyers, however, dig in their heels and refuse to give up. After being thwarted for so long, these tired but persistent purchasers tend to be grateful that the remedial work will finally be done to their house. But some builders compound the problem even more at this stage. The proper approach would be for builders to acknowledge the legitimacy of the complaints. Too often, though, purchasers are made to feel the builder is doing them a favor, that they are receiving special treatment they are not really entitled to. This "ignore, ignore and then reluctantly concede" approach does more than just create a poor impression about an individual builder. In the long run it ends up discrediting the entire new home building industry.

Once the deal has closed, the system actually works against purchasers of newly-built homes. They have very little bargaining power. Only in the rarest of cases has any money been retained by the purchaser to ensure the necessary service work is completed to the purchaser's satisfaction. More likely than not, the builder received the entire purchase price on closing. With no holdback of funds, many purchasers of newly-built homes feel there is less incentive for the builder to correct the defects and finish the uncompleted work as quickly as possible. Sometimes all purchasers feel they have to rely on is the good faith and integrity of the builder.

Many new home buyers feel that builders condition purchasers to accept less than perfection in their homes. A standard line builders use when a deficiency is raised is "It's not a custom built home." While this may be true, purchasers facing blatantly incompetent and shoddy workmanship, and construction deficiencies are entitled to a better answer than that. No purchaser of a newly-built home should have to face a leaky basement, uneven walls and floors, cold air infiltration and improperly operating windows, and then be criticized for asking that these items be fixed!

By shutting their eyes and ears to buyers' complaints, builders lose sight of who they are offending. Satisfied customers are still the best form of advertising in any field. Word does get around both when builders' service departments respond promptly to buyers' requests and when builders perpetually ignore buyers. Problems encountered with after-sales service eventually will come back to haunt the builder. To maintain good relations with his buyers, builders should be as concerned about the customer service department as they are with the actual construction of the house itself.

During strong sellers' markets, after-sales service inevitably suffers. There are only so many qualified tradesmen to go around. Where do builders send them first? To finish work on unbuilt homes so purchasers whose closings already have been delayed can move in? Or to remedy problems for those people already in possession? By rushing to complete the homes, it is inevitable that the final product delivered in most cases is not fully completed, certainly not to the standard purchasers expect. Therefore, there is more need for after-sales service in those homes than normally would be the case. But all this is happening at the very time when there is less manpower to attend to customer complaints, because the trades are struggling to complete other homes. Lengthy delays in having deficiencies fixed and uncompleted work finished become unavoidable.

Despite the inconvenience and the aggravation, purchasers may have no alternative but to bide their time in having problems rectified and uncompleted work finished during boom times. Undoubtedly their patience will run thin over time the more they are given the cold shoulder by the builder. All the more reason builders should be honest and tell purchasers that service will be slow, that they must be patient but yes, the work *will* be done. This is one of the trade-offs builders and new home buyers must make when business is brisk.

As part of their home-buying strategy, more and more people are asking about the builder's service department — how it operates and how it treats its purchasers — when checking out a builder's track record and reputation before signing any offer. Obviously it will have a great bearing in choosing a builder. Ask others who bought from the same builder if they encountered any serious service problems. Is there a local home owners' association that can inform you how the builder treats his buyers? Are prior purchasers satisfied customers or are they disillusioned, ready to heap scorn and contempt on the builder?

Ask this unique but very important question: Is the customer service department totally separate from the builder's construction department? The best answer is yes, but too often it's no. Unless different people man each department, the construction trades — the people responsible for a construction defect — are the ones being asked to correct their own mistakes! How could this ever be done effectively? If the construction crew can't complete the job properly once, why would anyone think they will do a better job the second time around? With an independent service department, buyers have a greater chance of having their complaints properly rectified.

Looking ahead to potential problems with after-sales service, how can you best protect yourself after closing? Where problems remain unresolved, what is the best strategy to effectively deal with the builder's service department? How can you ensure the work you feel must be done will eventually be completed? First, be persistent without becoming a nuisance. Fight for your rights, for what you bargained *and paid for*. Above all, don't get frustrated and simply give up. The only person who gains from a purchaser who throws in the towel is the builder.

But be reasonable in your approach. Ignore minor inconveniences that you can live with, or that you can take care of yourself. Concentrate your activities on the major defects and the uncompleted work, the items you *really* want done. The longer the list of nitpicking items, the more resentful the builder will become.

Try to avoid confrontations. Instead, approach the builder with tact and diplomacy, stating calmly and cooly what is outstanding. Builders do not necessarily listen to purchasers who scream the loudest or who make threats. Excessive criticism will only put the builder on the defensive, perhaps causing even further tardiness and inaction.

Try to get a written commitment as to the date when the completion and corrective work will be done. Most purchasers are not too successful here, but there's no harm in trying. Despite difficult market conditions, if a builder will provide you with this type of timetable *and honor it,* that's an excellent reflection of how he values his buyers.

Expect emergency repairs for a defective furnace, an electrical malfunction or a serious plumbing leak to be fixed by the builder immediately. If that is not done, you have every reason to complain bitterly.

Be prepared to spend time with the builder and his service department straightening out problems once the deal has closed. Just as the new car will have defects that are only noticed during the break-in period, so too with a newly-built home. Get to know the head of the builder's service department and the members of his team on a first-name basis. They are the ones responsible for completing the outstanding work and correcting the defects.

Remember that it may be necessary to spend some time at work on the phone with the builder's service department to resolve any outstanding issues and arrange for the repairs to be done. You may have to take time off work occasionally to meet with the service rep or tradesmen on site in order to address the problem face to face. There is little you can do — it goes with the territory when buying a newly-built house.

Carefully consider this dilemma. Unlike a car, a house cannot be left at a service depot to be picked up after work! Servicing can only be done on site. Customer service reps and tradesmen must have access to the house during the day to repair and service defects and deficiencies. Too often getting them to come once is difficult enough. Imagine if they can't gain access to your house! Someone must be home to let them in whenever they arrive (and a precise time is never guaranteed). Are you prepared to take time off work every time repairs and adjustments are needed? If you do stay at home, be cautious. Ask the trades to show you identification before letting them into your home.

If that is not practical, what is the alternative? Leave a key to your house with the builder's service department? Granted, you don't want strangers trekking through your home when you're not present, but it may be the only viable solution. Unless someone is at home all day, most buyers of newly-built homes end up leaving a key with the service department, and hope for the best. Some builders even insist on receiving written permission from purchasers to enter the house in their absence at reasonable times after closing, before doing any outstanding work.

Expect the service department to deny that certain problems exist, and to refuse to correct other deficiencies. Instead of repairing something faulty, plan on the after-service rep telling you it's very minor, and that you can live with it. Instead of agreeing to repair a pre-existing defect, anticipate being told to fix it yourself, since you caused the problem. This is probably the most aggravating part of buying a newly-built house — being told that it won't be 100 percent perfect.

Still, whenever remedial work is done, acknowledge it with sincere appreciation. Many people are quick to criticize, but slow to express their thanks. After-sales people have probably heard all the criticism before in various forms, but little praise. It doesn't cost much, but a few words of thanks could go a long way towards getting other work done promptly.

Of course, the diplomatic approach won't always work. Sometimes it is necessary to pursue the matter as adversaries, either in conciliation with the New Home Warranty Program or in court. Either way, make sure you marshall all the necessary facts about the problem. Every action and inaction should be well documented, in anticipation of going to court. Become an excellent record keeper. Keep copies of every letter sent and received. Make notes on every telephone conversation immediately after it is concluded, and every message left unanswered. Record every promise made and broken by the builder. Have your ammunition ready. Leave nothing to speculation or chance.

If your house is protected by a new home warranty, make sure you notify the NHWP of the problems you have encountered *before* the one-year basic warranty expires. This way the builder or the Plan, if necessary, is responsible to fix them even after the warranty lapses.

Above all, never get yourself so worried about the problems to the point of anxiety. As annoying as it may be, it's not worth the strain on your health, your physical and your emotional well-being. Always be in control of the situation — never let the situation control you. Try to maintain a positive mental attitude throughout. Otherwise, your enjoyment and enthusiasm for that new home will be affected, something you most certainly don't want to happen.

As part of your home-buying strategy, anticipate having to cope with a certain level of aggravation after closing. Buying a newly-built house means some work will remain unfinished at closing, while defects will materialize as time goes on. Rarely will the repairs be completed when you want them done. Some problems may never be corrected to your total satisfaction. Headaches like these are some of the non-monetary costs purchasers of newly-built homes face after closing.

Tips and Pointers

- Never throw your hands up in despair at the slow response of after-sales service. Be persistent in having problems corrected to your satisfaction.
- Ask whether the builder has a separate after-sales service department; the better ones do.
- Always approach the builder initially in a diplomatic manner, but be a good record keeper in case you eventually need to take the builder to court.

31

Home Ownership Tidbits

Very quickly, buyers of newly-built homes must become knowledgeable about many different technical aspects of a purchase. Here is a crib sheet to help you along.

Title
Once the offer is accepted, one of your lawyer's first questions will be "How do you want to take title?" Translation: How do you want to be registered in the deed? For Mickey and Minnie simply to say "co-owners" is inadequate, since there are several different types of co-ownership. And then you must concern yourself with the impact of the provincial family law legislation where you reside.

i) Joint Tenants
Joint Tenancy has nothing to do with being a tenant. A well-established old English expression, it originated when feudal lords owned all the land, and a "landowner" simply was a tenant of the feudal lord.

It is most commonly used when a husband and wife like Mickey and Minnie decide to own a property together. Like a joint bank account, Mickey and Minnie both own the home. However, being joint tenants also provides them with the survivorship arrangement at the time of death most married couples want. If Mickey dies, Minnie automatically becomes the sole owner of the house simply because she survived Mickey. By law, property passes to the surviving joint tenant *before* the deceased's assets are distributed. This means the house would not even be considered as an asset of Mickey's estate, since Minnie received it by survivorship. If Minnie died while Mickey was alive, the reverse would be true.

While holding the title as joint tenants is not limited to married spousal situations, its practical use in most other situations is quite limited, with the possible exception of the common law relationship.

ii) Tenants in Common
Once again ignore the reference to "tenant." Taking title as tenants in common means the named parties both own equal shares of the home, to deal with as they see fit. If Donald and Daisy were the registered owners of the property as tenants in common, then each would own a 50 percent share of the property. Each could sell their 50 percent share to someone else if he or she wanted, subject to the terms of any written agreements between them.

The biggest distinction from joint tenancy is the fact the survivorship rules do not apply to a tenancy in common. If Donald dies, his share of the home passes to his beneficiary, either by will if one exists, or by law if it does not. It does not pass automatically to Daisy as it would if they were registered as joint tenants. Since Donald named Louie as beneficiary of his will, this means Donald's share of the property goes to Louie on Donald's death. Now Daisy and Louie own the house as tenants in common.

If the respective shares are not 50/50, the title should clearly show this. This would occur if Daisy owned 65 percent of the property, while Donald had a 35 percent interest in it.

"Tenants in common" is popular when two or more unrelated people own property together — common-law couples, business associates or people living together in shared accommodations.

iii) One Name Only
Where one of two married spouses is self-employed, it is quite common for title to the matrimonial home to be registered in the name of the other spouse. When Charlie and Lucy bought their house, Lucy took title in her name alone, since Charlie is self-employed. Why did they do this? With title in Lucy's name alone, the house is protected from creditors in case Charlie's business suffers a financial setback. If Charlie's business was in dire straits, the matrimonial home could not be lost to his creditors to pay off his debts. The house belongs to Lucy alone, not Charlie.

iv) Family Law Reform

Where family law reform has been introduced, it would be very difficult for Lucy, the spouse who owns the matrimonial home, to sell, mortgage or even lease it without Charlie's written consent. The fact that Charlie must consent to any transactions affecting the matrimonial home does not give him any *property* rights in it. All he has is a *personal* right to remain there until he consents to any sale, mortgage or lease.

In those provinces with family law reform in place, it is immaterial who is the registered owner of the property when the matrimonial home is being conveyed. Whether Lucy, Charlie or Charlie and Lucy are its registered owners, both spouses must sign all deeds, mortgages and leases affecting it. They may be signing as owner, or they may be signing to grant their spousal consent. Either way, two signatures are needed when the matrimonial home is involved to validate any transaction.

Spousal consent replaced the ancient English concept of dower. Instead of protecting only women, spousal consent is required from both men and women alike. Not all properties are affected this way, but only the matrimonial home. Any investment property Charlie owns in his own name can be sold without getting Lucy's written consent.

Family law reform legislation also treats matrimonial homes somewhat uniquely in the event of marriage breakdown — separation, divorce and death. Different rules apply depending on how the property was acquired and in whose name it was registered. Leave nothing to chance. If you have any questions or concerns about how to take title and the impact of your provincial family law act on that decision, consult your lawyer immediately.

The Metric House

With the passage of time, more and more Canadians are becoming familiar with the use of metric measurements. However, many Canadians still feel uneasy when dealing in metric. In the last few years the real estate industry has expanded its use of metric measurements. Surveys are now prepared with metric dimensions, as are subdivision plans and lot dimensions/room sizes in real estate listings. As metric real estate is not only a fact of life but the way of the future, it is important to feel more comfortable measuring in metric.

Thinking metric takes time. The following chart has been designed for those who still need help in converting to and from metric:

Metre (m): — The basic unit of length in the metric system.
Square Metre: — The basic unit measuring area in the metric system (for lot sizes and room dimensions).

Length
— 1 inch = .0254 m. To convert metres to inches, divide the number of metres by .0254.

— 1 foot = .3048 m. To convert metres to feet, divide the number of metres by .3048.

— 1 yard = .9144 m. To convert metres to yards, divide the number of metres by .9144.

— 1 metre = 39.37 inches. To convert inches to metres, divide the number of inches by 39.37.

— 1 metre = 3.28084 feet. To convert feet to metres, divide the number of feet by 3.28084.

—1 metre = 1.09361 yards. To convert yards to metres, divide the number of yards by 1.09361.

Area
— 1 square foot = .092903 square metres. To convert square metres to square feet, divide the number of square metres by .092903.

— 1 square yard = .836127 square metres. To convert square metres to square yards, divide the number of square metres by .836127.

— 1 square metre = 10.7639 square feet. To convert square feet to square metres, divide the number of square feet by 10.7639.

— 1 square metre = 1.196 square yards. To convert square yards to square metres, divide the number of square yards by 1.196.

— For comparison, a room 15 feet by 10 feet, or 150 square feet, is equivalent to 13.935 square metres.

— A room 4.4 m by 3.1 m (14.436 feet by 10.171 feet) is equivalent to 13.64 square metres or 146.82 square feet.

— A 2,000-square-foot house is equivalent to 185.806 square metres.

— A 200-square-metre house is equivalent to 2,152.78 square feet.

Urea Formaldehyde Foam Insulation

Purchasers of resale homes are very concerned whether a particular property was insulated with urea formaldehyde foam insulation (UFFI). Anyone who buys a newly-built home today need not worry about UFFI for two reasons.

For a number of years, it has been illegal to use UFFI as a home insulator. Growing concerns about health problems caused by formaldehyde gas seepage led to the federal government banning its use on December 17, 1980. More importantly, UFFI was never used as a primary insulator for new homes. It was used to reinsulate the walls of older homes that lacked adequate insulation.

Construction Liens (Mechanics' Liens)

The buyer of a home being built is concerned about construction liens (or as they are sometimes called, mechanics' liens) for different reasons than the person whose house already exists. When work is done on the home you own, whether it be to install a new kitchen, construct an addition or finish the basement, the tradesmen and material suppliers have the right to place a lien against your property if they are not paid. The obligations and liabilities of home owners in this situation are examined in more detail in the companion volume to this book *Alan Silverstein's Home-Buying Strategies for Resale Homes.*

According to the provincial construction lien acts, when work is done or materials are supplied to a property, owners are to retain a set percentage of the value of the work done for a fixed number of days after the contract is substantially completed. Funds withheld this way are called the "holdback." It exists to benefit and protect subtrades by guaranteeing then some money in case the general contractor absconds with the other funds or goes bankrupt. Under the older acts, the holdback was 15 percent of the value of the work done and the holdback period was 37 days from the date of substantial completion. The newer legislation has changed the numbers to 10 percent and 45 days. Once the prescribed period expires the holdback can be released, provided no notice of any liens have been registered against the title to the property. What happens if you fail to comply with the holdback requirements? You are still responsible for paying the amount of the holdback to the subtrades. In effect, you could be forced to pay the holdback twice.

Purchasers of newly-built homes face a different type of dilemma than their resale counterparts. Richard and Francine bought a yet-to-be built home from Thebest Homes, the model type being "Thornwood." As is standard in most new home transactions, the Thornwood model they want to buy is just one of several models Thebest Homes offers in the subdivision. Richard and Francine's home will be built according to the builder's plans and specifications, which they approved. According to the construction lien legislation, Richard and Francine have bought this new house "according to sample," making them "owners" for purposes of the legislation. Like any other "owner," Richard and Francine must retain the statutory holdback on closing or else be in breach of the legislation.

One problem exists. Like most, their contract with Thebest Homes does not allow any holdback of funds on closing. All Richard and Francine will receive on closing is the builder's written "covenant of indemnity." In it, Thebest Homes agrees to reimburse Richard and Francine for any money they pay to satisfy any construction liens which are the responsibility of Thebest Homes. As good as it sounds, it may be a worthless piece of paper if Thebest Homes goes bankrupt. Then Richard and Francine would still have to pay the amount of the holdback from their own pocket, if a valid lien claim was made.

Some protection is available if they assumed the builder's mortgage. Rarely is the full amount of the mortgage advanced to the builder on closing. Funds are retained until the house, including the exterior work, is totally completed. Holdbacks by the lender and a delayed final advance are designed with possible lien claims in mind. The cost to Richard and Francine for this protection: the interest on the unadvanced portion of the mortgage, described in Chapter 15.

Recognizing how shocking it would be for buyers of newly-built homes like Richard and Francine to be saddled this way, Ontario has devised a scheme that protects most people in their situation. Provided two criteria are met, none of Thebest Homes' tradesmen can claim a construction lien against Richard and Francine and no money need be held back by them on closing. The criteria are:

a) the deposits paid must be less than 30 percent of the purchase price; and b) title to the home must not be transferred until either an occupancy certificate is issued by the local municipality or a Certificate of Completion and Possession is issued following the PDI under the mandatory New Home Warranty Program.

Realty Taxes

Most municipalities collect realty (or property) taxes in two stages, an interim bill followed by a final bill later in the year. The taxes on Doug and Aline's home were $1,200 in 1986. When the interim tax bill is issued in 1987, it will be for half this figure, or $600. Depending on the municipality, it will be payable in two, three or four equal instalments.

Once the local council sets the final taxes for the year, usually in late spring or early summer, the final tax bill will be issued, again payable over several instalments. With a 5.1 percent increase in taxes, or $61.20, their total 1987 taxes will be $1,261.20. As $600 has been paid already on account, the final tax bill will total $661.20.

Some municipalities, though, offer a discount for early payment of tax instalments. Prepaying your taxes this way will save you money. Check it out with the local tax office. To avoid interest penalties if payments are received late, some home owners send a series of post-dated cheques to the municipality, dated when each instalment falls due.

Until a few years ago, many people deliberately did not pay their realty taxes on time, because the interest penalty charged for over-due taxes was well below the consumer loan rate. It was a cheap way to borrow money. All this has changed. Overdue instalments now bear interest at current rates, making this scheme less economically viable.

When realty taxes remain unpaid, all taxpayers shoulder the financial burden of the municipality receiving less revenue than anticipated. To ensure that unpaid realty taxes do not place too great a strain on the municipality, they are given a special priority status in law. As a special lien against a property, unpaid realty taxes rank even higher than a first mortgage! Obviously lenders want to remain at the top of the heap, cutting out the municipality's chance to sneak in ahead. This explains why many lenders collect a portion of the estimated annual realty taxes with each mortgage payment. As the tax bills are issued, the lender pays the realty taxes from the tax account it maintains.

Utilities
Just like realty taxes, unpaid municipal hydro and water charges are enforceable as a lien against the property. This way the property benefitting from the utility must bear the burden. Otherwise all other users of the system would have to carry the cost. These lien rights do not exist in favor of privately owned utility companies — telephone, natural gas or cable TV systems.

32

The Beginning, Not the End

With a newly-built house, settling into it is rarely the end of the story. So much will be done, and needs to be done, in the weeks and months following closing.

Before long, that new development will begin taking on the appearance of an established community and neighborhood. The exterior will be cleaned up, sodded and graded. Trees will be planted and the sidewalks laid, followed by the final layer of asphalt on the streets. Then your immediate vicinity will begin to look like the picturesque residential community you expected to live in.

As more and more people move into the area, many of the services and facilities previously lacking will begin sprouting up, such as public transportation, schools and shopping centers, just to name a few. No longer are you a pioneer. Civilization is following you!

What about your own house? One of the first things you will have to get are drapes, blinds and other window coverings. After that, it won't take long before you decide to continue decorating the house to your individual taste, repainting and possibly wallpapering the walls. You may buy new furniture to fill the extra space you never had before; change the light fixtures; install additional shelving and closet organizers; purchase a central vacuum system; replace the shower curtains with a glass shower door. You might also plan to finish the basement, to maximize the use of the space in your house.

On the outside you will want to consider erecting a fence and landscaping the yards. You might add some external lights, especially around the patio. Electronic garage door openers are very popular, too.

As you can see, the possibilities are endless. The only limitation is your financial resources. But no one said it all has to be done at one time, right after closing.

In buying that house, you developed and applied your own unique home-buying strategy, the master plan that guided you from the pre-contract stage through to closing. Why stop now? Why not duplicate your success? To translate those four walls and a roof into a home that expresses your individual lifestyle, you need to establish a home ownership strategy. Just as with your home-buying strategy, draw up a needs and a wants list. Record what must be done immediately, and what you would like done as soon as possible. Organize the lists in order of priority. And then begin budgeting to do that work over the next few years.

Imagine what this will do for you. The excitement and enthusiasm of buying the house now can be applied to enriching it over the years to come. You will be anxiously looking forward to each year's changes and upgrades, all the more because you know you have budgeted for these improvements. The key to buying that newly-built house was advance preparation and and planning. The same holds true for owning it.

Always keep in mind that residential mortgages are expensive, no matter what the interest rate is. Interest paid on a mortgage arranged to finance the purchase is not deductible in Canada against other income earned. Part of your home ownership strategy should be to take the fullest possible advantage of the prepayment privileges appearing in your mortgage. By applying the POPS principle — Pay Off Your Principal Sooner — you will save thousands of dollars in mortgage interest costs and retire that loan years earlier than expected. To better understand the mechanics of the POPS principle, read my previous book *Hidden Profits in Your Mortgage*. Remember that the interest saved stays in your pocket, to be used elsewhere as part of your home ownership strategy.

A newly-built home is more than just a building. It's a new start for you and your family. The only other wish anyone can have is for good health. Without it, everything else is meaningless.